Read & Think
FRENCH

PREMIUM Second Edition

Read & Think
FRENCH

PREMIUM Second Edition

The editors of
Think French
magazine

New York Chicago San Francisco Athens London Madrid
Mexico City Milan New Dehli Singapore Sydney Toronto

4 5 6 7 8 9 10   QFR   21 20 19

ISBN   978-1-259-83629-9
MHID   1-259-83629-0

e-ISBN   978-1-259-83630-5
e-MHID   1-259-83630-4

McGraw-Hill Education books are available at special quantity discounts to use as premiums and sale promotions, or for use in corporate training programs. To contact a representative, please visit the Contact Us pages at www.mhprofessional.com.

McGraw-Hill Education Language Lab App

Audio recordings for select readings (see page 207 for full list) and flashcards for all vocabulary lists are available to support your study of this book. Go to www.mhlanguagelab.com to access the online version of this application. Also available for iPhone, iPad, and Android devices. Search "McGraw-Hill Education Language Lab" in the iTunes app store, Google Play or Amazon App store for Android.

Contents

Culture

Voyages

Tradition

Célébration

Biographie

Coutumes

Les Arts

Histoire

Géographie

Gastronomie

Introduction

Read & Think French is an engaging and non-intimidating approach to language learning. A dynamic at-home language immersion, *Read & Think French* is intended to increase French fluency while teaching you about life and culture in French-speaking countries.

This language learning tool is designed to build on and expand your confidence with French, presenting vocabulary and phrases in meaningful and motivating content emphasizing all four language skills: reading, writing, speaking, and understanding the spoken language.

Read & Think French brings the French language to life! Our diverse team of international writers is excited about sharing the language and culture with you. Read a travel narrative from Normandy and a documentary on Paris cafes. Discover the best markets of Provence with our insider tips, and explore the architecture on the colorful streets of Montreal. And don't forget, while you are enjoying these intriguing articles, you are learning French.

Read & Think French is used by educators and students of all ages to increase French fluency naturally and effectively. Using this as a complement to classroom study or as a self-study guide, you will actively build grammar and develop vocabulary.

The cultural information provided in each chapter helps readers develop a deeper understanding of the traditions and cultures in French-speaking countries, which creates greater interest and ultimately success with learning French.

Read & Think French accommodates a range of skill sets, from beginning to advanced:

• **Beginning:** We recommend that the student have the equivalent of one semester of college- or high school–level French. Your previous experience with French may have been through studies at a private or public school, self-study programs, or immersion programs. *Read & Think French* will allow you to immerse yourself in the language and the culture, and your understanding of sentence structure and use of verbs will be reinforced.

• **Intermediate:** As an intermediate student, you will learn new vocabulary and phrases. You will notice increased fluency and comprehension. You will also learn nuances about the language and the culture as you experience the authentic writing styles of authors from different countries.

• **Advanced:** The advanced student will continue to gain valuable information, as language acquisition is a lifelong endeavor. The diverse topics from a team of international writers offer you the opportunity to learn new vocabulary and gain new insight into the language and the people.

Whatever your current skill level, *Read & Think French* is an effective, fun, and accessible way to learn French.

Experience the enthusiasm that comes with learning a new language and discovering a new culture. Read, speak, enjoy . . . think French!

Guidelines for Success

Read & Think French is divided into chapters guiding you through the cultures and traditions of different French-speaking countries. At the end of each chapter is the "Test your comprehension" section. This section encourages development of reading comprehension and the understanding of written French in different voices.

It is not necessary for you to read *Read & Think French* from start to finish or in any certain order. You can read one chapter at a time or pick an article or chapter that is of particular interest to you. You can complete the test questions by article or by chapter. This flexibility allows you to go at your own pace, reading and re-reading when needed. The high-interest articles encourage enthusiasm as you study, making the material more enjoyable to read.

• Read through the article to get the general idea of the story line. Do not get frustrated if the first time through you do not fully understand the vocabulary.

• After you gain an understanding of the article, read through the story again and focus on vocabulary that is new to you. Notice how the vocabulary is used in context.

• Practice reading the article aloud.

• If you have access to an audio recorder, practice recording the articles or ask a fluent speaker to record them for you. Listen to the recording and notice how your listening comprehension improves over time.

Repeat, Repeat, Repeat! This is especially important for memorizing important parts and forms of words. Sometimes only active repetition will secure your memory for certain hard-to-retain items. Frequent vocal repetition impresses the forms on your "mental ear." This auditory dimension will help you recognize and recall the words later. With *Read & Think French* you have the opportunity to repeat different learning processes as often as you'd like and as many times as you want. Repeat reading, repeat listening, and repeat speaking will aide in your overall success mastering the French language.

Custom Bilingual Glossary

A custom bilingual glossary is provided next to each article to facilitate ease and understanding while reading in French. With uninterrupted reading, comprehension is improved and vocabulary is rapidly absorbed.

Every article contains new grammar, vocabulary, and phrases as well as repetition of previous vocabulary and phrases. The repetition throughout the articles enhances reading comprehension and encourages memorization. The articles are written in different perspectives. Most articles are written in third person while some are written in first person. This change of voice allows you to recognize verbs as they are conjugated in different tenses.

French instructors often recommend that students "create an image" or associate foreign words with something familiar to enhance memorization of new vocabulary. As you are learning new vocabulary with *Read & Think French*, however, you will not have to create these images. The images will be automatically created for you as the story unfolds. Take your time as you are reading and imagine the story as it is written, absorbing the new vocabulary. If a vocabulary word is particularly difficult, try focusing on an image in the story that the word represents as you say the word or phrase aloud.

Verbs in the glossary are written first in their conjugated form as they appear in the article, followed by their infinitive form.

For example: **offrent (offrir):** they offer (to offer)

conçu pour (concevoir): designed for (to design)

Test Your Comprehension

The test questions provided at the end of each chapter are designed to further develop your reading comprehension skills and ensure your overall success with French. In addition to determining the general meaning of the article by word formation, grammar, and vocabulary, you will also learn how to use context to determine meaning. Understanding context allows you to make educated "guesses" about the meaning of unfamiliar words based on the context of a sentence, paragraph, or article. Answers are provided at the end of the book and within each chapter.

About the Author

Read & Think French is based on articles from *Think French*, an online language learning membership published monthly by Second Language Publishing. The writers for *Think French* are native French speakers, including college and high school French instructors, travel experts, and journalists. Articles in this book were coordinated and compiled under the direction of Kelly Garboden, founder and editor-in-chief of Second Language Publishing. For membership information for *Think French* visit: www.thinkfrench.com.

Read & Think
FRENCH

PREMIUM Second Edition

Culture

Un dimanche en France

Le dimanche est **un jour particulier** en France. **Les magasins** sont **fermés**, mais **les boulangeries redoublent** d'activité. Pendant toute **la matinée**, **chacun** s'y **rend pour acheter** une baguette bien fraîche ou **les pâtisseries** qui **seront** servies en dessert **le midi**. Les fleuristes **ne chôment** pas **non plus** car le dimanche, c'est le jour **des repas en famille** et **il serait impoli** d'arriver **les mains vides**…

Quand j'étais **enfant**, **je redoutais** les dimanches parce que **je savais** que ce jour-là, **je passerais** avec mes parents **plusieurs heures** à table **chez** l'une de mes **grands-mères**. **D'abord**, il y avait l'apéritif : pastis, porto ou kir pour **les grands**, jus d'orange pour les enfants et, pour **tout le monde**, **cacahuètes**, olives, petits cubes de **fromage** à **grignoter**.

Le repas **suivait** avec une entrée, (**des fruits de mer**, par exemple), un plat principal, (de **la viande** et **des légumes**, généralement), du fromage (obligatoirement !), de la salade (**presque toujours**) et, **vers quatre heures** de l'**après-midi**, lorsque **les estomacs** étaient complètement **pleins** : le dessert (**enfin** !).

Le dimanche **soir**, **bien sûr**, **personne n'avait envie** de **manger**. Il ne restait qu'à **aller se coucher en se disant** qu'on avait **sans doute perdu** sa **journée**.

Et pourtant… Ma maman est **aujourd'hui** grand-mère et les dimanches chez elle, avec **ma femme** et **mon fils**, **n'ont rien d'ennuyant**. **Nous mangeons** bien, **mais pas trop** et, dès le dessert terminé, **nous sortons nous promener** tous ensemble **au bord de la mer** ou en **forêt**. Le dimanche soir, quand je couche mon fils, je me dis que la journée a été magnifique. **Pourvu** qu'**il pense la même chose** !

---

le dimanche: Sunday
un jour particulier: a special day
les magasins (le magasin): stores
fermés (fermer): closed (to close)
les boulangeries (la boulangerie): bakeries
redoublent (redoubler): increase (to increase)
la matinée: morning
chacun: everyone
il y rend (y rendre): goes there (to go there)
pour acheter: to buy
les pâtisseries (la pâtisserie): pastries
(elles) seront (être): they will be (to be)
le midi: lunchtime, noon
ne chôment pas (chômer): are not idle (to be idle)
non plus: either
des repas en famille: family meals
il serait impoli: it would be rude
les mains vides: empty hands

un enfant: child
je redoutais (redouter): I dreaded (to dread)
je savais (savoir): I knew (to know)
je passerais (passer): I would spend (to spend)
plusieurs hueres: many hours
chez: at the home of
grand-mères: grandmothers
d'abord: first
les grands (le grand): adults (adult)
tout le monde: everybody
cacahuètes (la cacahuète): peanuts
fromage: cheese
grignoter: to snack

suivait (suivre): followed (to follow)
des fruits de mer: seafood
la viande: meat
des légumes (un légume): vegetables
presque toujours: almost always
vers quatre heures: around four o'clock
après-midi: afternoon
les estomacs... pleins: bellies ... full
enfin: at last

le soir: evening
bien sûr: of course
personne n'avait envie: no one wanted
manger: to eat
aller se coucher: to go to bed
en se disant: saying to oneself
sans doute perdu: no doubt lost
la journée: day

aujourd'hui: today, nowadays
ma femme: my wife
mon fils: my son
ils n'ont rien d'ennuyant: there's nothing boring about them
nous mangeons (manger): we eat (to eat)
mais pas trop: but not too much
nous sortons (sortir): we go out (to go out)
nous promener: we go for a walk
au bord de la mer: on the beach, seaside
la forêt: woods
pourvu: let's hope
il pense (penser): he thinks (to think)
la même chose: the same thing

La France et la religion

Officiellement, la France est **un état laïc, il est d'ailleurs interdit de porter des signes** religieux visibles dans les établissements scolaires. **Il existe cependant** une exception pour une région, c'est l'Alsace-Moselle. **En effet**, lors de la séparation **des pouvoirs** politique et religieux en 1905, **celle-ci n'était pas encore** française, mais **allemande**. C'est la raison du **traitement** de faveur dont **elle bénéficie**, l'état finance même certaines de **ses églises**.

De manière générale, si **on s'intéresse** aux religions que les Français pratiquent, **on se rend compte** que **le pays** est **non seulement** multiculturel, **mais aussi** multiconfessionnel. Ce qui **en fin de compte** est normal lorsqu'on **se souvient** du **passé** colonial de ce pays. **D'après** les statistiques de l'Institut français d'opinion publique 64% de Français sont catholiques, 27% se considèrent comme **athées**, 3% sont musulmans, 2,1% sont de confession protestante et 0,6% sont **juifs**.

Historiquement, la France est un pays catholique **tout au moins** après **les huit guerres** de religion qui l'**ont ravagée** durant le XVIème siècle. Cependant, après **la Deuxième Guerre Mondiale**, l'**engouement** pour la religion **chute** et l'**arrivée** massive d'immigrés issus des anciennes colonies françaises contribuent à diversifier le climat religieux du pays. **Il n'existe pas** de conflit entre les différentes religions et **chaque** Français a **le droit** de **pratiquer** la religion de son **choix** tout en respectant les droits religieux de ses compatriotes.

un état laïc: secular state, non religious state
il est d'ailleurs: it is moreover
interdit de (interdire): prohibited to (to prohibit)
porter: to wear
des signes (un signe): signs
il existe (exister): it exists (to exist)
cependant: however
en effet: indeed
des pouvoirs (un pouvoir): powers
celle-ci: the former, this one
n'était pas (être): wasn't (to be)
encore: still
allemande: German
traitement: treatment
elle bénéficie (bénéficier): she benefits (to benefit)
ses églises (une église): its churches

on s'intéresse (intéresser): one is interested (to be interested)
on se rend compte (se rendre compte): we realize (to realize)
le pays: the country
non seulement: not only
mais aussi: but also
en fin de compte: at the end
se souvient (se souvenir): remember (to remember)
passé: past
d'après: according to
athées (un athée): atheists
juifs (un Juif): Jewish

tout au moins: at the very least
les huit guerres (la guerre): the eight wars
ont ravagée (ravager): devastated (to devastate)
la Deuxième Guerre Mondiale: The Second World War
engouement: infatuation
chute (chuter): fall (to fall)
arrivée (arriver): the coming
il n'existe pas (exister): it doesn't exist (to exist)
chaque: each
le droit: the right
pratiquer: to practice
choix: choice

on pense (penser): we think (to think)
très fort: very hard
on peut (pouvoir): we can (can)
presque: nearly
sentir: smell
le parfum: scent, fragrance
sucré: sweet
la lavande: lavender
ravivée (reviver): revived (to revive)
par le soleil: by the sun
(il) offre (offrir): (it) offers (to offer)
les plus belles (beau): the most beautiful
étendues (une étendue): areas, stretches
parme: mauve

peintres (un peintre): painters
se sont recueillis (se recueillir): they reflected
   (to reflect)
ces lieux (un lieu): these places
capturer: to capture
au creux de: in the trough of
leur œuvre (une œuvre): their work
des couleurs (une couleur): colors
le vent: the wind
souffle (souffler): blows (to blow)
à travers: across
les champs (le champ): fields
nous entraine (entrainer): carries us away
   (to carry)
véritable: real
des sens (un sens): senses

depuis des millénaires (un millénaire): for
   thousands of years
dans un premier temps: first time
(elle) a fait: it has claimed (to claim)
des adeptes (un adepte): followers
parmi: among
nos plus vieux: our oldest
ancêtres (un ancêtre): ancestors

utilisée (utiliser): used (to use)
précieusement: very carefully
tout d'abord: at first, to begin with
durant: during
le bain: the bath
les linges (le linge): linens
elle sera utilisée (utiliser): it was used (to use)
les temps moyenâgeux: medieval times
renfermer: to contain
des vertus (une vertu): properties
calmantes (calmant): soothing
cicatrisantes (cicatrisant): healing

convoité (convoiter): coveted (to covet)
des composants (un composant): components
son parme (le parme): its mauve color
doux: soft
(ils) se retrouvent sur: it can be found in
les vaisselles (la vaisselle): bottles
vendues (vendre): sold (to sell)
font la joie: they delight
des potiers (un potier): potters
autres: other
maisons (une maison): houses

Parfum de nos enfances

Quand **on pense très fort** à la Provence, **on peut presque sentir le parfum sucré** de **la lavande ravivée par le soleil** méditerranéen. Le plateau de Valensole, en Drôme provençale, **offre les plus belles étendues parme** de lavande.

De très grands **peintres se sont** souvent **recueillis** sur **ces lieux** pour **capturer au creux de leur œuvre**, l'harmonie **des couleurs** offerte par la nature. Quand **le vent souffle à travers les champs**, le parfum **nous entraine** dans une **véritable** symphonie **des sens**.

La lavande, véritable mine d'exploitation provençale **depuis des millénaires** a **dans un premier temps fait des adeptes parmi nos plus vieux ancêtres**.

Utilisée précieusement tout d'abord par les Romains **durant le bain** et pour parfumer **les linges, elle sera utilisée** durant **les temps moyenâgeux** en tant que plante médicinale qui aurait la réputation de **renfermer des vertus calmantes**, antiseptiques, **cicatrisantes**... la lavande a toujours été un ingrédient suprême pour la beauté et l'hygiène.

Son parfum est **convoité** des savonniers, parfumeurs, créateurs d'ambiance régionaux et il reste un **des composants** de base de la parfumerie contemporaine. **Son parme doux** et sa forme atypique **se retrouvent sur les vaisselles vendues** dans les boutiques et **font la joie des potiers**, et **autres** décorateurs de **maisons** et de linges.

Il existe même du miel de lavande, et c'est un produit très recherché des gens de la région pour la douceur qu'il renferme. Ses étendues cultivées ou sauvages ont révélé les plus grands peintres provençaux.

La cueillette, autrefois réalisée à la faucille, a lieu en été entre le 15 juillet et le 15 août, dans les « baïassières » endroits où poussent les « baïasses » (nom provençal donné aux pieds de lavande) par des travailleurs saisonniers venant de toute la région et parfois même d'autres pays d'Europe.

La lavandiculture prit une grande place dans la vie des Provençaux. Si vous demandez aux cultivateurs de vous parler de lavande, ils vous diront d'abord de faire attention à ne pas confondre lavande et lavandin. La vraie lavande est l'espèce d'origine, elle se reproduit naturellement à l'état sauvage ou cultivé. On peut la reconnaitre à sa taille et sa couleur.

La distillerie de son essence offre un parfum plus fin, plus doux, et elle garde toutes ses vertus thérapeutiques sous forme d'huile essentielle. Le lavandin, lui, est déjà plus grossier par son aspect, plus long et aux bouts plus gros, sa couleur est plus « violette » que celle de la lavande, plutôt mauve. Le lavandin est stérile, il ne se reproduit pas naturellement et sa fabrication est d'origine industrielle. En effet il peut produire beaucoup plus d'essence que la vraie lavande. Son huile essentielle ne préserve aucune vertu et reste rarement utilisée en pharmacopée de nos jours. Son odeur est déjà plus « acre » et moins sucrée.

La lavande pure reste un produit très prisé à l'achat et demeure un véritable produit de luxe. Elle reste le produit de référence quand on parle de la Provence. C'est le parfum de nos enfances.

---

il existe (exister): there exists (to exist)
le miel: honey
recherché: much sought-after
des gens: by the people
la douceur: the sweetness
il renferme (renfermer): it holds (to hold)
ses étendues (une étendue): its areas
cultivées (cultiver): cultivated (to cultivate)
sauvages (sauvage): wild
(elles) ont révélé (révéler quelqu'un): they made famous (to make somebody famous)

la cueillette: harvesting, picking
autrefois: in the past
la faucille: the sickle
endroits (un endroit): the places
où ils poussent (pousser): where they grow (to grow)
donné (donner): given (to give)
aux pieds (un pied): to the plants
des travailleurs (un travailleur): workers
saisonniers (saisonnier): seasonal
venant (venir): coming (to come)
d'autres pays: from other countries

la vie: the life
si vous demandez (demander): if you ask (to ask)
vous parler: you speak
ils vous diront (dire): they will tell you (to tell)
d'abord: first of all
ne pas confondre: not to confuse
vraie (vrai): real
elle se reproduit (se reproduire): it reproduces (to reproduce)
cultivé (cultiver): cultivated (to cultivate
on peut (pouvoir): we can (can, to be able to)
sa taille (la taille): its size

plus fin: more subtle
elle garde (garder): it keeps (to keep)
ses vertus (une vertu): its properties
huile essentielle (une huile): essential oil
grossier: rough
aux bouts (un bout): ends
plutôt: rather
il ne se reproduit (se reproduire): it does not reproduce (to reproduce, to grow)
en effet: in fact
il peut produire: it can produce
(elle) ne préserve aucune (préserver): it preserves no (to preserve)
rarement: rarely, seldom
de nos jours: nowadays
moins: less
sucrée (sucré): sweet

prisé: valued
à l'achat: to buy
(il) demeure (demeurer): it remains (to remain)
on parle (parler): we talk (to talk)
nos enfances (une enfance): our childhood

Les marchés du Sénégal

Visiter les marchés est **sans doute le meilleur moyen** de **s'imprégner** de l'ambiance d'une ville. **N'hésitez pas** à **vous enfoncer** dans **les méandres** de leurs **étroites ruelles** et à **slalomer entre les étals**, **après avoir pris les** précautions d'usage **contre** les pickpockets. C'est sans doute aussi le meilleur moyen d'y **apprendre le marchandage**.

Les marchés de Dakar

A Dakar, **vous en découvrirez plusieurs**, avec **chacun** ses spécialités et son ambiance. Le plus classique est le grand marché Sandaga**,** au **croisement** de l'avenue Lamine Gueye et de l'avenue Emile Badiane. Un grand **bâtiment** de style néo-soudanais **abrite**, sur deux étages, tous **les produits alimentaires: légumes, viande, poisson.** L'avenue Emile Badiane **est bordée de** kiosques **tenus** en général **par** des « baol-baol » (originaires de la région de Diourbel) où **vous trouverez** surtout des appareils électriques, souvent **dernier cri:** hi-fi, télévision, vidéo, etc. Dans **les rues voisines**, beaucoup de boutiques de **tissus, vendus** à la pièce ou assemblés en **sacs, vêtements**…

Le plus touristique est le marché Kermel**,** petit marché **au cœur du vieux** Dakar, entre l'Avenue Sarrault et le port, qui abrite de **belles maisons coloniales**. Dans un très beau **bâtiment** de 1860, ravagé par **un incendie** en 1994, puis reconstruit en 1997, l'**on trouve** tous les produits alimentaires de type européen, **joliment présentés**. C'est **aux alentours** que **les vendeuses** de **fleurs** circulent **chargées de** bouquets, **à côté de** boutiques d'artisanat (**vannerie, sculpture sur bois, maroquinerie**) et de **magasins** modernes: **boucheries, épiceries**…

Le plus authentique est le marché Tilène, avenue Blaise Diagne, dans **le vieux quartier** de la Médina. A l'extérieur, des étals de fruits et légumes. A l'intérieur, tous les produits de consommation africaine : alimentation, épices, fruits, **bijoux**, tissus, **friperie**, **ustensiles de cuisine**…

Le plus éclectique est le marché du port, où les marchandises **proposées dépendent souvent** des arrrivages **des bateaux. On y trouve** de **la quincaillerie**, du matériel utilisé par **les pêcheurs (bottes, cirés, cordages, pesons)**, des appareils photos, des cigarettes…

Le plus exotique est le marché « Casamance », **situé sur le quai d'embarquement** pour Ziguinchor. On y trouve tous les produits du **sud** du **pays**, souvent difficiles à trouver **ailleurs: huile de palme, crevettes séchées, miel**, fruits et légumes.

Le plus **vestimentaire** est le marché aux **fripes, itinérant,** que l'on retoue à Gueule Tapée, Grand Mosquée, Front de terre: **des centaines** de **ballots** de **vêtements** et **chaussures** d'occasion, **à tous les prix**.

Enfin, **si vous êtes** en **brousse**, **ne manquez pas** les « lumas », les marchés **hebdomadaires**. Les habitants de tous les villages **avoisinants**, venus **en charrette, se rassemblent** pour **acheter, vendre, échanger, discuter**. Vous y trouverez des produits alimentaires et artisanaux de la région, du **bétail**, des vêtements, des ustensiles de cuisine… **Des gargotes** s'y **installent pour toute la journée.**

le vieux quartier: old district
bijoux (la bijou): jewels
une friperie: second hand clothes shop
ustensiles de cuisine: kitchenware

proposées (proposer): offered (to offer)
dépendent de: depend on (to depend)
souvent: often
des bateaux (un bateau): boats
on y trouve (trouver): we find (to find)
la quincaillerie: hardware
les pêcheurs (un pêcheur): fishermen
bottes (une botte): boots
cirés (un ciré): raincoats
cordages (un cordage): ropes
pesons (un peson): scales

situé sur: located on
le quai d'embarquement: loading dock
le sud: south
un pays: country
ailleurs: elsewhere
l'huile de palme (une huile): palm oil
des crevettes séchées (une crevette): dried shrimp
le miel: honey

vestimentaire: related to clothing
fripes (une fripe): second hand clothes
des centaines (une centaine): hundreds
ballots (un ballot): bundles
vêtements (un vêtement): clothes
chaussures (une chaussure): shoes
à tous les prix (un prix): at all prices

enfin: finally
si vous êtes (être): if you are (to be)
la brousse: the bush
(vous) ne manquez pas (rater): do not miss (to miss)
hebdomadaires (hebdomadaire): weekly
avoisinants (avoisinant): neighboring
en charrette: by cart
(ils) se rassemblent (se rassembler): they gather (to gather)
acheter: to buy
vendre: to sell
échanger: to exchange
discuter: to discuss
un bétail: cattle
des gargotes (une gargote): cheap restaurants
(elles) s'installent (s'installer): (they) settle (to settle)
pour toute la journée: for the whole day

il y a: there are
deux saisons (une saison): two seasons
une année: year
hivernage: winter
qui va de … à (aller de … à): that is going
  from … to (to go from … to)
le carême: Lent
qui commence (commencer): which starts
  (to start)
un mois: month
se terminer: it ends (to end)
donnent (donner): give (to give)
deux visages (un visage): two faces
une île: island
pendant: while, during
sec: dry
chaud: warm

sèche (sec): dry
laquelle: which
célèbrent (célébrer): celebrate (to celebrate)
fêtes religieuses: holidays
les Pâques: Easter
camper: camping
au bord de la mer: at the seaside
manger: eating
le mets: the dish
le crabe de terre: crab (of the ground) *this
  very specific crab does not live in the sea but
  at the seaside*

plusieurs: several
semaines (une semaine): weeks
rechercher: to look for
les meilleurs emplacements: the best spots
elles pourront installer (pouvoir): they will
  be able to install (to be able, can)
on parcourt (parcourir): we cover, we travel
  (to cover distance)
une plage: beach
on se dirige vers (se diriger): we make (our
  way) toward (to make toward)
repérer l'endroit: to check out a place
tentes (une tente): tents
les voitures (la voiture): cars
surtout: above all
la cuisson: the cooking
des repas (un repas): meals
il s'agit de (s'agir de): it is about (to be about)
une vie: a life
restent (rester): remain (to remain)
assez: rather
depuis: since
reçoivent (recevoir): welcome (to welcome)
ont pris la décision: have made the decision
des douches (une douche): showers
qui désirent (désirer): who desire (to desire)
un peu plus: a little bit more

Les mois du camping et du crabe

Il y a deux saisons dans l'année en Guadeloupe: l'**hivernage, qui va de** juillet **à** décembre et **le carême qui commence** au **mois** de janvier pour **se terminer** en juillet. Ces saisons **donnent deux visages** totalement différents à l'**île**: très humide et cyclonique **pendant** l'hivernage, très **sec** et **chaud** pendant le carême.

Le carême est la saison **sèche** pendant **laquelle** les catholiques **célèbrent** deux **fêtes religieuses** fondamentales: **les Pâques** et la Pentecôte. Sur l'île, ces deux fêtes religieuses sont l'occasion d'une célébration populaire (et pas vraiment religieuse): **camper** en famille **au bord de la mer** et **manger le mets** de saison, **le crabe de terre**.

Plusieurs semaines avant la période des vacances de Pâques (en avril) ou de Pentecôte (en mai), les familles commencent à **rechercher les meilleurs emplacements** où **elles pourront installer** leur campement. Ainsi, **on parcourt** des kilomètres de **plage** ou alors **on se dirige vers** sa plage habituelle pour y **repérer l'endroit** où l'on installera le nombre de **tentes** adéquat, **les voitures** et **surtout** tout le nécessaire pour **la cuisson des repas**. Pour le reste, **il s'agit** de camping et les conditions de **vie restent assez** difficiles. C'est pourquoi **depuis** deux ans, les municipalités de Guadeloupe qui **reçoivent** des campeurs **ont pris la décision** d'installer des toilettes ou **des douches** portables pour les familles **qui désirent un peu plus** de confort dans leur aventure.

Certaines plages de Guadeloupe, **comme** le Souffleur à Port-Louis, l'Anse à la Gourde à Saint-François ou la Perle à Deshaies **sont prises d'assaut** par les campeurs avant **le début** des vacances **car** elles sont très accessibles et **offrent** une végétation **accueillante** pour les campements. Elles sont **si réputées** pour leur tradition de camping, qu'elles sont même à **éviter** à cette période **lorsque** l'**on ne vient pas** camper. **En effet**, les campeurs y **prennent leurs aises**, y **mettent la musique**. C'est **une véritable vie qui se met en place en quelques jours** sur ces plages.

L'autre élément essentiel de cette période pour les Guadeloupéens est le crabe de terre.

Il vit exclusivement dans les mangroves et **les lieux humides**. Il est très **savoureux** car **il grandit** dans **les racines des arbres**. **Il se nourrit** de végétaux et de petites **crevettes** ou de petits **poissons** de mangrove. **Sa chaire** est très appréciée et **est utilisée** dans plusieurs mets caractéristiques de la saison: le **matété** ou le **calalou** de crabe.

Les Guadeloupéens **apprécient beaucoup** cet animal qu'**ils ne mangent** en général qu'en cette saison car c'est à cette période qu'il arrive à maturité. L'espèce est **protégée** le reste de l'année. **On ne doit alors pas l'« attraper » sous peine de mettre l'espèce en danger.**

comme: as, such as
(elles) sont prises d'assaut (être pris d'assaut): they are stormed (to be stormed)
le début: the beginning
car: because
(elles) offrent (offrir): (they) provide (to provide)
accueillante (accueillant): welcoming
si réputées (réputé): so famous
éviter: to avoid
lorsque: when
on ne vient pas (venir): we do not come (to come)
en effet: indeed
(ils) prennent leurs aises (prendre son aise): they stretched out (to stretch out)
(ils) mettent la musique (mettre): they put music on (to put)
une véritable vie: a real life
qui se met en place (se mettre en place): which is put in place (to be put in place)
en quelques jours: in few days

il vit (vivre): it lives (to live)
les lieux humides: humid places
savoureux: tasty
il grandit (grandir): it grows up (to grow up)
les racines (la racine): the roots
des arbres (un arbre): trees
il se nourrit (se nourrir): it feeds itself (to feed oneself)
crevettes (une crevette): shrimp
poissons (un poisson): fish
sa chaire (la chaire): its meat
est utilisée (être utilisé): it is used (to be used)
matété: crab pilaf
calalou: gumbo

apprécient (apprécier): like (to like)
beaucoup: very much
ils ne mangent... que (manger): they only eat (to eat)
protégée (protégé): protected
on ne doit pas (devoir): we must not (must, to have to)
alors: then
attraper: catch
sous peine de mettre l'espèce en danger: with the risk of endangering the species

Les vendanges

La vendange est **la récolte** du raisin **qui est destiné** à la fabrication du **vin**. **On utilise** ce terme en tant que verbe, « **vendanger** » (récolter le raisin sur **les pieds** de **vignes**), comme **nom**, « la vendange » (**pour désigner** la récolte), ou au pluriel pour **évoquer** la période de la récolte ; **on parle** alors du **temps**, ou de la période, « des vendanges ».

Les vendanges ont traditionnellement lieu en France **entre fin** août/début septembre et octobre **selon** les régions. **Les viticulteurs emploient des saisonniers** pour récolter les raisins. **La plupart du temps**, ce sont **des étudiants qui effectuent ces travaux** car cela leur procure un revenu intéressant sur un temps **très court**, tout en **les aidants** pour le financement de **leurs études**.

Auparavant, les viticulteurs **embauchaient** régulièrement des vendangeurs **au noir**. La réglementation actuelle en France **est devenue** très stricte et **a engendré** l'élaboration de **contrats de travail** spécifiques aux vendanges, permettant ainsi de limiter les fraudes et **les embauches** illégales de travailleurs. Ainsi, les viticulteurs emploient les vendangeurs pour **une durée** qui varie de 8 à 15 jours. **Ils signent** un « contrat vendanges », contrat saisonnier particulier **qui ne peut dépasser un mois**. Il est possible de **cumuler** ou d'**enchaîner** plusieurs contrats vendanges, mais la durée totale de tous les contrats **réunis ne peut excéder** deux mois. La durée de travail hebdomadaire varie selon les exploitations de 35 à 39 heures. Ce travail est **rémunéré** sur la base du Smic, **c'est-à-dire autour de** 8 euros de l'heure, (soit 50 à 60 euros nets pour **une journée**).

Le travail de base consiste à **couper les grappes** de raisin avec **un sécateur** et à les **déverser** dans **une grande hotte** où **sont stockés** les grains. Les hottes sont ensuite **vidées pour effectuer un tri** des grains, ce qui permet par exemple d'éliminer les grains **abîmés qui auraient pu être cueillis**. Le raisin est ensuite **amené** en **cuve** où **pourra commencer** le processus de vinification (macération du **moût** et fermentation alcoolique qui aura lieu sous l'action des levures qui transforment les sucres en alcool puis **mise en fût de chêne**).

Le travail de vendange peut être fait à **la main** (avec un sécateur), **mais également** par l'intermédiaire de machines spécifiques. **Dans ce cas,** la récolte **ne permet pas** une sélection des grappes aussi rigoureuse que celle effectuée avec la récolte manuelle, et **cela engendre** forcément une qualité **moindre** du vin car les grappes **qui seront cueillies** seront **plus ou moins mûres** et/ou plus ou moins abîmées.

Chaque méthode de vendanges **comporte pourtant** ses avantages et ses inconvénients. Avec une machine, on peut vendanger **aussi bien le jour que la nuit** et **réduire le coût** d'intervention du personnel **qui n'est pas négligeable.** C'est par **ailleurs** particulièrement intéressant pour vendanger le raisin blanc, plus fragile, qui sera récolté plus **frais** pendant la nuit. La durée d'une vendange effectuée à la machine est bien-sûr beaucoup **plus courte** qu'à la main. **En moyenne, il faudra** 2 heures pour vendanger un hectare **contre** 70 heures pour la **même** superficie à la main. Le coût de la vendange réalisée avec une machine est **à peu près de** 50% du coût de la vendange effectuée **manuellement.**

En revanche, avec une machine, il faut que la vigne soit **assez haute** car les grappes situées **à moins de** 30 cm du **sol ne seront pas** récoltées et les grains **sont** plus facilement **écrasés** que lorsqu'ils sont cueillis manuellement. La vendange manuelle est une méthode utilisée pour la production de vins de qualité supérieure et des vins effervescents, car **cela exige** une sélection très rigoureuse des **meilleures** grappes. **La cueillette** à la machine **n'atteint jamais** la précision d'une cueillette manuelle.

Enfin, quelle que soit la méthode utilisée, **il faut éviter** de vendanger pendant les heures les plus **chaudes** de la journée car cela peut **déclencher** une fermentation **précoce** du raisin **avant son transfert** dans la cave de vinification. Cela pourrait avoir des répercussions sur la qualité du produit final. En tant que vendangeur, faire les vendanges reste une expérience enrichissante et bien que cela nécessite une certaine résistance physique, **elle permet de faire de belles rencontres** et de se faire un salaire non négligeable dans **un laps de temps assez court.**

---

la main: hand
mais également: but also
dans ce cas: in this case
ne permet pas (permettre): does not allow (to allow)
cela engendre (engendrer): it generates (to generate)
moindre: lesser
qui seront cueillies (cueillir): that will be picked (to pick)
plus ou moins: more or less
mûres: mature

chaque: each
comporte (comporter): includes (to include)
pourtant: though
aussi bien … que: as well as
le jour: day
la nuit: night
réduire: to reduce
le coût: cost
qui n'est pas négligeable: that is not negligible
ailleurs: elsewhere
frais: fresh
plus courte: shorter
en moyenne: in average
il faudra (falloir): it will be necessary (to be necessary)
contre: against
même: same
à peu près de: approximatively
manuellement: by hand, manually

en revanche: on the other hand
assez haute (haut): rather high
à moins de: shorter than
le sol: ground
(elles) ne seront pas (être): (they) will not be (to be)
(ils) sont écrasés (écraser): (they) are crushed (to crush)
cela exige (exiger): it requires (to require)
la cueillette: picking, harvesting
meilleures: best
n'atteint jamais (atteindre): never reaches (to reach)

il faut éviter (falloir): it is necessary to avoid (to be necessary)
chaudes (chaud): warm
déclencher: to cause
précoce: early
avant son transfert: before its transfer
elle permet de faire: it allows to do
de belles rencontres (une rencontre): nice meetings, encounters
un laps de temps: period of time
assez court: rather short

Noël sur les marchés

Ah, la France et **ses marchés ! Qui n'a jamais entendu parler** de ces fameux marchés **hebdomadaires**, **où se vendent** pêle-mêle fruits, légumes, fromages, charcuteries, **poissons**, épices et **plats à emporter** ? Si ces marchés font **la joie** des visiteurs et de **mes grands-mères**, c'est un tout autre genre de marché que **j'apprécie**. Des marchés qu'**on attend toute l'année**, car **ils n'ont lieu qu'**en décembre: les marchés de Noël.

Ouverts tous les jours en décembre, les marchés de Noël sont originaires d'**Allemagne** et d'Alsace et **remontent au** XIVème siècle. **Aujourd'hui**, **ils se sont répandus** dans toute l'Europe, **depuis les** grandes **villes jusqu'à** certains villages de **campagne**. Pourquoi **autant** de succès ? **Parce que** ces marchés **mêlen**t avec **brio** traditions, ambiance de **fête** et **joies** de l'**hiver**.

Semblant sortir tout droit d'une carte postale, les marchés de Noël ressemblent à de petits villages. Les chalets **en bois se serrent les uns contre les autres**, comme pour **se protéger** du **froid**. **Les guirlandes**, **lumières**, **sapins** et décorations **contribuent à donner** un **air féerique** à la scène. **Promenez-vous** dans **les allées**… **Sentez-vous** cette **bonne odeur** ? Ce sont **des gaufres** accompagnées de **vin chaud** à **la cannelle**, une spécialité de ces marchés. **Plus loin**, **vous trouverez** probablement des crêpes ou d'autres pâtisseries, **des châtaignes grillées** ou des plats bien hivernaux, comme la **tartiflette**.

Mais **vous n'êtes pas venus** seulement pour **manger**, n'est-ce pas ? **Avancez encore** un peu et **regardez autour de** vous. **Les marchands**, bien **emmitouflés** dans leurs **manteaux**, bonnets et **mitaines**, n'attendent que vous. **Les étals débordent** d'artisanats locaux et exotiques: **santons** provençaux, poteries, **bougies**, **bijoux** originaux, ponchos péruviens, sculptures et **bibelots** divers, décorations de Noël, jouets traditionnels **en bois**…

Avec un peu de chance, **vous pourriez même voir** les artisans **à l'œuvre**, sculptant **un morceau de bois** ou **tricotant** une paire de **moufles**. Il devient souvent difficile de **choisir ses cadeaux**, tant le choix est grand !

Si vous êtes fatigués de vous promener, **venez** donc **profiter** des spectacles organisés. **Emmenez vos enfants** admirer **la crèche** grandeur nature ou **faites leur faire un tour de manège**. Ici, **tout est prévu** pour faire **le bonheur** des petits et des grands.

Envie de le voir pour de vrai ? Les marchés de Strasbourg, d'Alsace, de Paris et de Provence sont parmi les plus réputés de France. En Europe, **essayez donc** celui d'Aix-la-Chapelle en Allemagne ou de Vienne en Autriche. Et pour nos **amis** nord-américains, tout a été prévu à Québec, pour les Marchés de Noël Joliette-Lanaudière. **Alors amusez-vous bien** !

---

vous n'êtes pas venus (venir): you did not come (to come)

manger: to eat

avancez encore un peu (avancer): move forward a little more (to move forward)

(vous) regardez (regarder): look (to look at)

autour de: around

les marchands (le marchand): stallholders

emmitouflés (émmitouflé): wrapped

manteaux (un manteau): coats

mitaines (une mitaine): fingerless gloves

les étals (le étal): stalls

débordent (déborder): overflow (to overflow)

santons: *Christmas nativity figurines*

bougies (une bougie): candles

bijoux (un bijou): jewelry

bibelots (un bibelot): ornaments

en bois: in wood

vous pourriez même (pouvoir): you could even (can)

voir: see

à l'œuvre: at work

un morceau de bois: a piece of wood

tricotant (tricoter): knitting (to knit)

moufles (une moufle): mittens

choisir: to choose

ses cadeaux (un cadeau): one's gifts

si vous êtes fatigués de vous promener: if you are tired of walking

(vous) venez (venir): come (to come)

profiter de: to take advantage of

(vous) emmenez (emmener): bring (to bring)

vos enfants (un enfant): your children

la crèche: creche, manger

(vous) faites leur faire un tour de manège: have them take a ride on a carousel

tout est prévu (prévoir): everything is scheduled (to schedule)

le bonheur: happiness

envie de le voir pour de vrai (une envie): would you like to see it for real

(vous) essayez (essayer): try (to try)

donc: so, therefore, then

des amis (un ami): friends

Alors amusez-vous bien ! (s'amuser): Enjoy! (to enjoy)

La légendaire impolitesse

À l'étranger, les Français **ont encore** une image de personnes **un peu rustres** avec des clichés **datant** de l'**époque** de **la Deuxième Guerre mondiale**. **Afin de sortir** la France de ce stéréotype, **il faut prendre plusieurs faits** en considération.

Les Français **attachent** énormément d'importance à l'Histoire et la Culture de leur **pays** qui sont d'une grande richesse. C'est un pays très ancien, avec une Histoire **remplie de conquêtes**, de **découvertes** et **régi** par **des rois** influents. Avec la gastronomie, cela **fait partie de** la grande **fierté** française. Certains étrangers arrivent en France en pays « **conquis** » et **peuvent avoir** une attitude **méprisante vis-à-vis** d'un pays **qu'ils ne comprennent pas** toujours, car culturellement très différent. Ce que l'**on peut prendre** comme de l'impolitesse peut être une simple réaction de fierté vis-à-vis de ce qui est **non compris** et d'une histoire qui n'est pas considérée comme importante. La France **ne se limite pas** à Paris et ses restaurants ou à la Côte d'Azur. Le Français y est **très attaché**, et les étrangers ne peuvent pas toujours comprendre ce concept, **qui peut parfois engendrer des quiproquos**.

Comme dans **chaque** pays étranger, tout dépend **également** de **la façon** dont le touriste **aborde sa visite** sur le territoire. **Aller dans** un pays **sans chercher** à **comprendre** les coutumes locales **exposera** le visiteur à **des réticences** de la part du **peuple hôte**, quel qu'il soit. La France **ne déroge pas** à cette **règle**.

Vis-à-vis des personnes anglophones, les Français **ont souvent subi des moqueries** sur leur accent lorsqu'**ils parlent** anglais. Il est donc peu **étonnant** que le Français soit ensuite réticent à s'**exprimer** dans cette langue quand il est sujet à moqueries. Pourtant, **si vous abordez** une personne dans la rue et lui demandez de **façon polie,** en français, s'il peut **vous renseigner** en anglais, **il est fort à parier qu'il cherchera** à vous **aider** du **mieux** qu'il peut. Par contre, si vous vous exprimez de façon un peu brusque sans faire un minimum d'effort et **en considérant** que la personne à qui vous **vous adressez parlera forcément** anglais, **ne vous étonnez pas** de vous **voir répondre** de la même façon.

Les Français **enfin** sont considérés comme étant **râleurs** et **exigeants**. Comme dans tous les peuples, **on ne peut faire** d'une minorité une généralité ; **au sein** des Français comme de toutes les autres nationalités, il y a de nombreuses personnalités différentes, **des gens charmants,** des idiots, des râleurs, **des gentils** et **des méchants**…, c'est ce qui fait la variété et l'**intérêt** d'une population. **Ne dit-on pas** qu' « **il faut de tout pour faire** un **Monde** » ?

---

ont souvent subi (subir): have often undergone (to undergo)
des moqueries (une moquerie): some mockeries
ils parlent (parler): they talk (to talk)
étonnant (étonner): surprising (to surprise)
exprimer (exprimer): express (to express)
si vous abordez (aborder): if you approach (to approach)
façon polie: with courtesy
vous renseigner (renseigner): to inform you (to inform)
il est fort à parier: the chances are
qu'il cherchera (chercher): he will try to (to try)
aider: to help
mieux: best way
en considérant (considérer): considering (to consider)
vous adressez (s'adresser): speak to (to speak)
parlera forcément (parler): will inevitably speak (to speak)
ne vous étonnez pas (étonner): do not be surprised (to surprise)
voir répondre (répondre): being answered (to answer)

enfin: finally
râleur: grouchy
exigeants: demanding
on ne peut faire (faire): we can't make (to make)
au sein: among
des gens charmants: charming people
des gentils: kind (people)
des méchants: malicious, mean (people)
intérêt: interest
ne dit-on pas (dire): don't we say (to say)
il faut de tout (falloir): we need all (types) (to need)
pour faire: to make
un monde: world

CULTURE NOTE Truth is, there are no more rude people in Paris than in any other major city in the world. Rules of what is polite and what is rude are, by essence, very culture-specific. And as guests, we shouldn't expect our hosts to make the effort to adapt to our rules. If we make no effort to speak their language, or if we criticize the way they do things or don't show respect for their culture, we can't blame them for telling us off!

So make an effort to learn the basics of French (hello, please, thank you, excuse me, can you help me, good-bye), and people will be so flattered that you try that they might switch to English to make it easier for you. We can't guarantee that you won't encounter rude people on your travels. But if you follow the same simple rules of humble and responsible travel in France as you would in any other country, you will be pleased to find people who are happy to help and honored to have crossed your path.

Francophonie canadienne

Le Canada est **un pays bilingue** et près de 6,5 millions de Canadiens sont francophones. **Ils vivent** principalement dans la province de Québec, mais **on retrouve** aussi des populations francophones dans les provinces du **Nord** et les provinces **qui sont encore appelées** « provinces maritimes » du Canada.

Les populations francophones **avaient du mal** à **s'imposer** dans un pays en majorité anglophone, mais **depuis les années soixante** on observe une tendance inverse. **Les pouvoirs** publics **qui comprennent** l'intérêt à préserver la culture francophone **mettent en place** des programmes qui **ont pour** but **de mieux la faire connaître non seulement** à l'intérieur, **mais aussi** à l'extérieur du pays.

Depuis 1974, le français est **désormais** la langue officielle du Québec, bien que l'anglais reste la langue officielle du reste du pays. Les Canadiens francophones sont **les héritiers** d'une culture très riche de leurs **aïeuls originaires** de France et **n'hésitent pas** la faire connaître **à tous ceux qui le souhaitent.** L'art, la musique, la gastronomie **ne représentent** que certains aspects de cette culture.

Comme leurs ancêtres, beaucoup de Canadiens francophones **prennent au petit-déjeuner** du café ou du thé avec un croissant. **Ils aiment** aussi des sandwichs **faits** avec des baguettes de **pain,** du **fromage** et du **jambon.** Parmi les spécialités culinaires que les Canadiens francophones aiment, **on peut aussi citer** la soupe de **pois** et **le ragoût de boulettes.** Dans **la rue**, les vendeurs **proposent** la poutine. Ce sont **des pommes frites arrosées** de sauce.

Cette émancipation culturelle et linguistique **ne se passe pas** sans **retombées** sensibles, un mouvement séparatiste qui **exige** l'indépendance du Québec **vis-à-vis** du reste du Canada est **né dans** les années soixante-dix et **malgré** quelques **échecs** politiques **cuisants,** **il continue** d'exister, car la préoccupation essentielle de beaucoup de Canadiens francophones est la préservation de la culture et la langue française.

La mode, reflet de la culture

Qui ne s'est jamais extasié devant l'élégance **des femmes** françaises, devant leur allure sobre et raffinée ou devant cette petite touche d'excentricité que l'**on retrouve** dans les détails d'**une chaussure** ou d'**une écharpe savamment disposée sur** une petite **robe** toute simple? **La mode** est indissociable de la culture française, et à **chaque saison** les regards **se tournent vers** Paris où les grands **couturiers recréent** les tendances **qu'imiteront** avec **plus ou moins** de succès toutes les femmes du **monde**.

Des belles de l'Antiquité aux **égéries** de **notre époque**, les femmes, et **dorénavant les hommes**, **cherchent à confirmer** leur **pouvoir** de séduction ou **parfois même** l'appartenance à leur génération ou à un groupe particulier, en adoptant un style **vestimentaire qui les définit** et dont **ils peuvent être fiers**. Au XVIIIème **siècle**, **ce sont plutôt** les hiérarchies sociales qui étaient **mises en scène** avec excès et parfois même ostentation par le biais du costume. De **nos jours**, même si c'est l'individualisme qui prime, la mode demeure l'expression de conventions sociales auxquelles **nous adhérons** tous plus ou moins.

En France, Coco Chanel a été l'une des premières **créatrices de mode**. S'inspirant **des lignes dépouillées** des costumes masculins et **mettant** le corset au **rancart**, elle a **libéré le corps** de la femme si longtemps emprisonné, en créant un style élégant et épuré. Des couturiers comme Cacharel, Yves St-Laurent, Dior et Jean-Paul Gaultier **ont conquis** la seconde **moitié du vingtième** siècle en élevant **la confection** au rang de l'art, et **en faisant** des mannequins qui présentent leurs modèles des célébrités à **part entière**.

Quelques exceptions cependant : le jeans - né du bleu de **travail** porté par **les fermiers** et **les ouvriers** américains vers 1870 - le t-shirt et **le col roulé** représentent le style décontracté **qui domine** depuis **la fin des années cinquante** et échappe à tous les diktats de la mode, que **ceux-ci viennent** de Paris ou d'**ailleurs**.

---

qui ne s'est jamais: who has never
extasié (s'extasier): been raptured by (to be raptured, to rave about)
des femmes (une femme): women
on retrouve (retrouver): we could find (to find)
une chaussure: a shoe
une écharpe: a scarf
savamment: cleverly
disposée sur (disposer): arranged on (to arrange)
une robe: dress
la mode: fashion
chaque saison: each season
se tournent (se tourner): turn to (to turn)
vers: toward
des couturiers: fashion designers
recréent (recréer): recreate (to recreate)
qu'imiteront (imiter): that will be imitated (to imitate)
plus ou moins: more or less
un monde: world

des belles: beautiful (women)
égéries (une égérie): muses
notre époque: our time
dorénavant: from now on
les hommes (le homme): men
cherchent à confirmer (confirmer): try to confirm (to confirm)
pouvoir: power
parfois même: sometimes even
vestimentaire: way of dressing
les définit (définir): define them (to define)
ils peuvent (pouvoir): they can (can)
être fiers: be proud of
un siècle: century
ce sont plutôt: it is rather
mises en scène: staging
nos jours: these days
nous adhérons (adhérer): we adhere (to adhere)

créatrices de mode: fashion designer
des lignes dépouillées: simplified style
mettant (mettre): by putting (to put)
rancart: aside
libéré (libérer): free (to free)
le corps: the body
ont conquis (conquérir): have conquered (to conquer)
moitié du: half of
vingtième: twentieth
la confection: the clothing industry
en faisant (faire): by doing (to do)
part entière: fully

travail: work
les fermiers (le fermier): farmers
les ouvriers (le ouvrier): workers
le col roulé: the turtleneck
qui domine (dominer): that dominate (to dominate)
la fin: the end
des années cinquante: the fifties
ceux-ci viennent: they come from
ailleurs: elsewhere

Évaluez votre compréhension

Un dimanche en France, page 4

1. What shops might you visit on a Sunday in France?

2. What is the typical activity and destination on this day or in this story?

3. List some of the food enjoyed on this day.

Les marchés du Sénégal, page 8

1. In what city and what setting will you find the most touristy market?

2. Where will you find dried shrimp, palm oil, and honey?

3. Describe *les lumas*. What kind of business is typically conducted here?

Parfum de nos enfances, page 6

1. When and for what purpose was lavender first used?

2. When is the lavender harvest?

3. What are some characteristics of the "real" lavender?

Les mois du camping et du crabe, page 10

1. What was added to the campgrounds to add more comfort?

2. Where does *le crabe de terre* live? What does it eat?

3. Why do the people of Guadeloupe catch and eat this crab only one season per year?

Test your comprehension

Les vendanges, page 12

1. When are the *vendanges*?

2. Who do the winemakers hire to do the work?

3. What are some of the hiring rules for seasonal workers?

4. What are some of the advantages of harvesting with a machine?

Francophonie canadienne, page 18

1. When did French become the official language of Quebec?

2. What typical French food can you buy from street vendors?

Noël sur les marchés, page 14

1. Where did the markets originate?

2. What kind of food or drink might you enjoy at the markets?

3. What gifts might you find?

La mode, reflet de la culture, page 19

1. Who was one of the first fashion designers in France?

2. What is she known for creating or doing?

Voyages

La grande et la merveilleuse

La Normadie est une région tellement unique en son genre que **vous trouverez** énormément de locutions et expressions dans la langue française **qui lui sont consacrées**. **L'une d'entre elles** est **la suivante** : « Réponse normande ». **On qualifie** une réponse de normande lorsque la personne **qui l'a donnée** a **employé** des termes ambigus et **il faut dire** que cette expression est tout à l'image de la région **elle-même**.

La Normandie est une région qui est **née** et s'est développée grâce aux **guerres** interminables et très **sanglantes** qui l'**ont hantée**, mais paradoxalement, c'est aussi celle qui **a contribué** énormément à l'enrichissement littéraire et culturelle tant de la France que de l'Angleterre. Il est impossible de faire **le décompte** de poètes **célèbres**, tant dans le passé qu'au présent, qui étaient et sont d'origine normande. De même que l'**on compte** une quantité innombrable de **mots** dans la langue anglaise actuelle qui ont une origine normande.

Outre son passé houleux et sa culture très riche, la Normandie est aussi célèbre en France et de part **le monde** pour ses merveilles gastronomiques incomparables. **Des boissons telles que le calvados**, le cidre **ont conquis** le monde entier, il en est de même pour **des mets** tels que le soufflé de **crevettes**, **les galettes** à la pâte d'**amande**, **le gâteau de lait** ou la confiture de lait (création **des moines** normands).

En plus des plages merveilleuses **qui feront sans aucun doute le bonheur** de beaucoup de touristes, la Normandie met aussi à votre disposition des sites historiques et architecturaux **à couper le souffle**. Le seul Mont Saint-Michel **éblouira** et **ravira** tous **ceux qui auront pris la peine** de s'y **rendre**. Cet **îlot** sur lequel **se dresse fièrement** l'abbaye du mont Saint-Michel est classé monument historique sur la liste du patrimoine de l'UNESCO **depuis** 1979.

Les pâtisseries de Paris

Paris, la capitale française, **regorge de plaisirs nombreux** et éclectiques. Mais il en est un dont personne **ne voudrait se priver** : celui qui consiste **à humer** le parfum **envoûtant** de **beurre qui émane des boulangeries** et des pâtisseries.

Il est facile de trouver de fabuleux croissants à Paris et bien **qu'ils semblent** tout aussi délicieux les uns que les autres, **les meilleurs** se trouvent *Au Levain du Marais*. Les *palmiers* en forme de **têtes d'éléphants** et **fabriqués à partir d'une légère pâte feuilletée** sont aussi une pure merveille. **Un truc de connaisseur : choisir** les plus **foncés** dont **le dessus** est bien caramélisé.

Le **célèbre** *gâteau opéra*, est une pâtisserie française **parmi les plus appréciées**. C'est chez *Dalloyau* que l'**on associe**, pour **constituer** ce délice, une pâte délicate à du café, le tout dans **un enrobage** de chocolat noir.

Les meilleures glaces de la capitale sont **amoureusement** concoctées au *Berthillon*. **Ne désespérez pas si la file d'attente semble interminable**, ou si c'est **jour de fermeture**, il y a aux **alentours** de nombreuses petites **échoppes qui proposent également** des glaces **bien fondantes**.

C'est au *Blé Sucré* que l'on trouve les meilleures *madeleines*. Ces petits **gâteaux** tout simples ont fait les délices du mélancolique **écrivain** Marcel Proust. **Que vous les préfériez** telles quelles ou **légèrement trempées dans** votre **thé** ou votre café, **elles constituent un goûter parfait** en **fin d'après-midi**.

Enfin, **on déniche** les *financiers* les plus délicieux, **ces gâteaux spongieux** fabriqués **à partir de farine** d'amandes, chez *Éric Kayser*.

Vous planifiez un voyage en France **au printemps ? Songez alors**, tout comme les Français, à dénicher **le pain le plus savoureux grâce à** leur traditionnel *Grand Prix de la Baguette*, **remis** au mois de mars !

(elle) regorge de: (it) is packed with
plaisirs nombreux: numerous pleasures
(on) ne voudrait (vouloir): we do not want (to want)
se priver: to deprive onself
à humer: to smell
envoûtant: captivating
le beurre: butter
qui émane: that comes from
des boulangeries (une boulangerie): bakeries

il est facile de trouver: it is easy to find
qu'ils semblent: they look like
les meilleurs: the best
des têtes d'éléphants: elephants ears
fabriqués: made
à partir de: from
une légère pâte feuilletée: light puff pastry
un truc de connaisseur: a helpful tip
choisir: to choose
foncés: brown
le dessus: top

célèbre: famous
parmi: among
les plus appréciées: the most appreciated
on associe (associer): we associate (to associate)
constituer: to realize
un enrobage: coating

les meilleures glaces (la glace): best ice-cream
amoureusement: with love
ne désespérez pas: do not despair
si la file d'attente: if the waiting line
semble (sembler): seems (to seem)
interminable: endless
le jour de fermeture: closing day
aux alentours: around, in the neighborhood
échoppes (une échoppe): shops
qui proposent (proposer): that offer (to offer)
également: also
bien fondantes: which melts in your mouth

gâteaux (un gâteau): cakes
un écrivain: writer
vous les préfériez: you would rather like it
légèrement: lightly
trempées dans: dipped in
le thé: tea
elles constituent: they are
un goûter parfait: a perfect snack
fin d'après-midi: late afternoon

on déniche (dénicher): we track down (to track down)
ces gâteaux spongieux: sponge cakes
à partir de: from
la farine: flour
amandes (une amande): almonds

vous planifiez (planifier): you schedule (to schedule)
au printemps: at springtime
songez alors: think then (*like the French*)
le pain: bread
le plus savoureux: the tastiest
grâce à: thanks to
remis: given

Vocabulary	
sans égale (égal): unrivaled	
elle emprunte (emprunter): it borrows (to borrow)	
mélanges (un mélange): blends, mixtures	
au fil du temps: as time goes by	
bordée par (border): lined by (to line)	
les eaux (l'eau): waters	
le fleuve: river	
un cours d'eau: waterway	
ayant (avoir): having (to have)	
jadis: in bygone days	
ouvert (ouvrir): opened (to open)	
fondée (fonder): founded (to found)	
devint (devenir): became (to become)	
le poste: station	
fourrures (une fourrure): furs	
ce n'est qu': it was only in	
est cédée (céder): was given away (to give away)	
(elle) tombe (tomber): it falls (to fall)	
elle accueillera (accueillir): it will take in (to take in)	
plus tard: later	
vagues (une vague): waves	
qui contribueront (contribuer): who will contribute (to contribute)	
façonner: to shape	
un visage: face, aspect	

survolant (survoler): flying over (to fly over)
une île: the island
on peut (pouvoir): we can (can, be able to)
aussitôt: right away
apercevoir to catch sight of
la vie: life
une colline: hill
la verdure: greenery
résister: to resist, to hold out against
aujourd'hui: today
un poumon: lung
en plein cœur de: right in the heart of
un hiver: winter
les sentiers (le sentier): footpaths
à travers: through, across
la forêt: forest
escalader: to climb
décrocher: to get
saisissante (saisissant): striking
des gratte-ciels (un grate-ciel): skyscrapers
une toile de fond: backdrop
l'étendue: area
montérégiennes: "Montrealese," of Montreal
au loin: in the distance
(ils) viennent (venir): they come (to come)
découper: to cut out

marquants (marquant): striking, significant
il demeure (demeurer): it remains (to remain)
éclatant: spectacular
(ils) cohabitent (cohabiter): they cohabit (to cohabit)
des bâtiments (un bâtiment): buildings
on y découvre (découvrir): you find there (to find)
des églises (une église): churches
des immeubles: a block of apartments
au pied de: at the foot of
verre: glass

Le visage unique de Montréal

Montréal est une ville **sans égale** en Amérique du Nord. **Elle emprunte** son charme et son originalité aux nombreux **mélanges** dont elle a été l'objet **au fil du temps. Bordée par les eaux** du **fleuve** Saint-Laurent, principal **cours d'eau ayant jadis ouvert** le continent aux explorateurs, elle fut **fondée** dès 1642 par les Français et **devint le** principal **poste** de commerce de **fourrures** de la colonie. **Ce n'est qu'**en 1760 que la ville **est cédée** aux armées britanniques et **tombe** sous la domination anglaise. **Elle accueillera plus tard** de nombreuses **vagues** d'immigration internationales **qui contribueront** à **façonner** son **visage** multiculturel.

En **survolant l'île** de Montréal, **on peut aussitôt apercevoir** le Mont Royal, élément central de **la vie** montréalaise. Cette **colline** de **verdure** a su **résister** à l'urbanisation et constitue **aujourd'hui un** immense **poumon en plein cœur** de la ville. Été comme **hiver**, on peut y explorer **les** nombreux **sentiers à travers la forêt, escalader** son sommet pour y **décrocher** une vue **saisissante des gratte-ciels** du centre-ville. On y admire, en **toile de fond, l'étendue** des grands espaces de la vallée du Saint-Laurent et des collines **montérégiennes** qui **au loin, viennent découper** l'horizon.

Un des caractères **marquants** de la ville **demeure** encore le contraste **éclatant** par lequel **cohabitent bâtiments** anciens et architecture moderne. **On y découvre des églises, des immeubles** centenaires **au pied** des gratte-ciels de **verre**.

Le centre-ville a tout d'une ville nord-américaine, avec son asphalte et son **béton**, sa circulation automobile, ses boutiques **branchées**, ses **tours de bureaux** et **le fourmillement agité** de ses **citadins**. Montréal **jouit d'un** important **réseau** de tunnels souterrains **qui permettent** d'**accéder** à des kilomètres de boutiques et de **magasins** sans avoir à **braver le froid pendant les** longs **mois** d'hiver.

Montréal est également une ville **bouillonnante** et festive, surtout en période **estivale**, car elle est **l'hôte** de **plusieurs** événements internationaux: le Festival de Jazz, les Francofolies, le Festival Juste Pour Rire, et le Festival des Films du monde, pour n'en **nommer** qu'**une poignée**. Sa réputation de ville culturelle **n'est plus** à **faire**. Avec ses nombreuses productions cinématographiques, ses **musées**, ses expositions et son **nouveau** Quartier des Spectacles, elle constitue un terreau fertile pour l'expression du **génie** artistique québécois.

Même l'hiver il est possible de profiter des activités de **la** belle **saison blanche** avec le Festival Montréal en Lumières, l'Igloofest, la Fête des Neiges, ou les nombreux sports d'hiver sur le Mont-Royal. **À ne pas manquer**: l'île Ste-Hélène, le Jardin Botanique, le Stade Olympique et le Biodôme.

Bien que Montréal soit aujourd'hui francophone à 80%, les habitants y **parlent** généralement les deux **langues officielles. Au fil du temps**, son caractère international et cosmopolite a su **gagner** du terrain, ce qui **se reflète** également dans sa gastronomie. **Que ce soit** dans le Quartier chinois, la Petite Italie, ou le Plateau Mont-Royal, on peut y dénicher des cafés branchés et des restaurants **qui proposent** des cuisines des quatre **coins du monde**.

Montréal **nous offre** ainsi **un milieu** riche en histoire, une culture distincte, bouillonnante et **audacieuse**, **qui recèle** de **trésors** et qui **sauront plaire** à **chacun**, peu importe **leur âge. Si vous venez** à Montréal, vous apprécierez également le contact avec les Montréalais, **reconnus pour** leur **accueil** et leur **ouverture d'esprit. Ils vouent** un **amour fidèle** à leur ville et à leur culture, qu'**ils adorent partager** avec les étrangers.

un béton: concrete
branchés (branché): trendy
tours de bureaux: office towers
le fourmillement: swarm
agité: hectic
citadins (un citadin): city-dwellers
jouit (jouir): enjoys (to enjoy)
un réseau: network
qui permettent (permettre): which make it possible (to make it possible)
accéder: to access
magasins (un magasin): shops
braver: to brave
le froid: cold
pendant: during
les mois (un mois): months

bouillonnante (bouillonnant): bubbling
estivale (estival): summer
l'hôte: host
plusieurs: several
nommer: to name
une poignée: handful
ne... plus: no longer
faire: to make
musées (un musée): museums
nouveau: new
un génie: genius

la saison: season
blanche (blanc): white
à ne pas manquer: not to be missed

bien que: although
(ils) parlent (parler): they speak (to speak)
langues officielles: official languages
au fil du temps: as time goes by
gagner: gain
(il) se reflète (se refléter): it is reflected (to be reflected)
que ce soit: whether it is
qui proposent (proposer): that offer (to offer)
coins du monde: corners of the world

nous offre (offrir): offers us (to offer)
un milieu: environment
audacieuse (audacieux): bold
qui recèle (recéler): which holds (to hold)
trésors (un trésor): treasures
qui sauront (savoir): that will know how to (to know how to)
plaire: to please
chacun: everyone
leur âge: their age
si vous venez (venir): if you come (to come)
reconnus pour: famous for
un accueil: welcome
ouverture d'esprit: open-mindedness.
ils vouent (vouer): they give (to give)
un amour: love
fidèle: faithful
ils adorent (adorer): they love (to love)
partager: to share

Des îles pleines de richesses

Il existe en Amérique du **Sud un pays** où le français est la **langue officielle**, où l'Euro est **la monnaie** officielle et où le président **s'appelle** Nicolas Sarkozy. Ses **voisins** sont le Surinam à l'ouest et le Brésil à l'est. **Il se situe au milieu** de ces deux pays et **il** en **partage les paysages** très spécifiques.

Quel est ce pays ?

Et oui, c'est la Guyane (française, bien sûr). Le continent américain **compte** trois départements français d'**Outre-Mer, c'est-à-dire** trois régions administratives de France, à **plus de** 7 000 kms de distance: la Guadeloupe, la Guyane française et la Martinique.

La Guyane, **devenue** française en 1503, est le plus **étonnant** des départements français d'Amérique car il ne correspond pas au « **soleil, plage** et rhum », associé aux **deux autres**. Cet environnement **si** particulier est **composé de la forêt** tropicale présentae sur 96% du territoire et de **huit ou neuf fleuves qui le traversent, dont** le Maroni, l'Oyapock et le Sinamary. La Guyane **étonne aussi** par ses très nombreuses **espèces** d'**animaux** rares ou **en voie de disparition** et ses populations très diverses.

Mais comment ce **lointain** pays est-il devenu français? **Repérée** par Christophe Colomb, **lors** d'un voyage en 1498, **il trouva** dans les paysages au **vert d'émeraude**, de très nombreuses populations amérindiennes, dont **beaucoup** y **vivent encore**. Peuplée dès 1503 par les Français, la Guyane devient en 1792 **un bagne**, où étaient exilés les criminels et les ennemis politiques français et ce **jusqu'**en 1946.

Les Guyanais d'**aujourd'hui** sont un peuple aux origines très diverses, ceci **grâce à** l'histoire **mouvementée** du pays :

Il y a une majorité de « Créoles » descendants d'esclaves ou d'Africains arrivés après l'**esclavage qui forment** environ 50% de la population, 14% sont des Européens, 12% des Amérindiens de diverses tribus comme les Arawaks et les Ka'linas. Les 28% **restants** sont composés d'Asiatiques comme les H'Mongs venus de Chine, du Laos ou du Vietnam, de Libanais, d'Indiens **mais aussi** d'une très **forte** immigration du Brésil et du Surinam.

Cette population de 200 000 habitants qui **augmente** très **vite**, **vit** dans **les** trois grandes **villes** du pays : Cayenne, Kourou et Saint-Laurent du Maroni, mais a aussi développé **une vie autour** des fleuves.

La Guyane est un pays **qui regorge** d'**atouts** et d'activités :

A Kourou **se trouve** le Centre Spatial **d'où est lancée la fusée** Ariane, qui **transporte** de nombreux satellites européens dans l'espace.

Au **mois** de **janvier**, de **février** et **parfois** jusqu'en **mars**, les visiteurs **peuvent** vivre avec les Guyanais au rythme du carnaval, qui est un événement culturel très important où **se mêlent** les traditions française, africaine et brésilienne. Le carnaval guyanais est très **célèbre** pour ses « Touloulous ». Ce sont **des femmes** déguisées entièrement et qui ne peuvent être **reconnues par personne** et **même pas leurs époux**. C'est alors **un jeu pour elles d'aller** inviter des hommes à danser, incognito.

Pour finir, les Guyanais **utilisent** aujourd'hui ce qui **était autrefois** négatif, pour **promouvoir** leur pays : on peut visiter **les bagnes**, faire des expéditions en **pirogue** sur les fleuves et aller à **la découverte** de la forêt amazonienne, qui **faisait si peur** autrefois. Ce **dernier outil** touristique sert aussi à **sensibiliser** la population **mondiale** aux problèmes de la déforestation, de **la disparition** d'espèces rares et aussi à **la survie** des Amérindiens et de leurs traditions.

---

aujourd'hui: today
grâce à: thanks to
mouvementée (mouvementé): eventful

il y a: there is
un esclavage: slavery
qui forment (former): that make up (to make up)
restants (restant): remaining
mais aussi: but also
forte (fort): strong

augmente (augmenter): increases (to increase)
vite: fast
(elle) vit (vivre): it lives (to live)
les villes (le ville): cities
une vie: life
autour: around

qui regorge (regorger): which is full of (to be full of)
atouts (un atout): assets

se trouve (se trouver): is found (to be found, to be situated)
d'où: from where
(elle) est lancée (lancer): it is launched (to launch)
la fusée: skyrocket
transporte (transporter): carries (to carry)

un mois: month
janvier: January
février: February
parfois: sometimes
mars: March
peuvent (pouvoir): can (can, be able to)
se mêlent (se mêler): they mingle (to mingle)
célèbre: famous, well-known
des femmes (une femme): women
reconnues (reconnaître): recognized (to recognize)
par personne: by no one
même pas: not even
leurs époux: their spouses
un jeu: game
pour elles: for them (feminine)
d'aller: to go

utilisent (utiliser): use (to use)
il était (être): it was (to be)
autrefois: in the past
promouvoir: to promote
les bagnes (la bagne): prisons
une pirogue: canoe
la découverte: discovery
faisait si peur: it was so frightening
dernier: last
un outil: tool, medium
sensibiliser: to raise awareness
mondiale (mondial): world
la disparition: (here) extinction
la survie: survival

Aix-en-Provence

L'un **des** simples **plaisirs** que **j'ai** à **vivre** dans la région dans laquelle **je vis**, est que **je me situe à peine** à 20 minutes **au sud** d'Aix-en-Provence.

Il s'agit d'une petite cité **pleine de** charme, **qui propose un mélange parfait** de l'ancien et du **nouveau**. Les touristes affluent **du monde entier** pour **arpenter** ses **petites ruelles sinueuses**, et en **profitent** pour explorer tous ses petits **commerces qui offrent** un mix atypique de **la mode** et de l'artisanat.

Mais tout le monde **n'est quand même** pas là que pour **se détendre** à Aix. La ville est **également animée** par **un quartier d'affaire** très dynamique. **Avocats**, **agents immobiliers**, **comptables**, **banquiers**…. Eux aussi **viennent** des quatre **coins** de la France pour **travailler** dans une ville **décrite** par certains comme étant l'une des **plus belles** villes françaises. **On y travaille** dur mais pas **sans oublier** de **vite apprendre** qu'ici, en Provence, **on prend** toujours **le temps** de **se détendre** en **buvant un café chaud au cœur du matin** et un apéritif **rafraîchissant l'après-midi**.

Le résultat en est que **peu importe l'heure** de la journée, les nombreux cafés et pubs qui **s'alignent** dans les rues, **se peuplent** d'un éventail de touristes et de **locaux parlant** toutes sortes de langues.

Moi, **j'adore venir** à Aix **durant** la matinée, et plus spécialement **au printemps** et en **été**, lorsque **les beaux jours reviennent**. Il n'est alors pas **surprenant** de **rencontrer** un musicien dans la rue **qui nous fait revivre** l'un des classiques français ou italiens avec un accordéon. **Je m'arrête** souvent pour **acheter le quotidien régional** « La Marseillaise », puis **je trouve un endroit sympa** pour boire mon café crème, et absorber **un peu de toute** cette atmosphère qui circule à travers le vieux village, **en même temps** que **les passants**.

Les touristes **ne viennent pas** à Aix simplement pour ses cafés du coin ou ses boutiques. Aix est une ville d'histoire, qui date de **plusieurs millénaires**. De magnifiques **chapelles** et **églises** médiévales sont **nichées au détour** des ruelles et, lorsque l'**on** y **rentre, on peut ressentir** toute leur histoire.

Aix en Provence est particulièrement **connue** pour son grand nombre de fontaines. La région est riche en **eaux**, **chaudes** et **froides**, et les ingénieurs romains **ont construit** de splendides fontaines approvisionnant toute la ville d'eau **fraîche**. Ces fontaines **apportent** aux touristes et aux photographes du monde entier **le besoin** de capturer cette image **parfaite** de « La Rotonde » ou même de juste rester **pendant quelques** minutes à la **contempler**.

Pour toutes ces raisons Aix reste la ville provençale que **je préfère**. **Je me sens chanceuse** lorsque **je m'y promène**. C'est une ville qui inspire ses habitants et ses touristes, tout comme elle inspirait de grands artistes comme Cézanne qui y **a passé** une grande partie de **sa vie**.

---

j'adore (adorer): I love (to love)
venir: to come
durant: during
au printemps: in the spring
un été: summer
les beaux jours: nice weather days
reviennent (revenir): come back (to come back)
surprenant: surprising
rencontrer: to meet
qui nous fait revivre: that brings back to life for us
je m'arrête (s'arrêter): I stop (to stop)
acheter: to buy
le quotidien régional: the regional daily newspaper
je trouve (trouver): I find (to find)
un endroit: a spot, a place
sympa: nice
un peu de toute: a bit of all
en même temps: at the same time
les passants (le passant): passers-by

ne viennent pas (venir): don't come (to come)
plusieurs: several
millénaires: thousands of years
chapelles (une chapelle): chapels
églises (une église): churches
nichées (nicher): nestled (to nestle)
au détour de: around the bend of
on rentre (rentrer): we go in (to go in)
on peut (pouvoir): we can (can)
ressentir: to feel

connue (connaître): well-known (to know)
eaux (une eau): waters
chaudes (chaud): hot
froides (froid): cold
ont construit (construire): built (to build)
fraîche (frais): fresh
apportent (apporter): bring (to bring)
le besoin: the need
parfaite (parfait): perfect
pendant: during
quelques: a few, some
contempler: to gaze at, to admire

pour toutes (tout): for all
ces raisons (une raison): these reasons
je préfère (préférer): I prefer, like best (to prefer)
je me sens (se sentir): I feel (to feel)
chanceuse (chanceux): lucky
je m'y promène (se promener): I walk around there (to walk around)
(il) a passé (passer): he spent (to spend)
sa vie (une vie): his life

Le quartier de la Croix-Rousse

Pour moi, le quartier de la Croix-Rousse **évoque d'abord des souvenirs d'enfance** : **la vogue aux marrons**, le petit **marché quotidien** de la place de la Croix-Rousse, **la maison des canuts**, le gros caillou ou encore **la « ficelle ».   Cela ne vous dit rien** ? Alors en route pour une visite **à la fois** touristique et historique de l'un des quartiers **les plus originaux** de **la ville** de Lyon.

D'un point de vue géographique, le quartier de la Croix-Rousse **se situe entre** la Saône et le Rhône, au nord de la Presqu'île de Lyon. **Il s'agit d'une colline** composée d'un plateau, le 4ème arrondissement, et **des pentes**, le 1er arrondissement.

J'ai vécu la majeure partie de mon enfance sur le plateau de la Croix-Rousse. Pour moi, c'est comme un village **au milieu** d'une grande ville avec ses restaurants et bistrots traditionnels, le petit marché de la Place de la Croix-Rousse où **ma grand-mère allait faire tous les jours ses courses**, la vogue aux marrons **qui s'installait** tous **les ans** à **l'automne**. Cette **fête foraine** était l'occasion pour moi de **manger des marrons chauds**, de **la barbe à papa rose** et de **conduire mes premières autos tamponneuses**. Mais le plateau, c'est aussi et **surtout** la maison des Canuts de la Rue d'Ivry, où l'on peut tout **apprendre** sur l'histoire de **la soie, voir des métiers à tisser d'antan fonctionner** et **comprendre** le **mode de vie** des canuts, **les ouvriers** de la soie.

Un autre symbole du quartier est le Gros Caillou. Cet **énorme rocher a été déterré** en 1892 lors de la construction de la « ficelle », **un funiculaire qui relie** la Croix-Rousse à **la Presqu'île** de Lyon. Le Gros Caillou se situe **désormais** sur les pentes de la Croix-Rousse.

Le quartier des pentes **se caractérise** comme son **nom l'indique** par un **très fort dénivelé. Les rues** sont étroites et sinueuses, **parfois** encore **pavées. Elles se transforment** souvent en **escalier** et **relient** ainsi **plus facilement** le plateau au centre ville de Lyon. **Je me rappelle** ainsi **avoir descendu quatre à quatre** des marches qui **me semblaient** immenses pour **rejoindre en moins** d'**une demi-heure** le parc de la **tête d'Or** sur **les rives** du Rhône. **Il est à noter** que les pentes de la Croix-Rousse font partie du territoire classé au patrimoine **mondial** de l'UNESCO.

Au début du XIXème siècle, **la soierie** est présente à Lyon dans les quartiers de Saint-Nizier sur la Presqu'île ou de Saint Jean, **au pied de** la Colline de Fourvière. La création d'une **nouvelle** génération de métiers à tisser **de taille imposante rend impossible** leur utilisation dans **les logements** traditionnels **des ouvriers.** Les nouvelles machines à tisser **nécessitent des plafonds hauts.** Les premières mécaniques **seront alors déménagées** dans les anciens couvents de la Croix-Rousse dont l'architecture permet de **les recevoir.** C'est ainsi que les premiers canuts et leurs familles s'installent sur la colline de la Croix-Rousse. Puis, **pour faire face à la venue sans cesse** croissante des ouvriers de la soie, **des immeubles adaptés à la taille** des métiers à tisser **vont y être construits.** Il s'agit en général de constructions composées de cinq à six **étages, divisées en** appartements **dotés de** hauts plafonds et **hautes fenêtres** ainsi que d'une mezzanine adaptée à **la vie de famille.** Entre les immeubles, **des passages étroits** qui vont dans **le sens** de la pente **sont créés** : ce sont les **fameuses traboules.**

Si vous visitez le quartier de la Croix-Rousse, **vous ne pourrez pas manquer** ces caractéristiques architecturales. Bonne visite !

---

se caractérise (se caractériser): is characterized (to be characterized)
un nom: name
il indique (indiquer): it indicates (to indicate)
très fort: very strong
un dénivelé: a difference in height/level
les rues (le rue): streets
étroites (étroit): narrow
parfois: sometimes
pavées (pavé): paved with cobblestones
elles se transforment (se transformer): they turn into (to turn into)
un escalier: a stairway
(elles) relient (relier): they link (to link)
plus facilement: more easily
je me rappelle (se rappeler): I remember (to remember)
avoir descendu: going down
quatre à quatre: four at a time
me semblaient: seem to me
rejoindre: to get back to
en moins de: in less than
une demi-heure: half an hour
le parc de la tête d'Or: *Lyon's famous park*
les rives (la rive): shores
il est à noter: it has to be said
mondial: world

au début du: at the beginning of
la soierie: silk industry
au pied de: at the bottom of
nouvelle (nouveau): new
de taille imposante: huge, imposing size
(elle) rend impossible (rendre): it makes it impossible (to make)
les logements (le logement): accommodations
des ouvriers (un ouvrier): workers
(ils) nécessitent (nécessiter): it requires (to require)
des plafonds hauts: high ceilings
seront alors déménagées: so they will be moved
les recevoir: to receive them
pour faire face: to face up to, deal with
la venue: arrival
sans cesse: constantly
des immeubles (un immeuble): buildings
adaptés à: adapted to
la taille: size
(ils) vont y être construits: they are going to be built
des étages (un étage): floors
divisées en: divided into
dotés de (doter): equipped with (to equip)
hautes fenêtres (une fenêtre): high windows
la vie de famille: family life
des passages étroits: narrow alleys
le sens: way
sont créés (créer): are created (to create)
fameuses (fameux): famous
traboules: passage between houses

si vous visitez (visiter): if you visit
vous ne pourrez pas manquer: you cannot miss

il existe (exister): there is (to exist, to be)	
très vieux: very old	
la ville: city	
il s'agit de (s'agir de): it is about (to be about)	
la cité phocéenne: the Phocaean city	
un lieu: a place	
incontournable: unmissable	
les grands férus (le féru): buffs, fans	
bâtie (bâtir): built (to build)	
un siècle: century	
autour: around	
la auberge: hotel	
elle regorge (regorger): it is packed with (to be packed with)	
artisans-commerçants: craftsmens and retailers	

Le vieux Marseille : le panier

Il existe un **très vieux** village dans **la ville** de Marseille. **Il s'agit** du plus ancien quartier de **la cité phocéenne** et aussi de son centre historique. C'est **un lieu incontournable** pour tous **les grands férus** d'histoire et de culture. **Bâtie** au XVIIème **siècle autour** de l'**auberge** du « Logis du Panier », la place du petit village du Panier **regorge** de petits **artisans-commerçants**.

si vous vous promenez (se promener): if you walk (to walk)
une découverte: discovery
vous sentirez (sentir): you will smell (to smell)
bonne (bon): good
une odeur: smell
un savon: soap
un savonnier: soap maker
ouvre (ouvrir): opens (to open)
propre: clean
(elle) se propage (propager): it spreads (to spread)
la rue: street
il a fini (finir): he finished (to finish)
ses derniers savons: his last soaps
cela se sent: you can smell it

Si vous vous y **promenez**, vous irez de **découverte** en découverte! En arrivant, **vous sentirez** la **bonne odeur** du **savon** de Marseille ! L'artisan **savonnier ouvre** sa boutique à 13h et l'odeur du **propre se propage** dans toute **la rue** : **il a fini** de confectionner **ses derniers savons** et **cela se sent** dans tout le village.

chaque fois: each time
je passe par là (passer): I go that way (to go)
je ne peux pas m'empêcher: I cannot stop myself
acheter: to buy
je ne suis pas la seule: I am not the only one
une foule: a crowd
venant (venir): coming (to come)
des coins (un coin): corners
(elle) se déverse (déverser): it pours (to pour)
qui passe par là: that goes through there

À chaque fois que **je passe par là**, **je ne peux pas m'empêcher** d'en **acheter** un ou deux... Et **je ne suis pas la seule** ! **Une foule** de touristes **venant des** quatre **coins** de France et d'Europe **se déverse** dans les rues : ils descendent du petit train de la ville **qui passe par là**.

plus loin: further
son nom (un nom): his name
(il) est déjà paru (paraître): it has already appeared (to appear)
célèbre: famous
il adore (adorer): he loves (to love)
inventer: to invent
nouvelles recettes: new recipes
l'huile d'olive: olive oil
le gingembre: ginger
le poivre: pepper
tout ce que l'on peut imaginer: everything we can imagine
il l'a déjà réalisé (réaliser): he has already created it (to create)
un atelier: workshop

Plus loin, il y a le chocolatier du Panier. **Son nom est déjà paru** plus d'une fois dans un très **célèbre** journal national. **Il adore inventer** de **nouvelles recettes** à base de chocolat : chocolat à **l'huile d'olive**, au **gingembre**, au **poivre** … **Tout ce que l'on peut imaginer**, il **l'a déjà réalisé** dans son humble **atelier** de chocolatier.

Puis **vous trouverez** l'atelier de céramique d'**un ami** à moi. Il a le statut d'artiste car **il fait** des pièces uniques. **Il conçoit les carrelages** de **salles de bain** ou autres poteries aux réminiscences provençales. **Il décore** sa boutique de ses **œuvres** et **reçoit** des **commandes** en provenance du sud de l'Europe.

Enfin, au centre de tout, vieille de plus de 500 ans, **se dresse** la Vieille Charité de Marseille. Au tout début de son existence, **elle abritait les orphelins** et vagabonds. Le Corbusier, grand architecte de **renommée mondiale**, sera à l'origine de sa restauration **qui s'achèvera** en 1986.

Aujourd'hui, la Vieille Charité représente un des plus grands centres multiculturels de la ville de Marseille. **Désormais entretenue** par **la mairie**, elle est le lieu de **plusieurs** expositions **mondialement connues**. Par exemple, l'exposition de **peintres provençaux** intitulée « **Sous le soleil** » en hommage à **la** fameuse **chanson** de Serge Gainsbourg, a fait plus de 10 000 entrées en 2005. Cette exposition a été **assurée** à plus de 700 millions d'euros car elle présentait **des tableaux venant des** quatre coins du monde.

Le panier est **également au cœur** d'**un essor** touristique. **En effet**, **sa renommée** lui a valu **le tournage** d'une série française « Plus Belle La Vie », **diffusée** dans les pays francophones. Les touristes **viennent** aujourd'hui visiter les rues qu'**ils voient si souvent** sur leur petit **écran**.

Le petit village du Panier est **un endroit** emblématique de la ville de Marseille ! **Si vous vous rendez** sur la place, au centre du village, **vous pourrez siroter** un bon 51 ou un bon Ricard **selon les goûts. Cela aide** quand l'été arrive et que le soleil **cogne sec**. Les Marseillais y **sont attroupés** comme au cœur d'un petit village de Provence. **C'est assez surprenant** et **en même temps** très agréable **lorsque** l'**on sait** qu'il est **situé** au centre d'une des plus grandes métropoles de France.

---

vous trouverez (trouver): you will find (to find)
un ami: a friend
il fait (faire): he does (to do)
il conçoit (concevoir): he designs (to design)
les carrelages: tiled floors
salles de bain: bathrooms
il décore (décorer): he decorates (to decorate)
œuvres (une œuvre): works (of art)
(il) reçoit (recevoir): he receives (to receive)
commandes: orders

(elle) se dresse (se dresser): it stands up (to stand up)
elle abritait (abriter): it sheltered (to shelter)
les orphelins (le orphelin): orphans
renommée mondiale: world renowned
qui s'achèvera (s'achever): that ended (to end)

désormais: from now on
entretenue (entretenir): maintained (to maintain)
la mairie: the town council
plusieurs: several
mondialement connues (connaître): known worldwide (to know)
peintres (un peintre): painters
provençaux (provençal): from Provence
sous le soleil: under the sun
la chanson: song
assurée: insured
des tableaux (un tableau): paintings
venant des (venir): coming from (to come)

également: also
au cœur de: in the middle of
un essor: development
en effet: indeed
sa renommée (la renommée): its reputation
le tournage: filming
diffusée: broadcasted
viennent (venir): come (to come)
ils voient (voir): they see (to see)
si souvent: so often
un écran: screen

un endroit: a place
si vous vous rendez (se rendre): if you go (to go)
vous pourrez siroter (pouvoir): you will be able to sip (can, to be able to)
selon: according to
les goûts (le goût): tastes
cela aide (aider): it helps (to help)
il cogne sec (cogner): (the sun) hammers down (to hammer down, pound)
(ils) sont attroupés (attrouper): they are gathered (to gather)
c'est assez surprenant: it is rather surprising
en même temps: at the same time
lorsque: when
on sait (savoir): we know (to know)
situé: located

je devais avoir (devoir): I must have been (must)	
une dizaine d'années: about ten years old	
la première fois: the first time	
je suis allée (aller): I went (to go)	
j'en ai toujours gardé (garder): I have always kept (to keep)	
un souvenir: a memory	
lumineux: bright	
je suis retournée (retourner): I went back (to go back)	
plusieurs: several	
depuis: since	
la semaine dernière: last week	
j'ai accompagné (accompagner): I went with (to go with)	
une amie (un ami): a friend	
québécoise (québécois): from Québec	
de passage: passing through	

d'abord: firstly
prendre: to take
le bateau: a boat
partir: to leave
le plaisir: pleasure
voir: to see
prendre de l'ampleur: to increase, to gain
au fur et à mesure: as
on s'approche de (s'approcher): we approached (to approach)

passées à bord (passer): spent on board (to spend)
nous débarquons (débarquer): we land (to land)
(ils) iront (aller): they will go (to go)
visiter: to visit
a commencé (commencer): started (to start)
un siècle: century
en ce qui me concerne: as far as I'm concerned
savourer: to savor

des loueurs de voitures: people who rent cars
vélos (un vélo): bikes
vous y attendent (attendre): they wait for you (to wait)
vous pouvez (pouvoir): you can (can)
parcourir: travel all over
mieux encore: better than this
à pied: by foot
longue: with a length of
compte (compter): has (to have, count)
près de: almost
sentiers (un sentier): trails
côtiers (côtier): coastal

se régaler: to enjoy
bonnes chaussures: good shoes
une bouteille d'eau: a bottle of water
des lunettes de soleil: sunglasses
un coupe-vent: a windbreaker
vous serez équipés: you will be equipped
parfaitement: perfectly
découvrir: to discover
qui surplombe (surplomber): which overhangs (to overhang)
la mer: sea
une quarantaine: about forty

Belle-Île-en-Mer

Je devais avoir une dizaine d'années la première fois que **j'y suis allée** et **j'en ai toujours gardé un souvenir lumineux**… J'y suis retournée plusieurs fois **depuis**, et, **la semaine dernière, j'y ai accompagné une amie québécoise de passage** dans la région.

D'abord, il y a la joie de **prendre le bateau**, l'impression de **partir** à l'aventure, et puis **le plaisir** de **voir** l'Île **prendre de l'ampleur au fur et à mesure** qu'**on s'approche d'**elle, comme hypnotisé.

Après environ 45 minutes **passées à bord, nous débarquons** au petit port de Palais. Les amateurs d'histoire **iront visiter** la citadelle dont la construction **a commencé** au XVIème **siècle**… **En ce qui me concerne,** mon plaisir, à Belle-Île, c'est … **savourer** Belle-Île !

Des loueurs de voitures (dont certaines électriques), scooters et **vélos vous y attendent**, mais **vous pouvez** aussi **parcourir** l'île en bus ou, **mieux encore**, **à pied**. **Longue** de 17km, large de 9km, Belle-Île **compte près de** 100 km de **sentiers côtiers**.

Voilà de quoi **se régaler** ! Avec de **bonnes chaussures**, un sac à dos, un petit pique-nique, **une bouteille d'eau, des lunettes de soleil** et **un coupe-vent, vous serez parfaitement équipés** pour **découvrir** les nombreux points de vue qu'offre cette île **qui surplombe la mer** d'**une quarantaine** de mètres.

Il n'y a ici **pas** (ou pratiquement pas) de **grosses** structures hôtelières. Dans les ports **principaux**, de **jolies boutiques** et de **charmants** petits restaurants (où l'**on mange** très bien !) s'**alignent sagement** face à la mer. La côte **a conservé** un caractère **sauvage** et pur dont **on ne peut se lasser**. L'air est **vif**, les odeurs de **fleurs**, d'**embruns** et d'**aiguilles de pin séchées** au **soleil** sont **enivrantes**.

On se sent vivre, revivre, ressourcer…

Pour **accéder** aux **plages** et aller **vous baigner** (attention, l'eau est **limpide**, mais **fraîche** !) **vous devrez descendre des pentes souvent raides, si vous arrivez** par le sentier, mais l'effort est **toujours récompensé** car si les odeurs de Belle-Île sont irrésistibles, les couleurs de cette île le sont **tout autant**. Une infinie palette de bleus et de **verts cerne l'île tandis que la terre** est **couverte de fleurs jaunes**, roses, **rouges**, **blanches**, d'une végétation variée et **parfois étonnante puisque** l'île bénéficie d'un microclimat qui lui permet d'**abriter** des espèces habituellement **inconnues** en Bretagne.

Véritable petit **bijou** de l'océan Atlantique, Belle-Île n'a pas encore **perdu** son âme à la fois **douce** et **indomptée**. **Pourvu que ça dure** !

il n'y a pas: there are no
grosses (gros): big
principaux (principal): main
jolies boutiques: pretty shops
charmants (charmant): charming
on mange (manger): we eat (to eat)
(ils) s'alignent (s'aligner): they are in line (to be in line)
sagement: wisely
a conservé (conserver): has kept (to keep)
sauvage: wild
on ne peut (pouvoir): we cannot (can)
se lasser: get bored
vif: bracing
des fleurs (une fleur): flowers
des embruns (masc): spindrifts
des aiguilles de pin: pine needles
séchées (sécher): dried (to dry)
le soleil: sun
enivrantes (enivrant): exhilarating

on se sent (se sentir): we feel (to feel)
vivre: alive
revivre: revived
ressourcer: recharged
accéder: to access
plages (une plage): beaches
vous baigner (se baigner): to swim
limpide: clear
fraîche (frais): cold
vous devrez (devoir): you will have to (to have to)
descendre: to go down
des pentes (une pente): slopes
souvent: often
raides (raide): steep
si vous arrivez (arriver): if you arrive (to arrive)
toujours: always
récompensé: rewarded
tout autant: as much
verts (vert): greens
(il) cerne (cerner): it surrounds (to surround)
l'île: the island
tandis que: while
la terre: the ground
couverte: covered
fleurs (une fleur): flowers
jaunes (jaune): yellows
rouges (rouge): reds
blanches (blanc): whites
parfois: sometimes
étonnante (étonnant): surprising
puisque: since
abriter: to shelter
inconnues (inconnu): unknown

véritable: real, true
un bijou: jewel
perdu: lost
une âme: soul
à la fois: at the same time
douce (doux): soft, sweet
indomptée (indompté): uncontrolled
pourvu que ça dure: let's hope it lasts

Saint Tropez

Si vous ne connaissez pas cette ville, cela signifie probablement que **vous êtes** indifférents à **la vie** des célébrités de notre planète. Cet oppidum du XVème **siècle** qui est actuellement l'une **des stations balnéaires les plus huppées** du **monde** est capable d'**offrir** à ses visiteurs plus que l'image mythique **imposée par** de nombreux magazines de **mode** et **luxe**.

C'est une commune française **située non loin d'une autre ville** côtière Marseille dans la région Provence-Alpes-Côte d'Azur **qui met** à votre disposition **non seulement** ses **plages** merveilleuses, **mais aussi** de nombreux monuments historiques. **Citons** entre autre l'**Église** de Saint-Tropez du XVIIIème siècle, la chapelle Sainte-Anne du début du XVIIème siècle, la chapelle de l'Annonciade, actuellement aussi Musée du **même nom**, qui date du XIVème siècle.

Commençons toutefois par les plages. C'est évident **parce que** la majorité des touristes **se rendent** principalement dans la station balnéaire et non dans la ville historique. **Les amoureux** de **bain de soleil** et de sports aquatiques **pourront se livrer** à leur activité favorite sur l'une des six plages publiques, car Saint Tropez c'est douze kilomètres de plages **dorées** et absolument sublimes. Saint Tropez, c'est aussi de nombreux magasins où les amateurs de shopping **se sentiront** comme au paradis ainsi que des restaurants où l'**on vous servira** de véritables délicatesses culinaires, trésors de la gastronomie française et internationale.

Une fois bronzé, **détendu** et **rassasié**, **vous pourrez enfin faire connaissance** avec l'histoire de la ville. **Toutefois**, même **si vous n'êtes pas** amateur d'histoire, **vous devez** visiter Saint-Tropez **tout au moins** pour vous livrer au sport favori de cette ville splendide « **voir et être vu** ». C'est logique dans une ville qui a pour devise « Ad usque fidelis » ce qui **se traduit** du latin comme « **Fidèle jusqu'au bout** ».

Le Sud-Ouest de la France

Nichée au cœur du Sud-ouest de la France, à quatre heures de Paris en TGV (Train à Grande Vitesse), à **quarante** minutes à peine **des plages** de l'Atlantique et à deux heures de l'Espagne, Bordeaux est **une ville pleine d'attraits**. De nombreuses petites communes **des alentour**s comme *Pessac, Bègles* ou *Mérignac* **sont regroupées sous l'égide de** la *Communauté urbaine de Bordeaux* **qui compte** plus de **sept-cent mille** habitants.

Non contente de **représenter dignement le monde** de l'œnologie auprès des amateurs de **vin** du **monde entier, elle possède** une histoire riche et **parfois même douloureuse** et une architecture classique **qui lui a permis** d'être **inscrite** au *Patrimoine de l'Humanité de l'Unesco.*

La ville de Bordeaux est **située au bord de** la Garonne, ce **fleuve** qui a vu remonter **les navires s'adonnant à la traite des esclaves** d'Afrique. **De nos jours**, elle accueille plutôt les plus gros bateaux de croisière du monde, **qui ne manquent pas** d'y **faire une escale estivale**.

Venus pour visiter les vignes et les châteaux **qui pullulent dans** les villes environnantes, les touristes **sont ébahis** par la beauté de son architecture et par l'accueil de ses habitants. **Qu'il s'agisse** du Grand Théâtre, de la majestueuse Place de la Bourse **qui domine les quais**, de la Grosse Cloche ou de son jardin public, **le promeneur** est **ravi par** la majesté et la sérénité **des lieux**.

Ville étudiante par excellence, c'est dans le *quartier St-Michel* et à la *Place de la Victoire,* où un obélisque gigantesque domine la rotonde devant laquelle **s'arrête** le tramway tout neuf, que **les jeunes s'attardent** aux terrasses des cafés.

On va y faire **ses courses** à *Mériadeck*, mais c'est au Lac, situé en périphérie, que l'**on aime passer** son **dimanche** ou à *Lacanau*, l'une des plus belles plages de France.

nichée: nestled, located
au cœur du: in the heart of
quarante: forty
des plages (une plage): beaches
une ville: city
pleine de: full of
attraits (un attrait): attractions
des alentours: surroundings
(elles) sont regroupées (regrouper): (they) are gathered (to gather)
sous l'égide de: under the control of
qui compte (compter): that counts (to count)
sept-cent mille: seven hundred thousand

non contente de: not happy to
représenter: to represent
dignement: with dignity
le monde: world
le vin: wine
monde entier: the whole world
elle possède (posséder): it has (to have)
parfois même: sometimes even
douloureuse: painful
qui lui a permis (permettre): that allows it (to allow, to permit)
inscrite: registered

située: located
au bord de: on the shore of
le fleuve: river
les navires (le navire): ships
s'adonnant à: doing
la traite des esclaves: slave trading
de nos jours: nowadays
elle accueille plutôt (accueillir): it rather welcomes (to welcome)
plus gros: biggest
les bateaux de croisière: cruise ships
qui ne manquent pas (manquer): that do not miss (to miss)
faire une escale: to make a cruise stop
estivale: in the summer months

venus pour (venir): came to (to come)
visiter: to visiter
les vignes (la vigne): vineyards
qui pullulent dans: that are swarming with
(ils) sont ébahis (ébahir): (they) are dumbfounded (to dumbfound)
qu'il s'agisse: whether it involves
qui domine (dominer): that dominates (to dominate)
les quais (le quai): quays
le promeneur: walker
ravi par: delighted by
des lieux (un lieu): places

ville étudiante: college town
(il) s'arrête (s'arrêter): it starts (to start)
les jeunes (un jeune): young people
s'attardent (attarder): stay until late (to stay until late, to linger)

on va (aller): we go (to go)
ses courses (une course): shopping
on aime passer: we like to spend
un dimanche: Sunday

Évaluez votre compréhension

La grande et la merveilleuse, page 24

1. Normandy is a region born from war. However, what did the wars contribute to France?

2. What treat will you find in Normandy, made by the monks?

Les pâtisseries de Paris, page 25

1. What tip is given for picking out the best "elephant ear" pastry?

2. Where will you find the best *madeleines*? And what is this treat perfect for?

Le visage unique de Montréal, page 26

1. Montreal was founded in what year and what commerce started the city?

2. What is one of the striking characteristics of the city?

3. The underground tunnels in Montréal allow you to shop while avoiding what?

4. If you visit Montréal you will find the people are famous for what?

Des îles pleines de richesses, page 28

1. How and when was the island of *La Guyane* founded?

2. *Le carnaval guyanais* is famous for what?

Test your comprehension

Le quartier de la Croix-Rousse, page 32

1. Where is the *Le quartier de la Croix-Rousse* located?

2. What are some things the author looked forward to at the "fun fair"?

3. What is the *le Gros Caillou*?

Le vieux Marseille : le panier, page 34

1. If you go for a walk, what will you discover?

2. What purpose did *La Vieille Charité* serve? What is it now?

3. *Le panier* is in the heart of the touristic district. What made this area especially popular with tourists?

Belle-Île-en-Mer, page 36

1. Lovers of history will especially love to visit what?

2. How does the author prefer to travel around the island? And what should you be equipped with?

3. How do you access the beach?

Saint Tropez, page 38

1. Name three historical monuments.

2. How many kilometers of beaches does Saint Tropez have?

Tradition

Un jour, un chocolat

Le calendrier de l'Avent **n'est pas n'importe quel calendrier** ! Contrairement à **tous les autres**, **il ne comporte pas** 30 ou 31 **jours**, **ni même** 28. Ce calendrier si spécial **compte** en effet les jours **restants avant** Noël. Traditionnellement, **il commençait le** premier **dimanche** de l'avent, **quatre semaines** avant Noël, mais **l'usage veut maintenant qu'il commence** le 1er décembre et se finisse le 24, **le soir** de Noël.

Le calendrier de l'Avent a très probablement **été créé pour faire patienter les enfants** jusqu'à Noël. **Il est apparu en Allemagne** au début du XIXème siècle, quand des familles ont **commencé** à **dessiner des traits** de **craie** pour compter **les journées écoulées** avant le grand jour. Le premier véritable calendrier de l'avent, **tel qu'on le connaît aujourd'hui**, **n'a** cependant **été fabriqué qu'**en 1851.

Il se présente maintenant **comme un** grand rectangle de **carton** dans lequel **sont découpées**, **dans le désordre**, 24 petites **fenêtres**. **Derrière** ces petites fenêtres… **on trouve des trésors**. Images religieuses ou dessins de Noël, biscuits, chocolats, décorations de Noël miniatures et même de petits **jouets**. Ces « trésors » n'ont aujourd'hui comme limite que l'imagination **des fabricants**. **On voit** maintenant **fleurir** les calendriers Lego, Lindt, Playmobil ou même Barbie.

Mais pour nous, les enfants, qu'importe **le cadeau** ! L'important, c'est ce sentiment d'impatience au **creux** du **ventre**, ce sentiment qui grandit jour après jour. Ce sentiment qui **nous donne envie** d'**ouvrir** toutes les fenêtres **d'un coup** pour **accélérer le cours du temps**… Mais **il faut être patient**. Alors **on se console** avec un chocolat, un par jour, en attendant le jour où le Père Noël **arrivera enfin**.

Les vacances à la française

Dites à un Français **qu'il ne pourra** bénéficier que de **deux semaines** de vacances par **année** et **vous verrez** sa mine s'**allonger** considérablement, et l'**entendrez entamer** une diatribe dont **vous vous souviendrez**. Les longues vacances font tellement partie **des mœurs** françaises que nombreux sont ceux **qui n'hésiteraient pas à sortir** leurs **bannières poussiéreuses** pour **manifester** dans **les rues** si **les congés annuels** **étaient écourtés**.

C'est en 1920 que l'idée de **payer** des vacances aux employés **a germé** pour **la première fois au sein d'un quotidien** politique et économique parisien. En 1936, la victoire du *Front populaire*, un parti politique socialiste, **a fait éclore de** nouvelles revendications de la part **des travailleurs**. C'est suite à **la pression** des employés **qui se sont mis en grève** et ont pratiquement paralysé **le pays**, que **le droit** à des vacances payées a été **accordé à tous**.

La durée des vacances annuelles **n'a cessé de s'accroître** de manière exponentielle depuis cinquante ans, **passant** de deux semaines à cinq semaines annuellement. Au contraire, le nombre d'**heures** de la semaine de travail suit la tendance inverse, tournant, dans l'Hexagone, autour d'un petit trente-cinq heures. Les Français, **loin d'être paresseux**, sont de **bons vivants qui ont su conserver**, à l'âge adulte, **le doux souvenir** des longues journées de vacances de leur enfance passées à **la plage** ou à **la montagne**.

Souhaitant ardemment retrouver l'insouciance de leur **jeunesse** où les responsabilités étaient l'**apanage** exclusif des adultes, les Français voient dans les vacances prolongées l'occasion de **prendre un bain de jouvence** qui leur permet de **refaire** leur plein d'énergie pour l'année entière. **Mais non contents d'être parmi** les plus favorisés **en matière de congés** payés en Europe et dans **le monde, ils se permettent souvent quelques** « ponts » supplémentaires (addition des jours de **fin de semaine** et autres congés pour **étirer** les vacances) dès qu'ils en ont l'occasion.

qu'il ne pourra (pouvoir): that they will not be able (can, to be able)
deux semaines (une semaine): two weeks
une année: year
vous verrez (voir): you will see (to see)
allonger: to stretch
entendrez entamer (entendre): you will hear ....start (to hear)
vous vous souviendrez (se souvenir): you will remember (to remember)
des mœurs: customs
qui n'hésiteraient pas à: who would not hesitate to
sortir: to take out
bannières poussiéreuses: dusty flags
manifester: to demonstrate
les rues (la rue): the streets
les congés annuels: the annual holidays
ils étaient écourtés (écourter): were shortened (to cut short)

payer: to pay
a germé (germer): was formed (to form)
la première fois: the first time
au sein de: among
un quotidien: daily newspaper
a fait éclore de: was at the origin of
des travailleurs (un travailleur): workers
la pression: pressure
qui se sont mis en grève: who went on strike
le pays: the country
le droit: the right
accordé à tous: granted to all

la durée: the length
n'a cessé de (cesser): has kept (to keep doing)
s'accroître: to increase
passant (passer): going from ... to
heures (une heure): hours
loin d'être paresseux: far from being lazy
bons vivants: "bon vivant" *a person who enjoys luxuries, literally: good living*
qui ont su conserver (savoir): who managed to keep (to manage)
le doux souvenir: the happy memory
la plage: the beach
la montagne: the mountain

souhaitant ardemment retrouver: keenly wishing to recover
jeunesse: younger days
apanage: prerogative
prendre un bain de jouvence: to have a taste from the fountain of youth
refaire: to recuperate
mais non contents d'être: not only are they
parmi: among
en matière: in terms of
de congés: holidays
le monde: in the world
ils se permettent:: they indulge in
souvent quelques: often some
fin de semaine: weekend
étirer: to stretch

Le temps des sucres

C'est vers **la fin** du mois de mars et **au début** du mois d'avril, après **un hiver** rude et hostile, que les premières **chaleurs printanières annoncent enfin des jours meilleurs.** Quand **le mercure remonte au-dessus** de zéro, **la fonte des neiges s'amorce. On peut** enfin se **dépouiller** de nos **lourds habits** d'**hiver** et s'abandonner à **la chaleur rayonnante** du **soleil** qui **scintille de nouveau** avec force. Ce moment privilégié annonce également **le retour** du **temps des sucres**, période festive où l'**on récolte la sève** de l'**érable** à sucre (**l'eau d'érable**) qui est à l'origine du fameux **sirop d'érable**.

Des milliers de Québécois **se rendent** alors dans **les érablières,** qu'**on appelle** communément « **cabanes à sucre** », pour **se régaler** d'**un bon repas** copieux, en famille ou entre **amis**, et se « sucrer le **bec** ». Le menu, typique de la cuisine du **terroir**, est **composé d'aliments** riches en calories: **jambon, soupe aux pois**, omelette, **fèves au lard**, crêpes au sirop d'érable, tarte au sucre, et des célèbres « oreilles de Christ », **faites de couenne de lard frite** et **salée**. Un véritable **repas de bûcheron** ! **Après avoir dansé**, au son festif de la musique traditionnelle, **on se prépare** à savourer **la tire d'érable, servie** dans **des** grands **bacs de neige. Plus épaisse** et plus concentrée que le sirop d'érable, **elle durcit** au contact de la neige. **On peut alors l'enrouler autour** d'**un bâtonnet** et la **déguster** comme **un suçon**.

Mais la récolte de l'eau d'érable **ne date pas d'hier.** Ce sont les Amérindiens qui ont **découvert** les premiers **son goût** sucré et **prirent l'habitude** de la **faire bouillir** pour en **extraire** le sucre. **Ils enseignèrent** cette technique aux premiers colons **venus de** France qui l'**adoptèrent** et en firent, **avec le temps**, un élément essentiel des traditions québécoises.

Aujourd'hui, la technique a **quelque peu évolué**, mais le principe reste **le même.** Pour récolter l'eau d'érable, **il faut attendre les** premières **journées** de dégel. **C'est à ce moment** que les réserves de sucre de l'érable, **emmagasinées** dans ses **racines pendant** l'hiver, **commencent** à **remonter** dans **le tronc. On fait** alors **une entaille à environ** 1 mètre du **sol** et on y **enfonce un chalumeau, qui permet l'écoulement** de l'eau d'érable dans **une chaudière suspendue plus bas.** L'eau d'érable est ensuite **filtrée,** et **vidée** dans **un évaporateur,** qui permettra d'**augmenter** la concentration de sucre en éliminant l'excédant d'eau. **C'est ainsi** qu'**on obtient** le sirop d'érable. **Au départ,** l'eau d'érable **ne contient que** 2 à 3 % de sucre. Ainsi, pour produire un litre de sirop d'érable, il faut près de 43 litres d'eau d'érable. **Pourtant, on ne prélève qu'une partie minime** des réserves de sucre de l'arbre, ce qui **ne menace pas sa santé**.

Le temps des sucres **dure** environ un mois, et **s'achève** lorsque la sève est remontée dans le tronc jusque dans **les feuilles** et que son goût **est devenu âcre.** 75% de **la production mondiale** de sirop d'érable **est réalisée** au Québec. 85% en est exporté, majoritairement vers les États-Unis. Tout comme pour **le vin, il y a de bonnes et de mauvaises années** pour la récolte de l'eau d'érable. En 2009, les cycles de **gel** et de dégel ont été particulièrement favorables aux acériculteurs (les producteurs de sirop) et 2009 s'annonce excellente en termes de volumes et de qualité. Les produits de l'érable **se conservent bien** et sont **disponibles tout au long de l'année.** Mais il est **plus facile** et **plus amusant** de se rendre dans une cabane à sucre au **printemps** pour **boire** l'eau d'érable à même la chaudière et déguster la tire d'érable **servie** sur la neige.

le nouvel an (un an): the new year
une fête: a party
païenne (païen): pagan
qui vit le jour (voir): that originated
 (to originate)
vers: around
46 avant notre ère: 46 BC
qui décida (décider): who decided (to decide)
(il) était (être): (he) was (to be)
le Dieu: God
des portes (une porte): doors
des commencements (un commencement):
 beginnings
il donna (donner): he gave (to give)
un nom: name
des douze mois (un mois): twelve months

le changement: change
la tradition voulait que: traditionally
l'on s'échange (echanger): we exchange
 (to exchange)
des pièces (une pièce): coins
des médailles (une médaille): medals
perdure (perdurer): lasts (to last)
au travers: through
des fameuses (fameux): famous
des étrennes: gift of money
qui sont remises (remettre): that are given
 (to give)
l'époque (une époque): time
le réveillon: New Year's Eve party
indiquait (indiquer): indicated (to indicate)
à venir: next, still to come

une dizaine: about ten
après: after
des vœux (un vœu): wishes
copieux: copious
le repas: meal
des offrandes (une offrande): offerings
rameaux (un rameau): branches
verts (vert): green
confiseries (une confiserie): candies
(elle) était clôturée (clôturer): (it) was
 brought to an end (to bring to an end)
célèbres: famous
jeux du cirque: circus games

Noël: Christmas
consacré (consacrer): devoted (to devote)
(il) est passé (passer): (it) is spent (to spend)
entre: among
les amis (le ami): friends
fêter: to celebrate
très bon: very good
la veille: eve
c'est-à-dire: that is to say

Le réveillon de la Saint Sylvestre

Le nouvel an est **une fête** d'origine **païenne qui vit le jour vers 46 avant notre ère**. C'est Jules César **qui décida** que le 1er janvier serait le Jour de l'An. Janus **était le Dieu** païen **des portes** et **des commencements, il donna** ainsi son **nom** à janvier, premier **des douze mois** de l'année.

Dans la Rome antique, à l'occasion du **changement** d'année, **la tradition voulait que l'on s'échange des pièces** et **des médailles**. Cette coutume **perdure** de nos jours **au travers des fameuses étrennes qui sont remises** aux enfants le 1er janvier. A l'**époque** déjà, les Romains organisaient de gigantesques banquets à l'occasion du **réveillon** du Jour de l'An: le nombre de plats **indiquait** l'opulence de l'année **à venir**...

Une dizaine de jours **après**, les échanges **de vœux** étaient réalisés à l'occasion de **copieux repas** qui s'accompagnaient d'**offrandes** de **rameaux verts** et de **confiseries**. Cette période de fête **était** ensuite **clôturée** par les **célèbres jeux du cirque**.

En France, alors que le réveillon de **Noël** est souvent **consacré** à la famille, celui du 31 décembre **est** généralement **passé entre amis**. Il est de coutume de **fêter** le nouvel an par un **très bon** repas **la veille, c'est-à-dire** le 31 décembre au soir.

C'est l'occasion de faire la fête. Le repas, commencé **tardivement**, **est prévu pour durer** jusqu'à minuit, **heure à laquelle le décompte** des secondes sera fait **en chœur**, jusqu'à ce que **les douze coups de minuit retentissent**. A ce moment là, quelle que soit l'activité en cours, **tout le monde s'arrête** pour **s'embrasser** et chacun **se souhaite** bonne année **de façon joyeuse**. La phrase traditionnelle reste: « Bonne année et bonne **santé** » !

Les échanges de vœux, sont souvent associés à **des lancers** de **cotillons**, de **boules** et **rubans** de papiers… **cris** de joie, chants, concerts de **klaxons**, **défilés** et **farandoles** dans **la rue**….

Tout est prétexte à **se souhaiter** bonne année. La tradition veut également que l'on s'embrasse sous un bouquet de **gui suspendu**, afin de **se porter chance**. Ensuite, la fête continue jusqu'à « **épuisement** » **des convives**.

La période de la Saint Sylvestre est également un moment pour **faire preuve** de bonnes résolutions. Chacun **dresse la liste** des bonnes résolutions qu'**il compte entreprendre** dans l'année…. **arrêter de fumer**, faire un régime, **mieux travailler à l'école**…. sont autant de résolutions qui, tout le monde le sait, sont rarement **tenues**. Mais cela reste **un petit plaisir** auquel tout Français s'**adonne** avec innocence, histoire de faire le point sur ce qui doit être **amélioré** dans sa **vie**.

De nombreuses **villes** en France **célèbrent** la nouvelle année en organisant **des feux d'artifice la nuit du** 31 décembre.

tardivement: late
(il) est prévu (prévoir): (it) is scheduled (to schedule)
pour durer: to last
heure à laquelle (une heure): hour at which
le décompte: the count down
en chœur: in unison
les douze coups de minuit: the last stroke of midnight
(ils) retentissent (retentir): (they) rang out (to ring out)
tout le monde: everybody
s'arrête (s'arrêter): stops (to stop)
s'embrasser: to hug
(il) se souhaite (souhaiter): (they) wish each other (to wish)
de façon joyeuse: in a merry way
la santé: health

des lancers (un lancer): throws
cotillons (un cotillon): petticoats
boules (une boule): balls
rubans (un ruban): ribbons
cris (un cri): cries
klaxons (un klaxon): horns
défilés (un défilé): parades
farandoles: farandoles (dances)
la rue: street

se souhaiter: to wish
un gui: mistletoe
suspendu (suspendre): hung up (to hang up)
se porter chance: to be lucky
épuisement: exhaustion
des convives (un convive): guests

faire preuve: to show
(il) dresse la liste (dresser): (he) makes a list (to make a list)
(il) compte entreprendre (compter): (he) plans to undertake (to plan)
arrêter de fumer: to stop smoking
mieux travailler: to work harder
à l'école: at school
tenues (tenir): kept (to keep)
un petit plaisir: a little pleasure
(il) s'adonne (s'adonner): (he) devotes (to devote)
améliorer: to improve
la vie: life

villes (la ville): cities
célèbrent (célébrer): celebrate (to celebrate)
des feux d'artifice: fireworks
la nuit du: the night of

Des chants sacrés

De toutes **les fêtes** guadeloupéennes, la plus fêtée est celle de **Noël que ce soit par** les chrétiens ou les non-chrétiens. **En effet, depuis longtemps**, Noël en Guadeloupe **est devenue autant** la fête des familles et du **partage qu'**une fête religieuse.

Pour une grande partie des Guadeloupéens, la tradition de Noël en Guadeloupe est symbolisée par **la nourriture** locale **consommée** en famille: plat d'igname (**tubercule** locale), de **riz** accompagné de **pois d'angole** en sauce, de porc en **fricassée** et de **jambon** de Noël **épicé**.

Pourtant, pour la majorité d'**entre eux**, ce qui symbolise avant tout la période de Noël, ce sont les « Chanté Nwel ». Cette expression **qui désigne** en créole les réunions où l'**on chante en cœur** et à **tue-tête les cantiques** de Noël, représente l'un **des temps forts** de Noël dans les Antilles françaises.

Le Chanté Nwel est donc une tradition **ancrée au cœur de** la célébration de Noël car depuis **la fin du mois** de novembre, **jusqu'à la veille** de Noël, **des anonymes**, des associations ou **des entreprises invitent le plus grand nombre** de personnes à **venir**, avec leur **recueil** de cantiques, afin de **chanter ensemble**.

Lors de ces Chanté Nwel, les **mêmes** cantiques **reviennent** régulièrement, si bien que toutes les générations **les connaissent**, **même s'ils subissent parfois** des modifications dans leurs airs ou leurs accompagnements **musicaux**. Il est parfois **assez surprenant pour les non-initiés** d'**entendre** « Michaux veillait » ou « Oh la bonne nouvelle », chants religieux à l'origine, ainsi chantés à tue-tête, avec **un verre de** punch à **la main**. Mais depuis longtemps, les cantiques de Noël **ont trouvé** leur place dans le folklore et la culture antillais, bien au delà de leur dimension **sacré**.

D'ailleurs, l'**engouement** de la population pour les Chanté Nwel **devient** même un argument commercial car les Chanté Nwel sont **enregistrés** et **gravés** sur des CD ou alors des associations et autres formations musicales **se spécialisent** dans l'animation des grands Chanté Nwel et **font payer** leurs prestations, comme **n'importe** quelle prestation artistique. **Il faut croire** alors que les Chanté Nwel **ont encore** de **beaux jours devant eux**.

---

lors de ces: during those
mêmes: same
(ils) reviennent (revenir): they are often sung (to sing)
les connaissent: know them
même si (s'): even if
ils subissent (subir): they undergo (to undergo)
parfois: sometimes
musicaux: instrumental
assez surprenant pour: quite puzzling for
les non-initiés: the untrained
entendre: to hear
un verre de: a glass of
la main: the hand
(ils) ont trouvé (trouver): they found (to find)
sacré: sacred, religious

d'ailleurs: by the way,
engouement: infatuation
devient (devenir): has become (to become)
enregistrés (enregistrer): recorded (to record)
gravés (graver): burnt (to burn)
se spécialisent: get specialized into
(elles) font payer (faire): they charge (to charge)
n'importe: whatever
il faut croire: here is the proof that
ils ont encore (avoir): they still have (to have)
beaux jours: good times
devant eux: ahead of them

CULTURE NOTE Christmas carols first appeared in France in the 15th century as part of religious drama. At the beginning of the 18th century, Christmas songs came to include dances such as gavottes and minuets. The 19th-century carols have a rather pompous character. Typically performed in cathedral squares at Christmas, these dramas give rise to the French theater. Puppet shows are also given every year at Christmas and are often combined with Christmas carols, especially in Paris and in Lyon. One of the most famous Christmas puppet plays, written by de Marynbourg, is called "Bethlehem 1933" and is considered a masterpiece of popular art.

Some of the most popular French Christmas carols are:

* *Minuit Chrétiens*, also known as *Cantique de Noël*. This is a traditional French Christmas carol. It is equivalent to the English carol "O Holy Night," though the lyrics are different.
* *Ah ! Quel grand mystère !* is a traditional French Christmas carol from the 19th century.
* *Douce nuit* is the French equivalent of "Silent Night" and is sung to the same tune.

La tradition du pastis

Le pastis est l'une des plus fameuses liqueurs **produites** en Provence. Très **célèbre aujourd'hui** dans toute l'Europe, le pastis est **une boisson** alcoolisée **parfumée** à l'anis. Il est produit **à partir de la macération** de **la réglisse** et du **fenouil**, qui est une plante parfumée typiquement provençale. **Il fait** donc **partie de** la grande famille des boissons **anisées** dont la plus célèbre **reste** l'absinthe, 72% d'alcool.

En 1915 **la loi** de la prohibition de la consommation d'absinthe et de tous les produits similaires **est votée**. **Il faudra attendre** 1920 pour que les alcools anisés **soient fabriqués de nouveau** à condition qu'**ils ne contiennent pas plus** d'un certain pourcentage d'alcool, mais **ce ne sera qu'en** 1938 que **le vrai** pastis **sera inventé** avec 45%.

Les Marseillais **adorent siroter** leur pastis en été sur **les terrasses ensoleillées**. Cette boisson qui **renferme** un **étonnant pouvoir désaltérant**, **se boit** lors de l'apéritif **en fin d'après midi**. Sa couleur à l'origine **plutôt ambrée** s'**éclaircit** beaucoup avec **l'eau jusqu'à donner** une couleur **jaune** très pale.

Dans **le sud**, le pastis est utilisé dans de **nombreuses recettes** de cuisine dont **ma préférée est** : **les gambas** flambées au pastis. C'est un délice ! Les poissons de Méditerranée **sont souvent cuisinés** avec les aromates anisés, **badiane**, fenouil, ou pastis, pour parfumer les préparations. **Il y a encore plus** simple comme l'omelette au pastis.

Les boissons anisées sont de **façon** générale **très appréciées** dans **le pourtour** méditerranéen. En Espagne, par exemple, **il s'agira** plutôt de **l'aguardiente** ou encore en Italie, de la sambuca.

---

produites (produire): produced (to produce)
célèbre: famous
aujourd'hui: today
une boisson: a drink
parfumée: flavored
à partir de: from
la macération: soaking
la réglisse: licorice
le fenouil: fennel
il fait partie de (faire partie): it is part (to be part of)
anisées (anisé): flavored with aniseed
reste (rester): remains (to remain)

la loi: the law
est votée (voter): was voted (to vote)
il faudra (falloir): it was necessary (to be necessary)
attendre: to wait
soient fabriqués (fabriquer): to be made (to make, to manufacture)
de nouveau: again
ils ne contiennent pas plus de (contenir): they do not contain more than (to contain)
ce ne sera qu'en (être): it will be only in (to be)
le vrai: the real
il sera inventé (inventer): it will be invented (to invent)

ils adorent (adorer): they love (to love, adore)
siroter: to sip
les terrasses (la terrasse): terraces
ensoleillées (ensoleillé): bathed in sunlight
renferme (renfermer): contains (to contain)
étonnant: surprising
un pouvoir: power
désaltérant: thirst-quenching
(il) se boit (boire): it is drunk (to drink)
en fin de: at the end of
un après-midi: afternoon
plutôt: rather
ambrée (ambré): amber
il s'éclaircit (s'éclaircir): it gets lighter (to get lighter)
l'eau: water
jusqu'à: until
donner: to give
jaune: yellow

le sud: the South
nombreuses (nombreux): numerous
recettes (une recette): recipes
ma préférée: my favorite
les gambas: jumbo shrimp
ils sont souvent cuisinés (cuisiner): they are often cooked (to cook)
la badiane: star anis
il y a encore plus: there are even more

une façon: a way
très appréciées (apprécier): very appreciated (to appreciate)
le pourtour: region
il s'agira: it will be about
l'aguardiente: firewater

La tradition **remonterait au temps des Romains** qui, eux, **buvaient** du vin d'anis aux plantes. Au XIIIème siècle, **une confrérie** produit différents **onguents** et élixirs à base d'anis, **utilisés** pour **guérir** de multiples **maladies**. **Les Maures** et **plus tard les croisés introduisent** l'anis en France et notamment à Marseille. Avec le temps la plante est adaptée, **raffinée** et **donne naissance** à l'ancêtre du pastis: l'absinthe.

Aujourd'hui, il existe **un véritable culte** autour du pastis. **Non seulement** le tout Marseille réinvente la cuisine avec les nombreuses recettes à base de pastis mais **il innove également** dans la création de nouveaux cocktails, dont en **voici quelques** exemples:

- La *Mauresque* : à base de pastis et de **sirop d'orgeat**
- La *Tomate* : a base de pastis et de sirop de grenadine
- Le *Perroquet* : a base de pastis et de sirop de **menthe**
- Le *Mazout* : à base de pastis et de soda au cola
- Le *Diesel* : à base de pastis et de **vin blanc**

Mais le culte du pastis **va bien au-delà** encore. Aujourd'hui **on peut même trouver** un dictionnaire du pastis **qui fait sourire** les Marseillais et **les touristes avisés**.   Dans le dictionnaire **on trouve** : <u>Pastis</u> : Liquide indispensable à l'exercice de certaines activités sportives de **haut niveau**, la pétanque par exemple. (Définition Impertinente - Edouard Huguelet).

Plus qu'une boisson, **vous l'aurez bien compris**, le pastis représente **en lui** toute la grande tradition de l'apéritif marseillais. Il est **5 heures et quart**… **le soleil tape toujours** et **les cigales ne se sont pas** encore **arrêtées** de **chanter**. **Je suis** sur la terrasse d'un café **au cœur** d'un petit village au centre de Marseille… Il fait chaud mais ici, **on sait se désaltérer**. C'est l'heure de l'apéritif.

remonterait au temps de (remonter): goes back to the time of (to go back)
des Romains (un Romain): Romans
(ils) buvaient (boire): they drank (to drink)
un vin: wine
une confrérie: brotherhood
onguents (un onguent): salves, ointments
utilisés (utiliser): used (to use)
guérir: to cure
maladies (une maladie): diseases
les Maures: Moors
plus tard: later
les croisés: crusaders
ils introduisent (introduire): they introduced (to introduce)
raffinée (raffiné): refined
elle donne naissance (donner): it gave birth (to give)

un véritable culte: a real cult
non seulement: not only
il innove (innover): it is used innovatively (to innovate)
également: also
voici: here are
quelques: some
le sirop d'orgeat: orgeat syrup
la menthe: mint
le vin blanc: white wine

va bien au-delà (aller): goes far beyond (to go)
on peut (pouvoir): we can (can, to be able to)
même: even
trouver: find
qui fait sourire: that makes smile
les touristes avisés: informed tourists
on trouve (trouver): we find (to find)
un haut niveau: high level

vous l'aurez bien compris (comprendre): you will have understood (to understand)
en lui: in itself
5 heures et quart: a quarter past five
le soleil: sun
(il) tape (taper): is scorching, beats down (to be scorching, hot)
toujours: still, always
les cigales (la cigale): cicadas
ne se sont pas arrêtées (s'arrêter): have not stopped (to stop)
chanter: to sing
je suis (étre): I am (to be)
au cœur de: in the heart of
il fait chaud: it is warm
mais ici: but here
on sait se désaltérer (savoir): we know how to quench our thirst (to know)
c'est l'heure de: it is the hour of

les vins (le vin): the wines
les fromages (le fromage): the cheeses
font partie de (faire partie de): are part of
  (to be part of)
intégrante: integral
très peu de: very few
repas (un repas): meals
ne se passent sans (se passer): take place
  without (to happen, take place)

célèbres (célèbre): famous
comment voulez-vous: how do you want?
gouverner: to govern
un pays: a country
en fait: in fact, actually
plus de: more than
un dicton: a saying
il dit (dire): it says (to say)
un pour chaque jour: one for every day
l'année (une année): year
le nombre: the number
écrit (écrire): written (to write)
communément: generally
recensées (recenser): listed (to list, compile)

délivré au: given to
mais également: but also
il garantit (garantir): it guarantees
  (to guarantee)
non seulement: not only
ceci permet (permettre): it allows (to allow)
une traçabilité: traceability
facilement: easily
reproductibles (reproductible): reproducible

on distingue (distinguer): you can discern
  (to discern)
le lait de vache: cow milk
le lait de chèvre: goat milk
le lait de brebis: ewe milk
etant donné que (donner): given that (to give)
de nombreux adjectifs: a lot of adjectives
décrivent (décrire): that describe (to describe)
le goût: the taste
il peut être (pouvoir): it can be
  (can, to be able to)
pâte molle: soft
pâte pressée: pressed
une croûte naturelle: natural rind
dure (dur): hard
forts (fort): strong
ils méritent tous (mériter): they are all worth
  (to be worth, deserve)

portent (porter) le nom de: have the name of
  (to have)
appellation: designation
la ville: city
la feuille: leaf

Le vin et le fromage français

Les vins et **les fromages font partie intégrante** de la culture gastronomique française. **Très peu de repas** en France **ne se passent sans** qu'il n'y ait du vin et du fromage à table.

Une des citations **célèbres** du Général de Gaulle est : « **Comment voulez-vous gouverner un pays** où il existe 246 variétés de fromage ? » Il en existe **en fait plus de** 400 différents types. **Un dicton** célèbre **dit** qu'il en existe 365, **un pour chaque jour** de **l'année**, mais **le nombre** exact est absolument impossible à déterminer. Quant au vin, 340 Appellations d'Origine Contrôlées (**écrit communément** AOC) sont **recensées** sur le seul territoire français.

Ce label AOC, **délivré au** vin, **mais également** au fromage, est donné par l'Institut National des Appellations d'Origine (dépendant du Ministère de l'Agriculture). **Il garantit non seulement** la qualité, mais également l'authenticité de l'origine géographique du produit. **Ceci permet une traçabilité** et un respect de la labellisation des fromages et vins qui, de part leurs nombres, sont **facilement reproductibles**.

On distingue trois types de fromages : les fromages au **lait de vache**, ceux au **lait de chèvre** et ceux au **lait de brebis**. **Etant donné** qu'il existe un grand nombre de fromages en France, **de nombreux adjectifs décrivent** la texture, **le goût** et le type de pâte le caractérisant : le fromage **peut être** frais, à **pâte molle**, à pâte normale, à **pâte pressée**, à **croûte naturelle**, à croûte **dure**. .. Il y a des fromages **forts** (Roquefort, Maroilles, Cancoillote...), ou des fromages plus doux (Brie, Tomme...), mais **ils méritent tous** un détour.

Certains fromages **portent** dans leur **appellation** le nom de **la ville** d'origine de leur fabrication. Ainsi, le *St Marcellin*, le Brie de *Meaux*, **la feuille** de *Dreux* ou le bleu de *Sassenage* fournissent directement les informations sur la ville de provenance du fromage.

D'autres possèdent juste le nom d'une région, comme le *Cantal*, le carré du *Poitou*, la tomme de *Savoie*, ou l'Epoisses de *Bourgogne*.

De la même façon, la plupart des vins français sont issus de régions spécifiques du pays. Ces régions, de part leur climat, la caractéristique et la richesse de leurs terres, font les spécificités de chacun des vins et qui y sont produits. Par exemple, la Champagne et l'Alsace (régions du nord et nord-est) produisent des vignes très différentes de celles des régions de Bordeaux et de Provence (sud et sud-est). La région d'origine des vignes et l'un des facteurs les plus importants dans la production du vin. Ces caractéristiques sont déterminées sous le terme de « terroir ». Un terroir est donc un ensemble de vignobles d'une même région géographique, avec le même type de sol (terre) et de conditions climatiques. La dénomination du terroir garantit ainsi de retrouver un certain type de vin qui aura les mêmes caractéristiques générales, mais avec des subtilités de goût différentes.

Les vins français sont issus des 9 grandes régions suivantes : Alsace, Beaujolais, Bordeaux, Bourgogne, Côtes du Rhône, Languedoc Roussillon, Loire, Provence/Corse et Sud Ouest. Le casse-tête des non-initiés au savoir viticole est de pouvoir choisir le vin adéquat en accompagnement d'un repas. Ainsi, la majorité des recettes de cuisine publiées comporte une annotation sur le type de vin à servir avec le plat en question. En cas de doute, il vaut mieux laisser les choix du vin à quelqu'un qui s'y connait, ou demander conseil, plutôt que de tenter sa chance au hasard. Choisir un vin qui ne se marie pas du tout avec un plat est une faute de goût certaine à la table des Français et vu le nombre de vins disponibles, on ne peut laisser la chance décider pour soi sans prendre un certain risque.

Pour ce qui est de l'alliance du fromage et du vin, le top du top est de savoir marier le bon fromage avec le bon vin. Tout un art, mais quel délice pour le palais !

les feuilles (la feuille): leaves
l'érable (masc.): maple tree
les champignons (le champignon):
  mushrooms
des bois (un bois): woods
jaune: yellow
le soleil: sun
(il) se voile (se voiler): (it) veils (to veil)
marron: brown
le tronc: trunk
belles (beau): beautiful
l'automne: autumn

les arbres (la arbre): trees
la survie: survival
adapté: adapted
ils sont implantés (implanter): they are
  settled (to settle)
tempérées (tempéré): mild
froides (froid): cold
utilisent (utiliser): use (to use)
avec parcimonie: sparingly
(ils) déclenchent (déclencher): (they) start
  (to start)
la veille: (here) dormancy
un hiver: winter
les parties (la partie): parts
(elles) sont protégées (protéger): (they) are
  protected (to protect)
écorce: bark
un tissu: tissue
tendre: soft
qui ne résiste pas (résister): that cannot
  withstand (to withstand, resist)

dès que: as soon as
commencent à (commencer): start to
  (to start to)
baisser: to decrease
vers: around
la fin: end
le mois: month
la sève: sap
véhiculée (véhiculer): carried (to carry)
(elle) ne peut plus accéder (pouvoir): (it) can
  no longer access (can, to be able)
nourrir: to feed
arrivent (arriver): manage (to manage)
survivre: to survive
pendant: for
propre: own
mais: but
petit à petit: bit by bit, slowly
elles se déshydratent: they become dehydrated
(elles) se durcissent (durcir): (they) harden
  (to harden)
la perte: loss
n'est plus produite (produire): is no longer
  produced (to produce)

Le flamboyant automne

Rouge, **les feuilles** de l'**érable**.
Orange **les champignons des bois**.
Jaune le soleil qui **se voile**.
Marron, comme **le tronc**.
Belles sont les couleurs de l'**automne** !

Les arbres ont un système de **survie adapté** aux régions où **ils sont implantés**. Ainsi, dans les régions **tempérées** et **froides**, les arbres **utilisent** leur énergie **avec parcimonie** et **déclenchent** un système de **veille** en **hiver**. Alors que **les parties** solides de l'arbre comme le tronc et les branches **sont protégées** par l'**écorce**, les feuilles quant à elles ont **un tissu tendre qui ne résiste pas** aux basses températures.

Dès que les températures **commencent à baisser**, **vers la fin** du **mois** de septembre en France, **la sève**, **véhiculée** habituellement dans toutes les parties de l'arbre, **ne peut plus accéder** aux feuilles car le système de veille de l'arbre n'a plus suffisamment d'énergie pour **nourrir** ses extrémités. Les feuilles **arrivent** donc à **survivre pendant** une période avec leur **propre** réserve, **mais petit à petit, elles se déshydratent** et **se durcissent**. Cette déshydratation est symbolisée par **la perte** de leur couleur verte, représentant la chlorophylle qui **n'est plus produite**.

Ainsi, quand arrive l'automne en France, **les paysages** sont illuminés par des **couleurs féeriques plus flamboyantes les unes que les autres:** orange, jaune, violet, rouge, ocre, **mordoré, or** … Ce phénomène **dure** habituellement **trois à quatre semaines**, mais **la douceur** des températures de certains automnes prolonge souvent ces magnifiques **tableaux quelques** semaines de plus.

En automne, **les enfants se régalent à faire voler** les feuilles **mortes en donnant de grands coups de pieds** dans **les tas** de feuilles **qui se sont amassées par terre.**

Les feuilles, **châtaignes** et autres **trésors trouvés à même le sol**, dans les bois et **forêts** sont autant d'**outils précieux** pour la réalisation de tableaux et natures mortes dont **les enseignants s'inspirent souvent** pour **créer** des activités de **bricolage** avec **leurs élèves.**

A cette période, **des** petits **stands apparaissent un peu partout** dans **les rues** pour **vendre** des châtaignes grillées, à **déguster** sur place, **encore chaudes**. Ces châtaignes sont grillées dans **des poêles** spécifiques (avec **des trous au fond**), sur **des braises, afin que** l'écorce **se craquèle** et permette ainsi au **fruit de cuire** rapidement **tout en gardant** sa texture.

De Paul Verlaine (avec sa « Chanson d'automne »), à Jacques Prévert (avec son **œuvre** « Les feuilles mortes »), les thèmes de l'automne et des feuilles mortes ont inspiré plus d'**un auteur français** et de nombreux poèmes **ont été écrits** à ce sujet. **En voici deux**, pour **le plaisir des yeux.**

les paysages (le paysage): landscapes
couleurs féeriques: magical colors
plus flamboyantes les unes que les autres:
  each more fiery than the next
mordoré: golden brown
or: gold
(il) dure (durer): (it) lasts (to last)
trois à quatre semaines: three to four weeks
la douceur: mildness
ces tableaux (un tableau): scenes
quelques: some

les enfants (le enfant): children
 se régalent à (se régaler): enjoy (to enjoy)
faire voler: to make fly
mortes (mort): dead
en donnant de grands coups de pieds:
  by kicking their feet
les tas (le tas): heaps, piles
qui se sont amassées par terre: that have
  piled up on the ground

châtaignes (une châtaigne): chestnuts
trésors (un trésor): treasures
trouvés (trouver): found (to find)
à même le sol: right on the ground
forêts (une forêt): forests
outils (un outil): tools
précieux: precious
les enseignants (le enseignant): teachers
s'inspirent (inspirer): are inspired (to inspire)
souvent: often
créer: to create
le bricolage: arts and crafts
leurs élèves (un eleve): their students

des stands (un stand): stalls
apparaissent (apparaître): appear (to appear)
un peu partout: just about anywhere
les rues (le rue): streets
vendre: to sell
déguster: to taste
encore chaudes (chaud): still warm
des poêles (une poêle): pans
des trous au fond: holes in the bottom
des braises (une braise): embers
afin que: in order to
se craquèle (se craqueler): cracks (to crack)
le fruit: (here) nut
cuire: to cook
tout en gardant: while keeping

une œuvre: work
un auteur français: French author
ont été écrits (écrire): have been written
 (to write)
en voici deux: here are two of them
le plaisir: pleasure
des yeux (un œil): eyes

La cérémonie du mariage

se déroule (dérouler): takes place (to take place)
(elle) a lieu (avoir lieu): it occurs (to occur)
la mairie: town hall
alors que: whereas
la deuxième: the second one
selon: according to
les croyances (la croyance): beliefs
une église: church
le prêtre: priest
bénira (bénir): will bless (to bless)
unira (unir): unite (to unite)
les deux époux: husband and wife, the married couple

le passage: passing
devant: in front of
se fait (se faire): is done (to do)
assez rapidement: rather quickly
s'assure (s'assurer): makes sure (to make sure)
tels que (tel que): such as
entre autres: among others
se doivent (devoir): owe each other (to owe)
mutuellement: mutually
la fidélité: fidelity
le secours: help, rescue
(ils) assurent (assurer): (they) ensure (to ensure)
ensemble: together
ils pourvoient (pourvoir): they provide (to provide)
des enfants (un enfant): children
avenir: future

quant à: as for
en effet: indeed
il leur revient de choisir: it is for them to choose
ils souhaitent (souhaiter): they wish (to wish)
décider: to decide
qui sera jouée (jouer): that will be played (to play)
pendant: while
les étapes (la étape): steps
la marche nuptiale: the nuptial walk
la clôture: end

(elle) se fait (se faire): it is done (to be done)
souvent: often
sur un fond: with a background
solennelle: formal
(il) entre (entrer): (he) comes in (to come in)
autel: altar
qui fera son entrée (faire): who will make her entrance (to do, make)
le bras: arm
son père (le père): her father
un petit discours: small speech
un accueil: welcome
(il) s'en suivra (s'en suivre): (it) will follow (to follow)
des amis (un ami): friends
(ils) auront préparés (préparer): (they) will have prepared (to prepare)
le plus émouvant: the most moving
sans nul doute: without a doubt
des consentements: consents

En France, le mariage **se déroule** en général en deux cérémonies. La première **a lieu à la mairie alors que la deuxième** se déroulera **selon les croyances** et pratiques religieuses du couple à marier. Pour un mariage « traditionnel » français, la cérémonie religieuse a lieu dans **une église**, où **le prêtre bénira** et **unira les deux époux** selon les rituels de la religion catholique.

Le passage devant Monsieur le Maire **se fait** généralement **assez rapidement**. L'officier d'état civil s'**assure** de l'identité des deux futurs époux et procède à la lecture d'articles du code civil relatif au mariage **tels que, entre autres:**

- « Les époux **se doivent mutuellement fidélité**, **secours**, assistance ».
- « Les époux **assurent ensemble** la direction morale et matérielle de la famille. **Ils pourvoient** à l'éducation **des enfants** et préparent leur **avenir** ».

Quant à la cérémonie religieuse, elle nécessite un investissement plus important de la part des futurs mariés. **En effet**, pour la cérémonie à l'église, **il leur revient de choisir** les textes qu'**ils souhaitent** voir lire, de **décider** de la musique **qui sera jouée pendant** les différentes **étapes** de la cérémonie (l'entrée dans l'église, après la lecture des textes par le prêtre, **la marche nuptiale** et **la clôture** de la cérémonie).

L'entrée dans l'église **se fait souvent sur un fond** de musique classique et **solennelle**. Le marié **entre** en premier et attend devant l'**autel** sa future épouse **qui fera** son entrée au **bras** de **son père**. A l'arrivée des mariés, le prêtre formule **un petit discours** d'**accueil** à leur attention. **S'en suivra** la lecture de psaumes et de textes lus par des membres de la famille et **amis**, comme l'**auront préparés** les futurs mariés. Le moment **le plus émouvant** de la cérémonie religieuse est **sans nul doute** le moment où le prêtre procède à l'échange **des consentements**.

L'étape d'échange des consentements **terminée**, l'échange des alliances et la bénédiction concrétisent l'union **devant Dieu**. **Une fois** l'échange **des alliances** faites, le prêtre déclare « **Désormais, vous êtes unis** par Dieu par **les liens sacrés du mariage** ».

S'en suit **la bénédiction** nuptiale et la signature des registres, **pour laquelle les témoins rejoignent** les époux. **La sortie** de l'église se fait généralement sur une musique **entraînante et gaie**. Il est de coutume de **lancer des poignées de riz**, symbole de fertilité et de prospérité, **au-dessus** des mariés sur **les marches** de l'église.

Après cette cérémonie **un vin d'honneur** est généralement proposé. Il permet d'**inviter** les personnes avec qui les relations **ne sont pas suffisamment proches** pour **les convier** à **la soirée**. La soirée de mariage **se poursuivra** ensuite une grande partie de la nuit. Les mariés, qui sont généralement **les derniers** à partir, **passeront** la majeure partie de **leur temps** à aller de table en table **afin de pouvoir** parler et **profiter** de **chacun** des invités.

De nombreux mariages ont lieu en France **pendant les mois** de juin, juillet et août quand le temps est **clément** et **les journées plus longues** et **propices à la fête**. D'un point de vue pragmatique, **il faut donc** s'assurer bien à l'avance de **la disponibilité** des lieux que les futurs époux **ont choisi** pour leur soirée de mariage. En effet, **les salles sont** souvent **réservées plusieurs** mois à l'avance.

Une fois **unis** par les liens du mariage, **il ne reste plus qu'**à respecter **la dernière** tradition : la légende **raconte** que si la mariée **trébuchait en entrant** pour la première fois dans **la demeure conjugale**, alors son mariage **serait promis** à **un avenir** catastrophique ! Pour conjurer le sort et pour **éviter** cet incident, le marié **porte** donc la **nouvelle** épouse pour **franchir le seuil** de leur porte et la **ferme** afin d'éviter qu'**elle ne ressorte**.

Évaluez votre compréhension

Un jour, un chocolat, page 44

1. Where and when did the advent calendar originate?

2. How did the families mark the days leading up to Christmas?

Le temps des sucres, page 46

1. What is a *cabane à sucre* and what happens here?

2. How do you make *la tire d'érable*?

3. What is the technique to harvest the syrup?

Les vacances à la française, page 45

1. What new idea concerning vacations came about in 1920?

2. How did employees make this change happen?

3. In the last 50 years what has happened to the length of paid vacations in France?

Le réveillon de la Saint Sylvestre, page 48

1. In ancient Rome what gifts were exchanged?

2. At the Roman banquets what did the number of plates represent?

3. Why is the New Year's Eve meal scheduled later in the day?

Test your comprehension

Des chants sacrés, page 50

1. What are some of the traditional meals enjoyed at Christmas?

2. What represents the highlight of Christmas in Guadeloupe?

3. What is the tradition of *Le Chanté Nwel* and when does it start?

La tradition du pastis, page 52

1. Pastis is flavored by what seed?

2. What law was passed in 1915?

3. When is this apéritif generally enjoyed?

Le vin et le fromage français, page 54

1. What does the label AOC guarantee?

2. What does the term *terroir* guarantee or indicate?

3. How many main French wine regions are there?

La cérémonie du mariage, page 58

1. What does the author consider the most moving part of the wedding?

2. Exiting the church is done to what type of music?

3. When do most French weddings take place and why?

Célébration

Pâques en France

Pâques: Easter
des fêtes chrétiennes: Christian holidays
l'année (une année): the year
elle rappelle (rappeler): it commemorates (to commemorate)
trois jours (un jour): three days
sa mort (une mort): his death
la croix: the cross
ce jour (le jour): this day
marque (marquer): marks (to mark)
la fin: the end
le Carême: Lent
pratiquants (pratiquer): practicing (to practice)
qui veut dire (vouloir dire): which means (to mean)
les fidèles (le fidèle): the faithful, believers
doivent arrêter (devoir): must stop (to have to)
travailler: to work
aller: to go
la messe: mass
ils vont (aller): they go (to go)
se confesser: to confess
on appelait (appeler): one called (to call)
utilisée (utiliser): used (to use)

aujourd'hui: today
surtout: mainly
célèbre: famous
les œufs (le œuf): eggs
elle dit (dire): it says (to say)
les cloches (la cloche): bells
deviennent (devenir): become (to become)
le Jeudi Saint: Holy Thursday
le deuil: mourning
rappellent (rappeler): remind (to remind)
sont parties (partir): have gone (to go, leave)
elles reviennent (revenir): they come back (to come back)
leur passage: their passing through

le siècle dernier: last century
était encore (être): was still (to be)
cher: expensive
prenaient (prendre): would take (to take)
une poule: hen
les décoraient (décorer): they decorated it (to decorate)
revient (revenir): comes back (to come back)
lentement: slowly
à la mode: in fashion
un roi: king
on trouve (trouver): you can find (to find)
des lapins (un lapin): rabbits

vont (aller): go (to go)
les cacher: to hide them
une chasse: hunt
celui qui trouve: the one who finds
le plus: the most
gagne (gagner): wins (to win)
chercher: to look for
partager: to share
il arrive (arriver): it happens (to happen)
on rencontre (rencontrer): one comes across (to come across)
un coin: a corner
joyeuses (joyeux): happy
bonne chasse: happy hunting

Pâques est une **des fêtes chrétiennes** les plus importantes de **l'année**. **Elle rappelle** la résurrection de Jésus Christ, **trois jours** après **sa mort** sur **la croix**, et **ce jour marque la fin** du **Carême** pour les chrétiens **pratiquants**. C'est une fête « d'obligation », ce **qui veut dire** que **les fidèles doivent arrêter** de travailler pour **aller** à **la messe**, où **ils vont** généralement **se confesser**. **On appelait** cela « faire ses Pâques » mais l'expression n'est plus très **utilisée**.

Aujourd'hui, Pâques est **surtout célèbre** pour… **les œufs** en chocolat. La légende populaire **dit** que **les cloches deviennent** silencieuses **le Jeudi Saint**, en signe de **deuil**. Les parents **rappellent** aux enfants que les cloches **sont parties** à Rome pour célébrer la mémoire du Christ. **Elles reviennent** ensuite le jour de Pâques, distribuant des œufs sur **leur passage**.

Au **siècle dernier**, le chocolat **était encore cher**, alors les parents **prenaient** des œufs de **poule** et **les décoraient**. Ce phénomène **revient lentement à la mode**, comme activité familiale. Mais aujourd'hui, le chocolat est **roi**! **On trouve** des œufs, grands ou petits, mais aussi **des lapins**, des poules et des cloches en chocolat.

Les parents **vont les cacher** dans le jardin ou dans l'appartement pour **une** « **chasse** à l'œuf », au grand plaisir des enfants. Certains villages organisent aussi des « chasses à l'œuf » dans un parc, pour enfants et adultes. **Celui qui trouve le plus** d'œufs **gagne**… mais le plus grand plaisir est de **chercher** et de **partager**. Évidemment, tous les œufs ne sont pas trouvés et **il arrive** souvent qu'**on rencontre** des œufs abandonnés dans **un coin**. Alors, **joyeuses** Pâques et **bonne chasse** à l'œuf !

La fête du Travail

La Fête du Travail est une fête **connue qui rend hommage** aux **travailleurs** dans **le monde entier**. **Tout commence** aux États-Unis, le 1er mai 1884, quand **les syndicats décident** de commencer **une grève : ils demandent** la réduction du **temps de travail**. **Deux ans plus tard**, le 1er mai 1886, les patrons américains acceptent **la journée de huit heures**.

En 1889, les syndicats français **veulent** aussi une réduction du temps de travail et décident donc que, **chaque** 1er mai, **il y aura des manifestations** en France. Pendant la manifestation de 1891, **neuf ouvriers** sont tués par la police : le 1er mai **devient** alors un symbole de **lutte** pour les ouvriers. Les syndicats **continuent** les manifestations chaque année et **appellent** le 1er mai « la Fête des Travailleurs ».

Ce n'est qu'en 1921 que le Sénat français **ratifie** la journée de huit heures. L'année **suivante**, le Maréchal Pétain déclare le 1er mai « Journée du Travail et de la Concorde Sociale » mais la Fête du Travail devient **un jour férié seulement** en 1947, **peu après la guerre**.

Si vous vous promenez en France au début du **mois** de mai, **vous verrez beaucoup** de **gens vendre** du **muguet**. C'est une tradition associée au 1er mai car le muguet est **un porte-bonheur**. **Le roi** Charles IX a en effet **reçu un brin** de muguet en 1561 et il a décidé d'en **donner** aux **dames** de **la cour** chaque année, pour **leur porter chance**.

Depuis, on offre du muguet à **nos amis** et à nos familles le 1er mai. **Chacun peut** en **cueillir** dans **son jardin** et en vendre dans **la rue ce jour-là**, **sans payer** de taxes **à l'état**. **Si vous êtes** en France à cette période, **n'oubliez pas** d'offrir un brin de muguet à **vos proches** mais **faites attention**, car cette **jolie fleur** est aussi toxique.

La Fête du Travail: Labor Day
connue (connaître): well-known (to know)
qui rend homage (rendre homage): which pays tribute (to pay tribute)
travailleurs (un travailleur): workers
le monde entier: the whole world
tout commence (commencer): it all started (to start)
les syndicats (un syndicat): labor union
décident (decider): decided (to decide)
une grève: a strike
ils demandent (demander): they asked (to ask)
temps de travail: working hours
deux ans: two years
plus tard: later
la journée de 8 heures: the 8-hour (work) day

ils veulent (vouloir): they want (to want)
chaque: each
il y aura (avoir): there will be (to have)
des manifestations (une manifestation): demonstrations
neuf ouvriers (un ouvrier): nine workers
(il) devient (devenir): it became (to become)
la lutte: fight
continuent (continuer): carry on (to carry on)
ils appellent (appeler): they call (to call)

ce n'est qu' (être): it is only (to be)
ratifie (ratifier): ratifies (to ratify)
suivante (suivant): following
un jour férié: a public holiday
seulement: only
peu après: shortly after
la guerre: the war

si vous vous promenez (se promener): if you go for a walk (to go for a walk)
le mois: month
vous verrez (voir): you will see (to see)
beaucoup: lots
des gens: people
vendre: selling
le muguet: lily of the valley
un porte-bonheur: a lucky charm
le roi: the king
(il) a reçu (recevoir): he received (to receive)
un brin: a sprig
donner: to give
dames (une dame): ladies
la cour: the court
leur porter chance: to bring them luck

depuis: since then
nos amis (un ami): our friends
chacun peut (pouvoir): everybody can (can, to be able to)
cueillir: to pick
son jardin (le jardin): his garden (the garden)
la rue: the street
ce jour-là: on that day
sans payer: without paying
à l'état: to the state
si vous êtes (être): if you are (to be)
n'oubliez pas (oublier): don't forget (to forget)
vos proches (un proche): your relatives
faites attention: careful
jolie (joli): pretty
fleur (une fleur): flower

Le carnaval aux Antilles

Chaque année, les Caraïbes **vibrent** aux **sons** du carnaval et dans les **Antilles françaises**, Guadeloupe et Martinique, c'est une tradition très **vivante**. Aux Antilles, l'Épiphanie ou **la fête des Rois**, qui est le **premier dimanche** de **janvier** est aussi le premier dimanche du Carnaval.

Mais **comment expliquer** la force de cette tradition aux Antilles françaises? Le carnaval a des origines européennes très **lointaines**. *Carne levare* **qui signifie** en italien « **lever la chair** » était une célébration religieuse qui **précédait** le **Carême**, période d'abstinence où **les croyants ne mangent pas** de **viande**. Ainsi, pour compenser **les manques** du Carême, on mangeait en abondance et en **se faisant plaisir**.

Au delà de ces origines européennes, il faut aussi **rappeler** que les Antilles françaises, **ont été peuplées** par les Africains, venus comme **esclaves**, avec des traditions et des célébrations très **fortes** aux Antilles. Le Carnaval était une période où ils étaient **un peu plus libres** d'**exprimer** leurs cultures **par des chants** et des danses.

De nos jours, le Carnaval commence le premier dimanche de janvier, **jusqu'à** la date officielle du **Mercredi des Cendres**, avec **des défilés** tous les dimanches. Chaque dimanche, de très **nombreux groupes** carnavalesques défilent dans des costumes variés et colorés et au son d'une musique traditionnelle. **On les appelle** les « groupes **à pied** », parce que **les carnavaliers** défilent à pieds, sans **chars**. Il en existe trois catégories.

Il y a tout d'abord, les groupes qui s'inspirent d'un carnaval très coloré comme **celui** de Rio. **Ils se reconnaissent** à leur musique « à **caisse claire** » et à leurs costumes très colorés **faits** de **plumes**, de **tissus** très **chatoyants** et à leurs chorégraphies.

Ils font partie de la tradition du carnaval guadeloupéen. Ils participent aux **concours** de la saison pour déterminer **le meilleur** groupe du carnaval et **élisent** une **Reine** du carnaval.

Les « ti-mass » sont des groupes d'**enfants** ou de **jeunes** qui se déguisent d'un **même** costume, d'une même couleur et **qui se cachent le visage** avec des masques de **singes** ou de **sorcières** de manga. C'est une évolution du carnaval en Guadeloupe car ces groupes ont une musique très innovante et très appréciée par les jeunes.

Pour finir, **le troisième** type de groupe s'appelle les groupes « à peaux » qui portent le nom **des tambours** faits avec **une peau de cabri** très **tendue**. Ces groupes sont dits traditionnels et font un carnaval **plus proche** des traditions africaines **qu'**européennes. **Les déguisements** sont souvent **des éléments** recyclés: **feuillages**, tissus, **bouteilles** en plastique. Ils défendent une vision du carnaval et de la société.

Ils ne défilent pas mais **marchent**, ils ne font pas de chorégraphies mais **chantent en avançant** avec un rythme très **soutenu**, comme une d'activité physique et spirituelle. **Devant** les groupes, il y a **toujours** de l'encens pour **appeler** l'esprit des ancêtres et de **fouets** pour annoncer leur arrivée.

Si dans certains **pays** c'est le **dernier jour** du carnaval, en Guadeloupe, deux **semaines plus tard**, les défilés **reprennent** le **jeudi** de la mi-Carême. Ce jeudi est exactement à **la moitié** du **mois** du Carême. On défile en rouge et noir, couleurs qui symbolisent **la renaissance** du carnaval pour l'**année suivante**.

Le carnaval **dure parfois** un mois, un mois et demi et même deux mois selon le calendrier de l'année, **mais malgré tout** les carnavaliers **n'en ont jamais assez**.

ils font partie (faire partie): they are a part of (to be a part of)
concours (un concours): contests
le meilleur: the best
ils élisent (élire): they elect (to elect, choose)
une reine: queen

enfants (un enfant): children
jeunes (un jeune): young people
même: same
qui se cachent (cacher): that hide (to hide)
le visage: face
des singes (un singe): monkeys
sorcières (une sorcière): witches

pour finir: in the end, finally
le troisième: the third
des tambours (un tambour): drums
une peau de cabri: young goat skin
tendue (tendre): stretched (to stretch)
plus proche... que: closer than
les déguisements (le déguisement): costumes
des éléments (un élément): items
feuillages (un feuillage): foliage, leaves
bouteilles (une bouteille): bottles

(ils) marchent (marcher): they walk (to walk)
(ils) chantent (chanter): they sing (to sing)
en avançant (avancer): while moving forward (to move forward)
soutenu: steady
devant: in front of
toujours: always
appeler: to call for
des fouets (un fouet): whips

des pays (un pays): countries
dernier jour (un jour): last day
des semaines (une semaine): weeks
plus tard: later
reprennent (reprendre): start again (to start again)
jeudi: Thursday
la moitié: half
un mois: month
la renaissance: rebirth
la année: year
suivante (suivant): following

dure (durer): lasts (to last)
parfois: sometimes
mais malgré tout: despite all this
n'en ont jamais assez (en avoir assez): never have enough of it (to have enough of it)

Faites de la musique !

La Fête de la Musique est **aujourd'hui** un événement international, **célébré** dans **plus de cent pays**. **Mais tout a commencé** en France, en 1982. **Après** les élections présidentielles de 1981, Jack Lang **devient** Ministre de la Culture et **adapte** une idée de Joel Cohen, un musicien de Radio France – Radio Musique. La première édition de la Fête de la Musique est donc **lancée** le 21 juin 1982 et **rencontre** un grand succès: les éditions **se succèdent** alors **chaque année** et la Fête devient un des événements culturels les plus importants de l'année. **Au fil du temps, elle s'exporte** en Europe puis dans **le monde entier,** avec plus de 340 **villes** participantes.

La Fête **a lieu** le 21 juin, **jour du solstice** d'été. C'est **la nuit la plus courte** de l'année et **on en profite** aussi pour célébrer l'arrivée de **l'été** et des vacances. C'est donc le moment idéal pour **descendre dans les rues** et **s'amuser jusqu'au lendemain matin** !

À la Fête de la Musique, **faites de la musique** ! **Ce jour-là,** des concerts **improvisés** ont lieu dans **les écoles**, les hôpitaux, **les musées**, les bars, les restaurants, **les salles de spectacles**… **mais surtout** dans les parcs et dans la rue ! Tout le monde peut organiser un petit concert pour exposer son talent ou, tout simplement, pour **partager** sa passion de la musique. Musiciens professionnels, groupes amateurs, **élèves** d'écoles de musique, débutants complets: **au moins** un Français sur dix **a déjà participé** à la Fête de la Musique, **soit en jouant, soit en chantant.** C'est en effet une bonne occasion de se produire **sur scène** !

La Fête de la Musique: The Music Festival
aujourd'hui: today
célébré (célébrer): celebrated (to celebrate)
plus de: more than
cent: one hundred
des pays (un pays): countries
mais tout: but everything
a commencé (commencer): started (to start)
après: after
devient (devenir): becomes (to become)
(il) adapte (adapter): he adapts (to adapt)
(elle) est lancée (lancer): it is launched (to launch)
(il) rencontre (rencontrer): it meets (to meet)
se succèdent (se succeder): follow one another (to succeed, to follow)
chaque année: every year
au fil du temps: as time goes by
elle s'exporte (s'exporter): it is exported (to export)
le monde entier: worldwide
des villes (une ville): cities

a lieu (avoir lieu): occurs (to occur)
le jour du solstice d'été: summer solstice day
la nuit: night
la plus courte (court): the shortest
on en profite (profiter de): we take advantage of it (to take advantage of)
l'été: the summer
descendre dans les rues: to go into the streets
s'amuser: to have fun
jusqu'au (jusqu'à): until
le lendemain matin: the next morning

faites de la musique: we make music
ce jour-là: that day
inprovisés (improviser): improvised (to improvise)
les écoles (la école): schools
les musées (le musée): museums
les salles de spectacles: concert halls
mais surtout: but most of all
partager: to share
des élèves (un élève): students
au moins: at least
a déjà participé (participer): has already participated (to participate)
soit en jouant soit en chantant: either by playing or by singing
sur scène: on stage

Ce jour-là, la SACEM (Société des Auteurs Compositeurs et Éditeurs de Musique) **ne demande aucun droit d'auteur** pour les concerts **gratuits**. Les musiciens **jouent** donc bénévolement. Mais c'est l'occasion de **se faire connaître** et de **toucher** un large public. 80% des Français **ont en effet assisté** à l'événement **au moins une fois depuis** 1982 ! Pour les « simples » spectateurs, la Fête de la Musique est une occasion formidable pour assister à des concerts gratuitement mais aussi pour **découvrir** de **nouveaux** styles de musique. Jazz, rock, musique du monde, RnB, musique classique, rap, musique traditionnelle… Tous les genres sont représentés !

La Fête a **d'ailleurs servi de tremplin** à de **nombreux** groupes dans certains genres récents, comme le hip-hop ou la techno. C'est aussi l'occasion de **prouver** que certains styles, considérés « **ringards** » ou **dépassés**, sont **toujours** d'actualité et appréciés par le public. Mais, **on assiste surtout** à un **joyeux mélange** des genres, qui **témoigne** de la vitalité de la scène musicale française.

Malgré tout, la Fête a aussi **ses mauvais côtés** et **la polémique renaît** chaque année. **Les nuisances sonores** ont en effet été critiquées par les habitants de certains quartiers et des restrictions **ont dû être imposées** sur les **lieux et heures** des concerts, ainsi que sur **les niveaux sonores**. Plus que **le bruit**, l'alcool est **le trouble-fête** le plus important. La consommation excessive de **bière** a ainsi dégradé l'image de la Fête de la Musique dans certaines villes, où la soirée s'est **parfois terminée** dans **des affrontements**. Le nombre d'accidents de la route est en augmentation cette nuit-là, à cause de **la vente** d'alcool à une population **jeune** et **souvent insouciante**. Pour l'occasion, le métro et certains transports publics sont gratuits toute la soirée, **afin d'**encourager **les gens** à **ne pas utiliser leur voiture**.

Malgré ces désagréments, la Fête de la Musique est **en bonne santé**. Avec 18 000 concerts chaque année, 5 millions de musiciens et 10 millions de spectateurs, elle reste un **des événements majeurs** et **incontournables** du **paysage culturel français**.

ne demande aucun (demander): asks for no (to ask for)
un droit d'auteur: royalties
gratuits (gratuit): free
jouent (jouer): play (to play)
se faire connaître: to introduce oneself
toucher: to reach
ont assisté (assister): have attended (to attend)
en effet: indeed
au moins: at least
une fois: once
depuis: since
découvrir: to discover
nouveaux (nouveau): new

d'ailleurs: besides
(elle) a servi de tremplin (servir): it has served as as a springboard (to serve)
nombreux: numerous
prouver: to prove
ringards (ringard): tacky, out of date
dépassés (dépassé): old-fashioned
toujours: always
on assiste à (assister): one witnesses (to witness)
surtout: most of all
joyeux mélange: joyful blend
témoigner: to witness

malgré tout: regardless
ses mauvais côtés (un côté): its bad sides
la polémique: a debate
renaît (renaitre): starts again (to start again)
les nuisances sonores: noise pollution
ont dû être imposées: had to be imposed
lieux et heures: where and when
les niveaux sonores: noise levels
le bruit: noise
le trouble-fête: a spoilsport, killjoy
une bière: beer
parfois: sometimes
terminée (se terminer): ended (to end)
des affrontements (un affrontement): confrontations
la vente: sale
jeune: young
souvent: often
insouciante (insouciant): carefree
afin de: in order to
les gens: people
ne pas utiliser: not to use
leur voiture (une voiture): their car

en bonne santé: healthy, carefree
des événements (un événement): events
majeurs (majeur): main, major
incontournable: indispensable, unmissable
le paysage culturel français: the French cultural scene

Poisson d'avril !

une coutume: custom
offrir: to give
un cadeau: gift
appelé (appeler): called (to call)
les étrennes: New Year's Day present
ses proches (un proche): one's close relatives
ses amis (un ami): one's friends
le jour de l'An: New Year's day
souhaiter: to wish
la bonne année: Happy New Year
espérer: to hope for
la santé: health
le bonheur: happiness
douze: mois (un mois): twelve months
venir: to come

débutait (débuter): started (to start)
le Roi: King
institua (instituer): established (to establish)
se faisaient (se faire): took place (to take place)
mais: but
même: same
les plaisantins (le plaisantin): jokers
eurent (avoir): had (to have)
la idée: idea
faire des cadeaux: to give presents
le changement: the change
marquant (marquer): marking (to mark)
une moquerie: mockery
vis-à-vis: toward
instauré (instaurer): introduced (to introduce)

pour parfaire: to add the finishing touches to
ils eurent (avoir): they had (to have)
faux: false
puisque: since
vraie (vrai): real
fausse (faux): false
la valeur: worth, value
des blagues (une blague): tricks
farces (une farce): practical jokes
est restée (rester): has remained (to remain)

plus connue (connaître): better known (to know)
utilisée (utiliser): used (to use)
les enfants (le enfant): children (child)
(elle) consiste (consister): it consists (to consist)
accrocher: to hang
en cachette: in secret
un poisson: a fish
quelqu'un: somebody
se promène (se promener): walks around (to walk around)
s'aperçoive (apercevoir): to notice
réalisent (réaliser): create (to create)
découpant (découper): cutting out (to cut out)
coloriant (colorier): coloring in (to color in)
s'appliquent (s'appliquer): make an effort (to make an effort)
(ils) s'amusent (s'amuser): they have fun (to have fun)
se laissent (se laisser): let themselves (to let oneself)
prendre: to be taken in, fooled
leur faire plaisir: to please them

Pourquoi cette date ? Il est de **coutume** d'**offrir un** petit **cadeau** (**appelé les étrennes**) à **ses proches**, **ses amis**, **le jour de l'An** pour leur **souhaiter la bonne année** et leur **espérer santé**, **bonheur** et prospérité pour les **douze mois** à **venir**.

En France, jusqu'en 1564, l'année calendaire **débutait** le 1er avril, également jour de Pâques. **Le Roi** Charles IX (1550-1574) **institua** par ordonnance le début de l'année au 1er janvier. Jusqu'en 1564, les étrennes **se faisaient** donc le 1er avril. En 1565, la coutume des étrennes de bonne année se fit donc le 1er janvier. **Mais** en date du 1er avril de cette **même** année, certains **plaisantins eurent l'idée de faire des cadeaux**, pour faire comme avant **le changement** de date **marquant** le début de l'année. Ceci, soit par rébellion, soit par pure **moquerie vis-à-vis** du changement **instauré** par Charles IX.

Pour parfaire la plaisanterie, **ils eurent** l'idée de faire des **faux** cadeaux **puisque** la date n'était plus la **vraie**, mais la **fausse**. Les cadeaux furent donc sans **valeur** particulière, pour rire et faire **des blagues** à leurs amis et proches avec des présents ridicules. Depuis cette date, la tradition de faire des blagues et **farces est restée** au 1er avril de chaque année.

La blague la **plus connue, utilisée** par les plus petits **enfants, consiste** à **accrocher en cachette, un poisson** dans le dos de **quelqu'un**. La personne **se promène** donc avec un poisson accroché dans son dos sans qu'elle s'en **aperçoive**. Les petits plaisantins **réalisent** leurs poissons en **découpant** et **coloriant** du papier. Il y en a de très élaborés et multicolores. Les petits enfants **s'appliquent** souvent pour faire leurs poissons et **s'amusent** beaucoup de cette blague à laquelle les adultes **se laissent prendre**, pour **leur faire plaisir**.

Le 1er avril **n'est pas réservé** aux plus petits, et les adultes, qui sont de grands enfants, **se prennent** également **au jeu**. De nos jours, les blagues sont plus **variées** et les nouvelles technologies **permettent** de laisser **libre cours** aux imaginations les plus **débordantes**. Faux PV, e-mails informatifs erronés, faux **courriers des impôts,** sont **autant de** farces dont il faut **se méfier** le 1er avril. **Quelle que** soit la blague effectuée, le farceur **s'écrit** « Poisson d'avril ! » **en riant**, au moment où la personne **se rend compte** qu'elle a été la victime d'une plaisanterie.

Mais pourquoi un poisson ? **Il y a plusieurs** explications possibles. La première, et la plus **répandue**, consiste dans le fait que le 1er avril est la date **qui marque la fin** du **carême**. **Pendant** cette période il est **d'usage** pour **les chrétiens** de faire abstinence et de **remplacer la viande** par du poisson. Le « faux » poisson marque donc la fin de **la durée** de carême et **le retour** à la consommation de la viande. C'est une bonne blague d'offrir un poisson quand on peut **justement** ne plus en **consommer**.

Ensuite, la pêche est une activité très répandue en France, et cette **époque** de l'année est réservée **au frai** des poissons (**c'est-à-dire** à la reproduction des poissons). Pendant cette période, **la pêche** est donc **interdite**. Certains plaisantins **eurent** l'idée de **jeter des harengs** (qui sont des poissons **d'eau de mer**) dans **la rivière**, pour faire une bonne blague aux **pêcheurs**, d'où **le terme** de « Poisson d'avril ».

Enfin, **d'autres** attribuent aussi l'utilisation de cet animal au fait que le signe zodiacal de cette période est le poisson. Quelle que soit l'explication, le 1er avril reste un jour où **tout le monde** s'amuse en **se moquant des autres** et en **faisant de blagues**. Bon poisson d'avril !

n'est pas réservé (être réservé): is not just for (to be just for, set aside for)
ils se prennent au jeu: they get involved (to get involved)
au jeu (un jeu): in the game
variées (varié): varied
permettent (permettre): allow (to allow)
libre cours: free rein to
débordantes (débordant): wild
courriers (un courrier): mail, letters
des impôts (un impôt): taxes
autant de: as many
se méfier: to be wary of, watch out for
quelle que: whatever
s'écrit (s'écrier): exclaims (to exclaim)
en riant (rire): in laughter (to laugh)
se rend compte (se rendre compte): becomes aware (to become aware)

il y a (avoir): there are (to have)
plusieurs: several
répandue (répandu): widespread
qui marque (marquer): which marks (to mark)
la fin: the end
le carême: Lent
pendant: during
d'usage: usual
les chrétiens (le chrétien): Christians
remplacer: to replace
la viande: meat
la durée: period
le retour: the return
justement: actually
consommer: to eat

ensuite: then
l'époque (une époque): time
au frai: spawning
c'est-à-dire: that is to say
la pêche: fishing
interdite (interdit): forbidden
(ils) eurent (avoir): they had (to have)
jeter: to throw
des harengs (un hareng): herrings
d'eau de mer: sea water
la rivière: river
pêcheurs (un pêcheur): fishermen
le terme: the term

d'autres (un autre): others
tout le monde: everybody
se moquant de (se moquer de): making fun of (to make fun of)
des autres (un autre): others
faisant des blagues: playing tricks

a lieu (avoir lieu): takes place (to take place)
tous les étés (un été): every summer
attachée (attacher): linked to (to link)
en effet: in fact
elle commémore (commémorer): it commemorates (to commemorate)
la prise: the storming
qui a vu tomber (voir): which saw the toppling (to see)
la royauté: the monarchy
célébrée (célébrer): celebrated (to celebrate)
ce jour (un jour): this day

on se lève (se lever): people wake up (to wake up)
bonne heure: early
il ne faudrait pas rater: people should not miss
un défilé: parade
si l'on veut (vouloir): if one wants to (to want to)
rendre: to go
soi-même: oneself
il faut se déplacerr: they have to go around
des heures (une heure): hours
avoir: to have
se faire: to get
la barrière: the guard rail

on relève la tête (relever): one put their head up (to put)
on peut également (pouvoir): one can also (can, to be able to)
profiter: to enjoy
aérien: aerial
avions (un avion): planes
(ils) relâchent (relâcher): they release (to release)
la fumée blanche: the white smoke
les trois couleurs: the three colors
un drapeau: flag

on peut apercevoir: one can see
eux-mêmes: themselves
un discours unificateur: a unifying speech

le soir: in the evening
les rues (la rue): the streets
s'agitent (s'agiter): are busy (to be busy)
la foule: the crowd
qui ne travaille pas (travailler): who don't work (to work)
le droit: the right
un feu d'artifice: fireworks
vous pourrez admirer: you will be able to admire
mille feux: to sparkle brightly
ont préparé (préparer): prepared (to prepare)
éclater: to burst
aller danser: to go to dance

ont lieu des bals (avoir lieu): balls take place (to take place)
exploser: to burst
des rires (un rire): laughs
des cris (un cri): shouts, cries

Le 14 juillet

La fête nationale française **a lieu tous les étés**, lors du 14 juillet. Cette date est **attachée** à un sentiment certain de patriotisme. **En effet, elle commémore la prise** de la Bastille du 14 Juillet 1789 qui a été pris comme symbole de la Révolution. La Révolution **qui a vu tomber la royauté** en faveur du peuple. C'est l'unité du peuple **qui est donc célébrée** en **ce jour**.

On se lève de **bonne heure** le jour du 14 Juillet : **il ne faudrait pas rater** le début du **défilé** sur les Champs-Élysées. **Si l'on veut** s'y **rendre soi-même, il faut se déplacer** à **des heures** impossibles pour **avoir** la chance de **se faire** une petite place près de **la barrière**.

Si **on relève la tête** au bon moment, **on peut également profiter** du défilé **aérien** : plusieurs **avions** en formation **relâchent de la fumée blanche**, de la fumée bleue, et de la fumée rouge, pour symboliser **les trois couleurs** du **drapeau** français.

Si on est chanceux, **on peut apercevoir** les véhicules de l'armée et les soldats **eux-mêmes**, en uniforme. Le président de la République honore le peuple par **un discours unificateur**.

En attendant **le soir**, **les rues s'agitent** de **la foule qui ne travaille pas** ce jour-là. C'est jour de fête et ce soir, on aura **le droit** à **un feu d'artifice**. À Paris, **vous pourrez admire**r la Tour Eiffel s'illuminer de **mille feux**. Mais dans toute la France, même les plus petits villages **ont préparé**, pour ce jour-là, des festivités. On attend de voir les feux d'artifice **éclater**, puis, c'est l'heure d'**aller danser**.

Traditionnellement, le jour du 14 Juillet **ont lieu des bals**, des soirées dansantes qui voient **exploser des rires** et **des cris** de joie.

La fête de la Saint-Jean Baptiste

Le Québec **possède** un fort sentiment d'identité nationale. **Pays** francophone **noyé au milieu du** grand Canada anglophone, **il a gardé**, depuis **des siècles**, sa **propre** culture. Ainsi c'est avec **fierté** que Québécoises et Québécois **célèbrent** leur **fête nationale** le 24 juin de **chaque année**.

L'idée d'une fête nationale du Québec **naît** en 1834 dans l'esprit du journaliste Ludger Duvernay **qui organise** un grand banquet en **ce jour**. **Il pense** qu'il est important de **donner** au Québec un jour pour célébrer son unité, ce qui favorise l'union des Français-Canadiens.

La date du 24 juin a été **choisie** parce qu'elle correspond à la célébration du **solstice d'été**, le jour le plus long de l'année. Cette date correspond **également** à celle de la fête de la Saint-Jean Baptiste, célébrée traditionnellement par **un** grand **feu de joie**.

Bien que **célébrée** par les habitants du Québec depuis des années, cette fête **ne devient** officielle qu'en 1925. **Mais il faudra attendre** 1950 pour **voir** une évolution : cette célébration devient alors plus populaire et l'on organise **des soirées dansantes** avec **des chansons** traditionnelles. **Vers la fin des** années 1950 **apparaissent les défilés qui attirent des foules** de plus en plus importantes.

Petit à petit, la fête **perd** sa signification religieuse pour **devenir** davantage une représentation culturelle et artistique. Cependant, le feu de joie et **les feux d'artifices** illuminent toujours ses **nuits**, car **ils représentent le partage** et la solidarité.

Aujourd'hui, la fête nationale du Québec **compte plus de** 700 projets organisés dans autant de lieux différents. **On peut admirer** les plus grands feux de joie et des concerts impressionnants sur les Plaines d'Abraham à Québec et au parc Maisonneuve à Montréal.

---

possède (posséder): has (to have)
un pays: country
noyé: swallowed up
au milieu du: among
il a gardé (garder): it has preserved (to preserve)
des siècles (un siècle): centuries
propre: own
fierté: pride
célèbrent (célébrer): celebrate (to celebrate)
fête nationale: National Day
chaque année: every year

naît (naître): was born (to be born)
qui organise (organiser): who organized (to organize)
ce jour (un jour): this day
il pense (penser): he thought (to think)
donner: to give

choisie (choisir): chosen (to choose)
le solstice d'été: summer solstice
également: also
un feu de joie: bonfire

célébrée (célébrer): celebrated (to celebrate)
ne devient (devenir): only became (to become)
mais il faudra attendre: but it was not before
voir: to see
des soirées dansantes: dances
des chansons (une chanson): songs
vers: around
la fin des: the end of
apparaissent (apparaître): appeared (to appear)
les défilés: parades
qui attirent (attirer): which attracted (to attract)
des foules (une foule): crowds

petit à petit: little by little
perd (perdre): has lost (to lose)
devenir: to become
les feux d'artifices: fireworks
nuits (une nuit): nights
ils représentent (représenter): they represent (to represent)
le partage: sharing

aujourd'hui: nowadays
compte plus de (compter): there are more than (to count)
on peut admirer: people can admire

Le festival de musique créole

Si vous êtes aux Antilles **à la toute fin** du **mois** d'octobre, **voici l'événement incontournable** de **la saison**. Cette **année, comme toutes les autres depuis** 1997, **l'île anglophone** de la Dominique dans **les Caraïbes vibre** aux **sons** de la musique du "World Creole Music Festival" du 30 octobre au 1er novembre.

Malgré son nom, ce festival **n'a pas pour unique objet** la musique. **En effet**, les dates **choisies chaque** année ne le sont pas **au hasard**, elles **correspondent** à deux événements majeurs **pour l'île**: le 28 octobre, Journée Internationale du Créole et le 3 novembre, célébration de l'indépendance de l'île de la République Dominique. **Autour de** ces deux dates, le gouvernement de la Dominique **a décidé** de **mettre en place un événement artistique qui rend hommage** à **la diversité culturelle** de la population dominiquaise, ainsi qu'à **la langue** créole.

Le créole **n'est pas juste** un prétexte **mais** un élément fondamental qui **justifie** l'existence du festival. **Il faut rappeler** que les Dominiquais sont généralement anglophones et créolophones, **ce qui constitue** un pont linguistique avec **leurs voisins** antillais Guadeloupéens et Martiniquais qui sont eux francophones et créolophones.

La programmation du festival, qui en est à sa 13ém édition, **rappelle** le positionnement de l'île **par rapport** à ses voisins de la Caraïbe **mais aussi** la place centrale **réservée** au créole. **Si l'on peut** venir à la Dominique **pour écouter** des célébrités caribéennes **qui ont atteint une reconnaissance** internationale comme Kassav, Maxi Priest, Carimi ou Morgan Heritage, c'est aussi l'occasion de participer aux concerts de **nombreux** artistes antillais **moins connus** et **entre autres** de nombreux artistes créolophones **venant de** Guadeloupe, Martinique et Haïti.

Cet événement, qui **est devenu au fil des années un repère** pour les amateurs de musique, permet aux musiques **les plus diverses**, comme le « bouyon » de la Dominique, le reggae de la Jamaïque, le zouk des Antilles françaises ou le compas d'Haïti, de **se côtoyer. D'ailleurs**, **l'engouement qu'il suscite** est tel qu'**il faut** s'y prendre bien **à l'avance** pour **trouver un logement** pratique pour participer à toutes **les manifestations proposées autour du** festival.

(elle) rappelle (rappeler): (it) recalls (to recall)
par rapport: in relation
mais aussi: but also
réservée (réserver): kept (to reserve, to keep)
si l'on peut (pouvoir): if we can (can, to be able to)
pour écouter: to listen
qui ont atteint (atteindre): who have attained (to attain)
une reconnaissance: recognition
nombreux: numerous
moins connus: less known
entre autres: among others
venant de (venir): coming from (to come)

est devenu (devenir): has become (to become)
au fil des années: over the years
un repère: landmark
les plus diverses: the most diverse
se côtoyer: to mix
d'ailleurs: besides
engouement (masc.): passion
qu'il suscite (susciter): that it arouses (to arouse)
il faut (falloir): it is necessary (to be necessary)
à l'avance: in advance
trouver: to find
un logement: accommodation
les manifestations (la manifestation): events
proposées: suggested
autour du (autour de): around

French Vocabulary for Celebrations and Good Wishes!

Happy birthday! - Bon anniversaire !

Happy Bastille Day! - Joyeux quatorze juillet !

Happy Easter! - Joyeuses Pâques !

Happy Hanukkah! - Bonne fête de Hanoukka !

Happy Holidays! - Joyeuses fêtes !

Happy New Year! - Bonne Année !

Happy Saints' Day! - Bonne fête !

Merry Christmas! - Joyeux Noël !

Seasons greetings! - Joyeux Noël et bonne Année !

Best wishes - Mes/Nos meilleurs vœux

Cheers! - À ta/votre santé ! À la tienne/vôtre !

Congratulations! - Félicitations !

Good luck! - Bon courage !

To your new house! - À ta nouvelle maison !

Quid des Vieilles Charrues

ils étaient (être): they were (to be)

ils sont maintenant: they are now

plus de: more than

depuis: since

est devenu (devenir): became (to become)

désormais: from then on

tout a donc commencé (commencer): everything started (to start)

17 ans (un an): 17 years

ses amis (un ami): his friends

décident (décider): decided (to decide)

une fête: a party

le but: the goal

se faire une bonne bouffe: to have some good food

chanter: to sing

boire un coup: to have a drink

l'année suivante: the following year

de nouveau: again

cette fois: this time

ouverte (ouvrir): opened (to open)

viennent (venir): came (to come)

apprécier: to appreciate

au fil des années: over the years

connaît (connaître): has, enjoys (to have)

des chanteurs (un chanteur): singers

célèbres (célèbre): famous

comme: like, such as

ou encore: or even

il passé de … à (passer): it goes from … to (to pass)

trois jours (un jour): three days

pendant: during

le nombre des: the number of

cela va même doubler: it is even going to double

chaque: each

déménager: to move

il s'installe (s'installer): it settles (to settle)

il se célèbre (célébrer): it is celebrated (to celebrate)

maintenant: now

Ils étaient 500, **ils sont maintenant plus de** 200 000. **Depuis** sa première édition en 1992, le festival des Vieilles Charrues **est devenu** de plus en plus populaire. C'est **désormais** le festival de musique le plus fréquenté en France.

Tout a donc commencé il y a **17 ans**. Christian Troadec et **ses amis décident** d'organiser **une fête** à Landeleau, dans le Finistère. **Le but** était de « *se faire une bonne bouffe, de chanter et de boire un coup* ». **L'année suivante**, la fête est organisée **de nouveau**. **Cette fois**, elle est **ouverte** au public: 1 300 personnes **viennent apprécier** la musique de groupes locaux.

Au fil des années, le festival **connaît** un succès grandissant. On commence à y inviter des groupes et **des chanteurs** français **célèbres**, **comme** Miossec, Zebda, Les Innocents **ou encore** Maxime le Forestier. Le festival **passe** d'un à **trois jours**. **Pendant** les premières années, **le nombre des** festivaliers **va même doubler** à **chaque** édition ! Il faut donc rapidement **déménager** et le festival **s'installe** à Carhaix, où **il se célèbre maintenant** chaque année.

Carhaix est **une petite ville** de 8 000 habitants mais, chaque juillet, la ville **accueille environ** 200 000 festivaliers. Les concerts **ont** maintenant **lieu** sur la plaine de Kerampuilh, **en dehors** du centre-ville. Le camping, **gratuit**, s'organise sur 30 hectares **autour du** site et **des milliers** de tentes **poussent comme des champignons**. Il est évidemment possible de **dormir** à l'hôtel à Carhaix ou dans **les villes voisines**, **une aubaine** pour la région et le secteur touristique.

Aujourd'hui, le festival **s'étend** sur 4 **jours** mais **beaucoup** de festivaliers **ne viennent que** trois jours, **profitant ainsi** du week-end. **Les billets se vendent** sur Internet ou dans **des points de vente** spécialisés, comme La Fnac. **On peut acheter** des « pass 4 jours », les très populaires « pass 3 jours » à 75€ ou **se contenter** de tickets à **la journée**, à 32€. Et **il vaut mieux** s'y **prendre** à l'avance ! Car chaque année, les pass sont **très vite épuisés** et certains jours **se font à guichet fermé**.

Les Vieilles Charrues **sont devenues** le plus grand festival de rock français. Sa programmation est éclectique, avec des groupes locaux, français ou internationaux. **On y rencontre** des chanteurs de la *Nouvelle Scène* française, comme Raphaël ou Cali, **côte à côte** avec des grandes stars du rock, comme Placebo, Franz Ferdinand, R.E.M ou Muse. La programmation **n'oublie cependant pas d'inviter** des groupes **moins** célèbres **pour les faire ainsi connaître**.

Enfin, et **depuis quelques années**, les Vieilles Charrues accueillent aussi quelques **comiques** français, tels Jamel Debouze ou Gad Elmaleh, ce qui donne un petit air de **kermesse** au festival.

une petite ville: a small town
accueille (accueillir): welcomes (to welcome)
environ: approximately
ont lieu (avoir lieu): they take place
  (to take place)
en dehors: outside
gratuit: free
autour du: around
des milliers (un millier): thousands
poussent comme des champignons: they
  sprout up like mushrooms
dormir: to sleep
les villes voisines: the bordering cities
une aubaine: a good opportunity

aujourd'hui: today
s'étend (s'étendre): stretches out
  (to stretch out)
des jours (un jour): days
beaucoup: a lot
(ils) ne viennent que (venir): they only come
  (to come)
profitant ainsi: and so taking advantage of
les billets (le billet): tickets
se vendent (vendre): are sold (to sell)
des points de vente: points of sale
on peut acheter (pouvoir): we can buy
  (can, to be able to)
se contenter: to limit oneself
la journée: the day
il vaut mieux (valoir): it is better (to be worth)
prendre: to get
très vite: very quickly
épuisés: sell out
se font à guichet fermé: are sold out

sont devenues (devenir): became
  (to become)
on y rencontre (rencontrer): we come across
  (to come across, meet)
côte à côte: side by side
n'oublie pas (oublier): does not forget
  (to forget)
cependant: nevertheless
inviter: to invite
moins: less
pour les faire ainsi connaître: in order to
  make them known

enfin: finally
depuis quelques années: for some years
comiques (un comique): comic actors
une kermesse: fair

célébration **77**

Jours de mémoire

C'est **bien connu**. Nous, les Français, **on adore être en vacances**. **Malgré la semaine** des 35 heures, **on court toujours après les jours fériés**. Un jour de vacances en plus, c'est comme **Noël avant l'heure** !

Si mai reste **le mois des « ponts »** et des longs week-ends, novembre **annonce** aussi généralement quelques jours de **détente**. C'est une bonne occasion de **se débarrasser** de la dépression **automnale mais aussi** de « **se rappeler** ». Les deux jours fériés de novembre **nous invitent en effet** à nous **replonger** dans **le passé**…

Halloween n'est pas un grand succès en France. **Cependant, le lendemain** représente une tradition pour beaucoup de familles. Le 1er novembre, on **célèbre** en effet **la Toussaint**. C'est **une fête** catholique qui, **comme son nom l'indique**, **commémore** tous les saints **reconnus** par l'**Église** catholique. La Toussaint est un jour férié mais le lendemain, la Fête **des Morts, ne l'est pas**. Il est donc de coutume de « célébrer » **les deux le même jour**, le 1er novembre. Pour la majorité des familles, **c'est** alors **le temps d'aller nettoyer** et **refleurir les tombes de ceux qui sont déjà partis**.

À la Toussaint, les cimetières sont donc **noirs de monde : on ramasse les feuilles mortes, on passe un coup de chiffon** sur le marbre, **on arrose les fleurs, on se rappelle les bons souvenirs, on parle** avec **les voisins**… Le chrysanthème, **qui fleurit à cette époque**, est la fleur de prédilection pour **décorer** les tombes et est ainsi **devenu** un des symboles de la Toussaint.

---

bien connu: well known
on adore (adorer): we love (to love)
être en vacances: to be on vacation
malgré: despite
la semaine: the week
on court toujours après (courir): we always run after (to run)
les jours fériés: public holidays
Noël: Christmas
avant l'heure: early

le mois: the month
des ponts (un pont): long weekends
annonce (annoncer): announces (to announce)
détente: relaxation
se débarrasser: to get rid of
automnale (automnal): autumnal
mais aussi: but also
se rappeler: to remember
(ils) nous invitent (inviter): they invite us (to invite)
en effet: indeed
replonger: to dive again
le passé: the past

cependant: nevertheless
le lendemain: the day after
célèbre: celebrate
la Toussaint: All Saints' Day
une fête: celebration
comme son nom l'indique (indiquer): as its name indicates (to indicate, point out)
(elle) commémore (commémorer): (it) commemorates (to commemorate)
reconnus (reconnaître): recognized (to recognize)
la église: church
des morts (un mort): the dead
(elle) ne l'est pas (être): (it) is not (to be)
les deux: both
le même jour: the same day
c'est le temps d'aller: it is time to go to
nettoyer: to clean
refleurir: to flower again
les tombes (la tombe): graves
de ceux qui sont déjà partis (partir): of those who are already gone (to go)

noirs de monde: crowded
on ramasse (ramasser): we pick up (to pick up)
les feuilles mortes (une feuille): dead leaves
on passe un coup de chiffon: we wipe
on arrose (arroser): we water (to water)
les fleurs (une fleur): flowers
on se rappelle (se rappeler): we remember (to remember)
les bons souvenirs: good memories
on parle (parler): we talk (to talk)
les voisins (un voisin): neighbors
qui fleurit (fleurir): that flowers (to flower)
à cette époque: at this time
décorer: to decorate
(il) est devenu (devenir): (it) became (to become)

Le 1er novembre reste donc **plutôt un événement familial**, que **chaque** famille **aborde** à sa **manière**. Quelques jours **plus tard**, le 11 novembre **nous ramène** en 1918. Bien que cette journée reste un événement national important, **la plupart** des Français **ne se sentent plus connectés** à l'importance de cette journée.

Le 11 novembre 1918, à 5h15, l'Armistice signale en effet **la fin de la première guerre mondiale**. L'**Allemagne** capitule, **le cessez-le-feu est déclaré** et les églises des villages font **sonner les cloches** : c'est la fin d'un des plus grands massacres d'Europe, avec ses quinze millions de **morts** et ses vingt millions d'**invalides**.

Ironiquement, **ce jour-là**, il y a eu **un sursaut belliqueux** et **vengeur** de certains capitaines et compagnies : 11 000 personnes **vont mourir** ou **être blessées**, entre la signature de l'Armistice et le début du cessez-le-feu.

Aujourd'hui, les Français commémorent **toujours** la fin de la guerre chaque 11 novembre, appelé le « Jour du Souvenir ». **Pas de défilé**, comme pour le 14 juillet, mais des cérémonies dans de **nombreuses communes**. À Paris, sous l'Arc de Triomphe, le président **se recueille** généralement sur la tombe **du soldat inconnu**. Ce soldat français n'a **jamais** été identifié et représente ainsi tous les morts de la guerre.

Cependant, **le dernier** « **poilu** » français, Lazare Ponticelli, est mort en 2008. Avec lui, une page **se tourne**. La **nouvelle** génération **se sent de moins en moins concernée par** la Grande Guerre, **se contentant d'**en **apprendre** les événements pour **les contrôles** en classe d'histoire.

Espérons que ce jour férié **contribuera à préserver** la mémoire de ce qui a été un des événements **fondamentaux** de notre histoire commune.

La fête des Rois en France

Pour beaucoup de Français, **la fête des rois consiste à manger une bonne galette à la frangipane (la galette des rois)** ! En réalité, l'origine de cette tradition est religieuse et plus particulièrement **chrétienne puisqu'il s'agit** de l'Épiphanie. **Le sens** chrétien de cette fête réside dans **la visite** de l'enfant Jésus par **les trois rois mages qui s'appellent** Gaspard, Melchior et Balthazar.

Cette fête religieuse **est célébrée** le 6 janvier. Comme **il ne s'agit pas** d'**un jour férié** en France, elle est généralement fêtée **le deuxième dimanche** après Noël. Dans la pratique, c'est tout au long du **mois** de janvier que l'on fête les rois. **En effet**, il est possible de **trouver** durant toute cette période de magnifiques galettes à la frangipane dans **les pâtisseries** et **boulangeries** françaises … à la grande joie des enfants **qui peuvent ainsi** tirer les rois **plusieurs fois de suite**.

Mais que **signifie** « **tirer les rois** » et **pourquoi** les petits Français **adorent-ils cela** ? La tradition veut que l'Épiphanie soit l'occasion de tirer les rois : **une fève** est **cachée** dans une pâtisserie et la personne **qui l'obtient devient le roi** (ou **la reine**) **de la journée**. La fève a été progressivement **remplacée par** de petites **figurines** représentant un roi, une reine, l'enfant Jésus et **de nos jours** bien d'**autres choses**. Les galettes **sont** généralement **vendues** avec **des couronnes en carton dorée** ou **argentée**.

La personne **obtenant** la fève peut donc être symboliquement **couronnée** roi ou reine pour la journée et **choisir son partenaire royal**. L'usage veut aussi que s'il y a des enfants, **le plus jeune d'entre eux se cache** sous la table pendant que la personne **qui sert** la galette **la découpe** en parts. Avant que l'adulte ne serve une part, l'enfant **doit désigner qui sera** le destinataire de la portion. Ce rituel **très apprécié** des enfants permet de distribuer au hasard les parts de la galette.

La tradition culinaire de cette fête **diffère** aussi **selon que l'on se trouve** dans le nord ou le sud de la France. Dans **la moitié** nord du **pays**, on mange traditionnellement une galette des rois **réalisée** avec **une pâte feuilletée** et **garnie** d'une crème à la frangipane. Dans le sud de la France et plus particulièrement en Provence, on tire les rois en mangeant une brioche en forme de couronne décorée de **fruits confits** et de **sucre granulé**. Un **santon** minuscule **a tendance à remplacer** la fève traditionnelle.

Néanmoins, la galette des rois à la frangipane **gagne du terrain** puisqu'elle est **de plus en plus courante** en Provence. **Cela s'explique** par le fait que la galette est **moins chère** que la brioche aux fruits confits et aussi **plus facile** à **réaliser** et à **conserver**. **De surcroît**, de plus en plus de **gens** originaires de la moitié nord de la France s'**installent** en Provence **amenant** avec eux **leurs propres** traditions et **goûts** culinaires.

Si vous ne trouvez pas de galettes à la frangipane dans votre pays, rien de plus facile que d'en réaliser une **vous-même**. **Pendant ce temps**, vos enfants ou petits enfants **peuvent s'amuser** à **créer** de superbes couronnes colorées. **Bref, de quoi les occuper** pendant tout **un dimanche après-midi** !

Le Noël: Christmas
comme ailleurs: as elsewhere
une fête: a celebration
avant tout... mais aussi: mostly ... but also
haute en couleurs: colorful
chargée de: full of
le début: beginning
commencent (commencer): start (to start)
la fin de l'année: the end of the year

dit (dire): says (to say)
une jeune fille: young girl
qui souhaitait (souhaiter): who wished
  (to wish)
consacrer: to devote
sa vie (une vie): her life
Dieu: God
elle se fit baptiser: (she) was baptized
l'avis: the permission
son père (un père): her father
il l'a fit emprisonnée: he had her put in jail
mourir: to die
un énorme orage: huge thunderstorm
éclata (éclater): started (to start)
foudroya (foudroyer): struck (to strike)
ses bourreaux: her executioners
on fasse (faire): we make (to make)
germer: to sprout
des graines (une graine): seeds
le blé: wheat
trois soucoupes (une soucoupe): three saucers
couvertes (couvert): covered
humide: damp
on dépose (déposer): we set (to set)
le dessus: the top
la cheminée: hearth
pousser: to grow
faire des présages: to make predictions
suivante (suivant): following
les tiges (une tige): stalks
poussaient (pousser): (they) grew (to grow)
bien droites (droit): very straight
vertes (vert): green
les anciens (un ancien): elders
disaient (dire): said (to say)
les récoltes (une récolte): crops
seraient bonnes: would be good
une année de vaches maigres: lean year

aujourd'hui: today
(ils) placent (placer): (they) put (to put)
les carrés (le carré): squares
le réveillon de Noël: Christmas Eve feast

cinq temps forts: five signifiant times
allumer le feu: to light the fire
il s'agit de: it is about
allumage: lighting
la bûche de Noël: Yule log
au soir: at night
le benjamin: the youngest child
ils tiennent (tenir): they hold (to hold)
ils font le tour de: they go around
(ils) l'allument: (they) set fire to it
arrosée (arroser): watered (to water)
le vin cuit: fortified wine
prononçant (prononcer): saying (to say)
des paroles (une parole): words (word)

Noël en Provence

Le Noël en Provence est **comme ailleurs** en France **une fête avant tout** familiale **mais aussi** collective, **haute en couleurs** et **chargée de** symboles chrétiens. Dès **le début** du mois de décembre, les provençaux **commencent** à préparer les festivités de **la fin de l'année**.

C'est la Sainte Barbe, le 4 décembre, qui marque le début des festivités. La légende **dit** que Barbe était une magnifique **jeune fille qui souhaitait consacrer sa vie** à **Dieu**. **Elle se fit baptiser** sans **l'avis** de **son père**. **Il la fit emprisonner** et torturer. Alors qu'elle était sur le point de **mourir**, **un énorme orage éclata** et **foudroya ses bourreaux**. Depuis, la tradition provençale veut que l'**on fasse germer des graines** de **blé** ou de lentilles dans **trois soucoupes couvertes** de coton **humide** que l'**on dépose** sur **le dessus** de **la cheminée**. Les graines vont germer et **pousser** pendant le mois de décembre et le 25, il sera possible de **faire des présages** pour l'année **suivante**. Si **les tiges poussaient bien droites** et **vertes**, **les anciens disaient que les récoltes seraient bonnes**. Dans le cas contraire, cela serait **une année de vaches maigres**.

Aujourd'hui les provençaux perpétuent cette tradition et **placent** ces petits **carrés** de verdures soit dans la crèche familiale soit sur la table du **réveillon de Noël**.

Le Noël provençal traditionnel est marqué par **cinq temps forts**:

• Le cacho-fio: « Cacho-fio » signifie en provençal « **allumer le feu** ». **Il s'agit** donc **de l'allumage** de **la bûche** de Noël, le 24 décembre **au soir**. Ce sont **le benjamin** et le plus ancien de la famille qui procèdent à ce rituel. **Ils tiennent** la bûche ensemble et **font** trois fois **le tour de** la table puis **l'allument**. Elle est **arrosée** trois fois de **vin cuit** en **prononçant des paroles** qui varient d'une famille à l'autre mais qui ont pour thème commun la prospérité.

- **Le gros souper**: **il est servi** après l'allumage de la bûche et avant de **se rendre** à **la messe** de minuit. Il s'agit d'**un repas maigre** dont **la mise en scène** est essentielle. Il y a toute une symbolique et **les chiffres** sont très importants. Ainsi, le chiffre trois **fait référence à** la Trinité. La table **doit être recouverte** de trois **nappes blanches**, de **trois bougies** ou chandeliers **allumés** et des trois soucoupes de blé et lentilles germés de la Sainte Barbe. Les trois nappes **serviront** pour les trois repas des fêtes de fin d'année. **Un couvert** doit être **ajouté**: c'est le couvert du **pauvre**. Le menu **est composé de sept plats** maigres **en souvenir de**s sept **douleurs** de la Vierge Marie. Ils sont accompagnés de **treize petits pains** en référence à **la Cène**.

- **Les treize desserts**: La composition et le moment auquel **ils doivent** être servis varient d'**une ville à l'autre**. Certains **les mangent** avant la messe de minuit et d'autres **au retour de** celle-ci. Les treize desserts sont composés des produits **suivants: des figues sèches**, **des amandes**, des raisins secs, **des noix**, des dattes, du nougat blanc qui représente **le bien,** du nougat **noir** qui symbolise **le mal**, une fougasse, des fruits **confits** et **frais**.

- **La veillée** de Noël: c'est un moment de **recueillement** ou l'**on écoute** les anecdotes et les histoires des anciens. Il s'agit d'un moment de **partage** ou l'**on chante** et **discute** tout **en dégustant** de l'**anchoïade**.

- **La messe de minuit**: **parfois** en **langue** provençale dans certains villages, elle est **rythmée** par **des cantiques** provençaux, des pastorales et parfois la cérémonie du **pastrage**.

Si ces traditions **sont transmises** de générations en générations, **elles sont vécues** et organisées le plus souvent par les communautés locales et **en amont** des fêtes de Noël. **Si bien que** les familles provençales **peuvent vivre** leurs traditions mais aussi **fêter** Noël plus classiquement comme **la plupart** des Français.

---

le gros souper: the great supper
il est servi (servir): it is served (to serve)
se rendre: to go
la messe: mass
un repas maigre: meal without meat
la mise en scène: staging, set up
les chiffres (le chiffre): numbers
fait référence à: refers to
doit être recouverte (devoir): must be covered (to cover)
nappes (une nappe): tablecloths
blanches (blanc): white
trois bougies (une bougie): three candles
allumés (allumé): lit
serviront (servir): will be used (to use)
un couvert: place setting
ajouté (ajouter): added (to add)
pauvre: poor
est composé de (composer): is composed of (to compose)
sept plats (un plat): seven dishes
en souvenir de: in memory of
les douleurs (la douleur): pains
treize petits pains: thirteen bread rolls
la Cène: the Last Supper

ils doivent (devoir): they must (must)
une ville à l'autre: from one city to another
(ils) les mangent (manger): (they) eat it (to eat)
au retour de: back from
suivants (suivant): following
des figues sèches (une figue): dried figs
des amandes (une amande): almonds
des noix (une noix): walnuts
le bien: good
noir: black
le mal: bad, evil
confits: candied
frais: fresh

la veillée: the evening
recueillement: meditation, contemplation
on écoute (écouter): we listen to (to listen to)
partage: sharing
on chante (chanter): we sing (to sing)
discute (discuter): talk (to talk)
en dégustant: while tasting
une anchoïade: anchovy pate

parfois: sometimes
langue: language
rythmée: accompanied
des cantiques (un cantique): songs
pastrage: offering of a lamb

sont transmises (transmettre): are passed down (to transmit)
elles sont vécues (vivre): they are alive (to live, be alive)
en amont: before
si bien que: so well that
peuvent vivre (pouvoir): can keep alive (can, to be able to)
fêter: to celebrate
la plupart de: most of

Évaluez votre compréhension

La fête du Travail, page 65

1. What will you find vendors selling on this day?

2. Why and when did this tradition begin?

3. What word of caution does this story end with?

Le carnaval aux Antilles, page 66

1. The carnaval became a period for the Africans to express what aspect of their culture?

2. What are the costumes of the *à caisse claire* like?

3. What are the *ti-mass*?

Faites de la musique !, page 68

1. How many cities now particpate in this festival?

2. When does the festival begin and what is it celebrating?

3. What problem came about during the festival and how was it fixed?

Poisson d'avril !, page 70

1. This holiday was originally celebrated on what day?

2. What is the most common trick played on this day?

3. Why is the fish the symbol on this day?

Test your comprehension

Le 14 juillet, page 72

1. This holiday, also called Bastille Day, is attached to what sentiment? Why?

2. People wake up early on this day to do what?

3. The aerial show puts on a special display. What is it?

La fête des Rois en France, page 80

1. When does *La fête des Rois* usually take place?

2. Describe the tradition of the Twelfth Night Cake?

3. How does the recipe differ in the north and south of France?

Jours de mémoire, page 78

1. What holiday occurs on November 1st, and what does this holiday commemorate?

2. What holiday takes place on the day after? What is done on this day?

3. What flower is used to decorate graves and symbolizes All Saints' Day?

Noël en Provence, page 82

1. According to the *Sainte Barbe* tradition, what will happen if your seeds sprout straight green stalks?

2. Who carries out the tradition of lighting the Yule log?

3. *Le gros souper* is a meal without what type of food? What do the 13 bread rolls indicate?

Biographie

Ingénieur français célèbre

C'est sous ses **arches métalliques impressionnantes** et si caractéristiques que de nombreux **amoureux font initialement connaissance** avec le Paris romantique : la Tour Eiffel.

Son concepteur est l'**ingénieur** français Alexandre Gustave Eiffel, **né** le 15 décembre 1832 à Dijon (Côte-d'Or) **au sein** d'une famille **aisée**. Après **avoir été admis** à l'**École** centrale des arts et manufactures de Paris, Gustave Eiffel **entre** ensuite à l'École polytechnique où **il obtient,** en 1855, un diplôme d'**ingénieur chimiste**. Sa **rencontre** avec Charles Nepveu, entrepreneur spécialisé dans les constructions métalliques, dont l'**essor** suit l'évolution récente de la métallurgie, **changera** le cours de sa carrière professionnelle et **confirmera** son **intérêt** pour ce **matériau d'avenir**.

Avant d'**entreprendre** la construction de la Tour Eiffel, **qui fera sa renommée**, Gustave Eiffel **conçoit,** à **vingt-six ans**, la **passerelle** Eiffel à Bordeaux et contribue à la création de **la célèbre** statue de la Liberté de New-York. Après **avoir fondé sa propre société, il se lance** avec succès dans des projets d'**envergure** tels la construction de viaducs, de **ponts**, de **gares**, d'**églises** ainsi que de diverses **charpentes** métalliques.

La construction de la Tour Eiffel **découle** directement de l'**engouement** des ingénieurs et architectes de l'époque pour les structures **en hauteur, qui constituent** alors de **réelles prouesses** techniques. **Inaugurée** lors de l'Exposition universelle de Paris de 1889 après quelques polémiques, la tour Eiffel **s'élève** à **une hauteur de** 313 mètres et **pèse** plus de 10,100 tonnes. Il s'agit d'un des monuments **les plus visités** au **monde**.

Gustave Eiffel, dont le succès **ne se démentira jamais, s'intéressera par la suite** au développement de la technologie en faisant installer des antennes radio **au sommet** de la Tour Eiffel. **Il décédera** à Paris le 27 décembre 1923 et **demeurera à jamais** dans les esprits un ingénieur et un industriel de **génie**.

Une femme, une artiste

Peu de femmes ont connu un destin aussi exaltant et particulier que Camille Claudel. Sculpteure exceptionnelle, **dotée** d'une prescience peu commune, **elle connaissait** avec certitude, dès son **plus jeune âge**, l'orientation **que prendrait** son destin.

Ainée d'**une fratrie** de quatre enfants, **elle naît** le 8 décembre 1864 à Fères-en-Tardenois, une petite **bourgade** de l'Aisne **située** dans le nord-est de la France, **au sein d'**une famille bourgeoise. C'est à 17 ans que cette artiste à l'**esprit libre** et indépendant **décide** de **se consacrer** exclusivement à la sculpture. **Elle se rend** à Paris en 1882 **afin de suivre les cours** de l'Académie Colarossi où **elle fait la rencontre** du sculpteur Auguste Rodin, avec qui **elle entretiendra** une relation **amoureuse** au long cours.

Ses premières **œuvres** connues répertoriées, *La Vieille Hélène* ou *Paul à treize ans* **datent de** cette **époque bienheureuse** où **la puissante** influence du **maître n'avait pas encore** marqué son œuvre de son empreinte indélébile. **Toutefois**, son talent exceptionnel **ne tarde pas** à faire une **forte** impression sur Rodin **qui l'incite** à **se joindre** à son **atelier** de la rue Université en 1885. Cette collaboration fructueuse **donne lieu à** la réalisation du monument des *Bourgeois de Calais* et des **célèbres** *Portes de l'Enfer*.

Inextricablement liés par le talent et le cœur, Camille Claudel et Rodin **produisent** des œuvres dont il est **parfois** difficile d'identifier l'auteur avec certitude. Cette symbiose artistique **se produit malheureusement** aux dépends de la carrière de Camille. **Confrontée au refus de** Rodin de **quitter sa fidèle** compagne Rose Beuret, Camille Claudel **parvient à retrouver** une certaine autonomie en 1898, **ce qui la conduit** à la réalisation d'œuvres plus personnelles comme *La Valse* ou *La Petite Châtelaine*.

Souffrant de **paranoïa aiguë** et **accusant** Rodin de **s'approprier** ses œuvres, **elle sera internée** dans un hôpital psychiatrique où **elle finira ses jours** en 1943.

Albert Camus et l'absurde

Albert Camus (1913-1960) **compte parmi** les plus grandes figures de la littérature française du XXème **siècle**. C'est avec *L'Étranger*, **son roman le plus connu,** que **j'ai fait sa connaissance.**

L'Étranger **figurait** dans mon programme de littérature au **lycée. À 16 ans**, la musique m'intéressait plus que la littérature, **et pourtant**… **ce livre** m'a fascinée **de la première** à la **dernière** page.

J'y ai découvert le thème de l'absurde, **si cher à** Camus. **Athée, il définit** l'absurde comme « cette confrontation **entre l'appel humain** et le silence déraisonnable du **monde** ». Pour lui, **non seulement il n'y a pas** de **Dieu**, mais l'existence **n'a pas de sens**. Attention ! **Ce n'est pas pour autant** un appel au **désespoir** et au suicide !

En fait, **il faut considérer** l'absurde comme un générateur d'énergie. Si **on ne choisit pas** le suicide, **on doit** choisir l'exaltation de **la vie. Être solidaire des opprimés**, ou bien **profiter pleinement** de l'instant présent sont des formes de révolte **contre** l'absurde. Le monde n'a **peut-être** pas de sens, mais **ça ne l'empêche pas** d'être **beau** et ça n'empêche pas les humains d'être solidaires et **justes**. Au contraire.

D'ailleurs, en plus d'**être quelqu'un d'engagé (il a mené plusieurs** combats politiques, a été résistant…) Camus était **un homme sensuel**, qui avait une **véritable** passion pour **le soleil** et **la mer**.

Je me souviens que **la première fois** que **j'ai lu** *L'Étranger*, **j'ai été frappée par** la sensualité présente dans le livre. Meursault, le personnage principal, **semble impassible, passif**.

---

compte parmi (compter): figures among (to figure)
un siècle: century
son roman (un roman): his novel
le plus connu: the best known
j'ai fait sa connaissance (faire la connaissance): I met him (to meet)

figurait (figurer): was listed (to be listed)
un lycée: high school
à 16 ans: at the age of 16
et pourtant: and yet
ce livre (un livre): this book
de la première (premier): from the first
dernière (dernier): last

j'y ai découvert (découvrir): there I discovered (to discover)
si cher à: so important to
athée: atheistic
il définit (définir): he defines (to define)
entre: between
l'appel humain: the cry of humanity
le monde: world
non seulement: not only
il n'y a pas: there is no
Dieu: God
n'a pas de sens: there is no meaning
ce n'est pas pour autant: it is not necessarily
le désespoir: despair

il faut (falloir): one has to (to have to)
considérer: to consider
on ne choisit pas (choisir): we do not choose (to choose)
on doit (devoir): we must (to must)
la vie: life
être solidaire de: to stand united with
des opprimés: the oppressed
profiter: to profit
pleinement: fully
contre: against
peut-être: maybe
ça ne l'empêche pas (empêcher): it does not prevent it (to prevent)
beau: beautiful
justes (juste): fair

d'ailleurs: besides
être quelqu'un d'engagé: to be committed
il a mené (mener): he led (to lead)
plusieurs: several
un homme sensuel: a sensual man
véritable: true
le soleil: the sun
la mer: the sea

je me souviens (se souvenir): I remember (to remember)
la première fois: the first time
j'ai lu (lire): I read (to read)
j'ai été frappée par (frapper): I was struck by (to strike, knock)
(il) semble (sembler): he seems (to seem)
impassible: impassive, unmoved
passif: passive

On l'accuse même d'être insensible parce qu'**il ne pleure pas** à l'enterrement de **sa mère**. **Il ressent** pourtant de **façon très aiguë la chaleur, la lumière, les rayons** du soleil **sur sa peau**, **le goût du café au lait** et de la cigarette… **Il perçoit les bruits**, les odeurs…

Il semble en fait être en état d'« hyper conscience » permanente. C'est **sans doute** ce qui **l'empêche** de **se comporter** comme **les gens qui l'entourent**. C'est ça, l'absurde: une conscience aiguë du monde **qui ne laisse pas de place** aux mythes, aux **croyances** ou au kitsch.

Pas la peine de mentir, de **faire croire** ou de se faire croire **que tout va bien**. **Mais si s'obliger** à **voir** le monde tel qu'il est peut être une expérience **effroyable**, c'est aussi un exercice qui **peut nous rendre** plus humains, **plus à l'écoute des autres** et de la nature.

À vrai dire, cette vision du monde **me semble** particulièrement pertinente en 2009. **Nous vivons** dans **une époque confuse**. **L'avenir** est incertain et **parfois angoissant**, mais le fait de **se soucier** de l'environnement, de s'extasier **devant** la beauté d'**un paysage** ou de **militer** pour plus de justice **pourrait nous permettre**, **chacun à notre façon**, de combattre l'absurdité du monde **en donnant un sens** à notre vie.

Quoi qu'il en soit, je vous invite à découvrir ou à redécouvrir **les œuvres** de ce grand homme, **qu'il s'agisse** de *La Mort heureuse*, *L'Étranger*, *La Peste* ou *La Chute* … **Bonne lecture !**

Cinéaste français

À la fin des années 50, François Truffaut a été l'un des premiers, avec Jacques Rivette et Jean-Luc Godard, **à faire** des films dans un style qu'**un critique de cinéma baptisera** « **la Nouvelle Vague** ». D'un point de vue technique, ce style novateur **se caractérise entre autres** par **des éclairages** naturels (**au revoir**, les studios !) ainsi que l'introduction d'un équipement (son et caméra) **plus léger**, **moins bruyant**, **qui permet** donc de **se déplacer** et de **suivre les personnages**.

Une proximité et une connivence **s'installent** alors **entre** les personnages et le spectateur **qui n'est plus comme** au théâtre, mais **aux côtés des** acteurs et dans **la vie** des personnages. Le résultat est **plus réaliste**, les émotions plus palpables.

Dans *Les quatre cents coups,* par exemple, la caméra **suit pas à pas** la vie et **les malheurs** du **jeune** Antoine Doinel. **Souvent** mobile, **parfois** instable, cette caméra **semble** aussi imprévisible que la vie d'Antoine. **Nous sommes entraînés** dans l'histoire et **surtout** LES histoires du jeune garçon, **ses mensonges**, **ses espoirs**, ses interrogations…

Avec la Nouvelle Vague, **le montage évolue** lui aussi. **Il n'est plus contraint** de **respecter** des critères de continuité. Les images **nous apparaissent un peu comme des pensées** spontanées, dans **le désordre,** comme dans **la** « **vraie vie** ».

Il **faut dire** que les films de la Nouvelle Vague **reflètent une époque** de **bouleversements**, de jeunes **qui cherchent** à **se comprendre** et à comprendre **le monde dans lequel ils vivent**.

La seconde guerre mondiale est **terminée**, **le pays se reconstruit**, **on accède** à un plus grand confort matériel, les mouvements **étudiants**, anticolonialistes et féministes sont de plus en **plus actifs**, le modèle familial **évolue**…

On sent souvent, dans les films de François Truffaut, des personnages **en quête de sens**, **en décalage avec** la société ou leur environnement direct. C'est là que réside, **selon moi**, l'intérêt des films de Truffaut car ce décalage **est traité** avec humour, poésie et tendresse. Les personnages sont **parfois** ridicules… **presque toujours touchants et attachants**. Les **amoureux**, eux, sont toujours passionnés !

On dirait que dans ses films, Truffaut **nous signifie** que la vie est **trop précieuse pour ne pas être vécue pleinement**.

Pour cet **homme** qu'un cancer a **emporté à 52 ans seulement**, le cinéma aura **en tout cas** été une passion **dévorante**. De cette passion, **nous avons hérité** de petits bijoux cinématographiques dont, **je crois**, **nous ne sommes pas près de nous lasser**.

Quelques-uns des films de François Truffaut :

- *Vivement dimanche !* (1983)
- *La femme d'à côté* (1981)
- *Le dernier métro* (1980)
- *L'homme qui aimait les femmes* (1977)
- *L'histoire d'Adèle H.* (1975)
- *La nuit américaine* (1973)
- *Baisers volés* (1968)
- *Jules et Jim* (1962)
- *Les quatre cents coups* (1959)

il faut dire (falloir): it has to be said (to have to)
reflètent (refléter): reflect (to reflect)
une époque: a time
bouleversements: disruptions
qui cherchent (chercher): that look for (to look for)
se comprendre: to understand
le monde: the world
dans lequel: in which
ils vivent (vivre): they live (to live)

la seconde guerre mondiale: the Second World War
terminée (terminer): ended (to end)
le pays: country
se reconstruit (reconstruire): is rebuilt (to rebuild)
on accède (accéder): we reach (to reach)
les étudiants (le etudiant): students
plus actifs: more active
évolue (evoluer): evolves (to evolve)

on sent souvent (sentir): we can often feel (to feel)
en quête de sens: in quest of meaning
en décalage avec: at odds with
selon moi: according to me, for me
(il) est traité avec (traiter): it is dealt with (to deal)
parfois: sometimes
presque toujours: almost always
touchants (touchant): touching
attachants (attachant): engaging, endearing
amoureux: in love

on dirait (dire): it seems (to seem)
nous signifie (signifier): told us (to tell)
trop précieuse (précieux): too precious
pour ne pas être vécue: to not be lived
pleinement: fully

un homme: man
emporté: taken away
à 52 ans seulement: at just 52
en tout cas: in any case
dévorante: all-consuming
nous avons hérité (hériter): we have inherited (to inherit)
je crois (croire): I believe (to believe)
nous ne sommes pas près de nous lasser: we are not about to tire of them

Écrivain et philosophe français

On dit de lui **qu'il a été** le philosophe **le plus discuté** du 20ème **siècle**. Mais Jean-Paul Sartre **doit surtout sa renommée** à sa théorie de l'existentialisme et à ses nombreuses pièces de théâtre et **romans**, dont *l'Être et le Néant* et *La Nausée*, **publiés** respectivement en 1938 et en 1943.

Né à Paris, le 21 juin 1905 d'**un père** officier de la marine **qui décède** avant sa **deuxième année**, **il est élevé par sa mère** et son **grand-père** maternel **qui est apparenté** au docteur Albert Schweitzer, **récipiendaire** du **prix Nobel de la paix** en 1952. **Il s'est fait connaître** tant par **les polémiques suscitées** par **ses écrits** que par **sa vie amoureuse hors du commun**. Compagnon de **vie** de Simone de Beauvoir jusqu'à **sa mort**, c'est un ardent défenseur de **la gauche** radicale. **Il n'hésite pas** à **aller à contre-courant** des tendances de **son époque en rejetant**, notamment, le mariage et la paternité.

Sa théorie philosophique s'oppose au matérialisme, et à l'idéalisme traditionnel. **Elle propose** une vision de la vie humaine où **l'être doit agir** et s'**ouvrir** au **monde** pour exister. **Selon** son **postulat**, les éléments fondamentaux de l'existence de l'**homme se résument** à l'engagement, l'aliénation, l'ennui, **la peur**, **le néant**, l'absurde et à la liberté. L'éventualité du suicide **étant**, selon lui, **la seule** question véritable.

Jean-Paul Sartre a **échoué** en 1928 au premier **concours** d'agrégation de l'**École** normale supérieure de Paris **qui lui aurait permis d'enseigner**. **Il le réussit l'année suivante** et enseigne au Havre, à l'Institut français de Berlin et au lycée Pasteur à Paris. En 1944, **il fonde** la revue *Les Temps Modernes* puis **se tourne par la suite** vers le théâtre et **devient un auteur** très prolifique. **Il refuse** le prix Nobel de littérature **qui lui est attribué** en 1964, car **il s'est** toujours **fait un devoir** de décliner les honneurs. Il est mort à Paris le 15 avril 1980.

Prix Nobel de médecine

Né le 14 novembre 1891 dans **la ville** d'Alliston en Ontario, au Canada, et benjamin d'**une fratrie** de cinq enfants, Frederick Grant Banting **a bénéficié** d'**un destin peu commun**.

Connu comme le découvreur de l'insuline, conjointement avec le professeur J.J.R. Macleod, **il a débuté sa scolarité** en fréquentant **les écoles publiques** de sa ville natale. **Par la suite**, **il entre** à l'Université de Toronto avec **le désir** de poursuivre **une filière** d'**études** religieuses, mais **il s'oriente** finalement **vers** la médecine.

L'avènement de la Première Guerre mondiale **le conduit** sur **le front** en France en 1916 avec le Corps médical de l'Armée canadienne. **Blessé** à la bataille de Cambrai en 1918, **on lui octroie** la Croix Militaire pour **bravoure** en 1919. À son **retour de la guerre**, **il étudie la chirurgie** orthopédique et **œuvre** successivement comme praticien à London (Ontario) et chirurgien résident à l'Hôpital pour enfants **malades** de Toronto. **Il devient** par la suite professeur et conférencier en pharmacologie à l'Université de Toronto.

Le Dr Banting a toujours manifesté un grand intérêt scientifique **envers** le diabète et plus particulièrement par la possibilité d'**extraire** l'insuline directement **des ilots** de Langerhans **qui le sécrètent** dans le pancréas. Avec l'aide du Dr Macleod, **qui soutient sa démarche** expérimentale, et de son assistant, le Dr Charles Best, alors étudiant, **il parvient** à **vérifier** l'authenticité de sa théorie, **laquelle donne lieu** à la découverte de l'insuline.

On lui accorde, conjointement avec le Dr J.J.R. Macleod, **le prix Nobel** de médecine en 1923. **Il a également reçu** de nombreuses décorations honorifiques canadiennes et **étrangères**, et a **été ennobli** en 1934. **Marié** à **deux reprises**, **père** d'**un fils** et **peintre** de talent, il a également participé à une expédition artistique **le conduisant au-delà** du cercle arctique. **Il est mort** dans un accident d'**avion**, en février 1941, à Terre-Neuve, au Canada.

né (naître): born (be born)
la ville: the city
une fratrie: sibling
a bénéficié (bénéficier): enjoyed (to enjoy)
un destin: fate
peu commun: exceptional

connu comme (connaître): known as (to know)
le découvreur: the discoverer
il a débuté (débuter): he started (to start)
sa scolarité: his school years
les écoles publiques: public schools
par la suite: later
il entre (entrer): he got in (to get in)
le désir: the desire
une filière d'études: a course of study
il s'oriente vers (orienter): he turned toward (to turn)

l'avènement: the advent
le conduit (conduire): led him (to lead)
le front: battlefront
blessé (blesser): injured (to injure)
on lui octroie (octroyer): he was awarded (to award)
la bravoure: courage
retour de la guerre: back from war
il étudie (étudier): he studied
la chirurgie: surgery
(il) œuvre (oeuvrer): he worked (to work)
malades: sick
il devient (devenir): he became (to become)

envers: toward
extraire: to extract
des ilots: islets
qui le sécrètent (sécréter): which produce it (to produce)
qui soutient (soutenir): who supported (to support)
sa démarche: his process
il parvient (parvenir): he succeeded in (to succeed)
vérifier: to check
laquelle donne lieu: which led to

on lui accorde (accorder): he was awarded (to award)
le prix Nobel: the Nobel Prize
il a également reçu (recevoir): he also received (to receive)
étrangères: foreign
il a été ennobli (ennoblir): he was ennobled (to ennoble)
marié: married
deux reprises (une reprise): two times
un père: father
un fils: a son
peintre: painter
le conduisant (conduire): which led him (to lead)
au-delà: beyond
il est mort (mourir): he died (to die)
un avion: plane

La Môme

Connaissez-vous cette **chanteuse française née** le 19 décembre 1915 et **appelée** Édith Giovanna Gassion ? Non ? Et **si je vous dis** qu'**elle s'est rendue célèbre** dans **le monde entier** avec **des chansons** comme *La Vie en rose, Milord* ou *Non, je ne regrette rien* ? Oui, c'est Édith Piaf, **bien sûr** !

Voilà **une femme** qui, **un peu comme** Billie Holiday aux États-Unis, aura connu la gloire grâce à un immense talent et qui aura eu, **en tant que** femme, **une vie** particulièrement **douloureuse**.

Née d'un artiste de **cirque** et d'**une mère** chanteuse, Édith **vit** dans **la misère la plus absolue les deux premières années** de sa vie. **Son père est parti à la guerre**, sa mère **n'a pas les moyens** de s'occuper d'elle. **On la confie** donc à sa grand-mère maternelle, **mais celle-ci la néglige** totalement. **On la place** donc **un an et demi plus tard** chez sa grand-mère paternelle, **patronne** d'**une maison close** en Normandie. **Certes, on peut rêver d'un meilleur** environnement qu'une « maison de **débauche** » pour **élever une petite fille**, mais là, **au moins**, Édith est **bien nourrie** et **choyée** par sa grand-mère et toutes les prostituées **qui travaillent** pour elle. Édith **a sept ans** lorsque son père **vient la chercher** pour qu'elle travaille avec lui dans **des cirques itinérants**.

Petit à petit, **elle se rend compte** qu'elle a **une voix** et que ça peut lui **permettre** de **gagner de l'argent**. Accompagnée de **sa meilleure amie**, **elle chante** de plus en plus souvent et **quitte** son père à l'âge de 15 ans **pour tenter sa chance**, **seule**. À 17 ans, **elle tombe amoureuse** d'un certain Louis Dupont, avec qui **elle aura** une petite fille, Marcelle, **qui mourra** d'une méningite à l'âge de deux ans…

Si c'était un film, **on dirait** que c'est **exagéré**, mais la vie d'Édith Piaf est une succession de drames et de joies, tout aussi intenses. Édith chante pendant quelques années dans **les rues** de Paris avant d'être remarquée par Louis Leplée qui, **séduit** par sa voix, **l'engage** dans son prestigieux cabaret et **la baptise** « la môme piaf ». **Un piaf** est **un petit oiseau** et Édith **ne mesure qu'un mètre quarante-sept**. Le succès est immédiat et Édith **ne tarde pas** à **enregistrer** son premier **disque**.

En 1937, la môme Piaf devient définitivement Édith Piaf. Elle n'a que 22 ans, **mais déjà** toute une vie de femme **derrière** elle et toute une carrière d'artiste **qui l'attend**… Pendant la Seconde Guerre mondiale, elle continue à chanter, mais ses chansons **évoquent** la résistance et **elle s'efforce de faire travailler** des musiciens juifs.

C'est en 1945 qu'**elle écrit** seule la chanson *La Vie en rose*. **Sa vie amoureuse** est riche, mais pas toujours simple. Ses liaisons sont généralement de **courte durée**. Lorsque le boxeur Marcel Serdant, le grand amour de sa vie (pour qui elle écrit *L'Hymne à l'amour*) meurt en 1949 dans **un accident d'avion**, Piaf, d'un naturel **enjoué** et **rieur**, sombre dans une dépression **qui ne la quittera jamais vraiment**.

Deux ans plus tard, en 1951, **elle est impliquée** dans deux accidents de **voiture qui aggraveront** son état. **Sa santé** fragile, l'alcool et **une accoutumance** à la morphine **obligeront** Piaf **à délaisser** temporairement **le métier qu'elle aimait tant**. De cure de désintoxication en **tournées triomphales, elle parvient tant bien que mal** à tenir la route jusqu'en 1963.

Usée, épuisée, abîmée, elle meurt à 47 ans, le 10 octobre, **un jour avant** son ami Jean Cocteau **qui dira d'elle**: « **Je n'ai jamais connu d'être moins économe** de son âme. **Elle ne la dépensait pas**, elle la **prodiguait**, elle **en jetait l'or par les fenêtres**. »

si c'était (être): if it was (to be)
on dirait (dire): one would say (to say)
exagéré (exagérer): exaggerated (to exaggerate)
les rues (une rue): the streets
séduit (séduire): seduced (to seduce)
(il) l'engage (engager): he hires her (to hire)
(il) la baptise (baptiser): he named her (to name)
un piaf: a little bird, sparrow
un petit oiseau: a little bird
ne mesure qu' un mètre quarante-sept: she is only one meter forty-seven centimeters tall
ne tarde pas (tarder): does not take her long (to take long)
enregistrer: to record
un disque: record

mais déjà: but already
derrière: behind
qui l'attend (attendre): that is waiting for her (to wait)
évoquent (évoquer): evoke (to evoke)
elle s'efforce de faire (s'efforcer de): she tries hard (to try hard)
travailler: to work

elle écrit (écrire): she writes (to write)
sa vie amoureuse: her love life
courte durée: cut short
un accident d'avion: airplane crash
enjoué: cheerful
rieur: laughing
qui ne la quittera jamais vraiment (quitter): that will never really leave her (to leave)

elle est impliquée (impliquer): she is involved (to involve)
une voiture: car
qui aggraveront (aggraver): that will worsen (to worsen)
sa santé (une santé): her health
une accoutumance: addiction
(ils) obligeront (obliger): (they) will force (to force)
à délaisser: to abandon
le métier: profession
qu'elle aimait tant (aimer): that she loved so much (to love)
tournées (une tournée): tours
triomphales (triomphal): triumphant
elle parvient (parvenir): she manages (to manage)
tant bien que mal: more or less

usée (usé): worn down
épuisée (épuisé): exhausted
abîmée: hurt, run down
un jour avant: a day before
qui dira d'elle (dire): who will say about her (to say)
je n'ai jamais connu (connaître): I have never known (to know)
d'être moins économe: less stingy being
elle ne la dépensait pas (dépenser): she did not spend it (to spend)
elle la prodiguait (prodiguer): she gave it (to give, to lavish)
elle en jetait l'or par les fenêtres (jeter): she threw its gold out the windows (to throw)

grâce à: thanks to
ses romans (un roman): his novels
publiés (publier): published (to publish)
fait connaître comme : became famous as
une écrivaine: a female writer
le rayonnement: radiance
elle bénéficie (bénéficier): she enjoys
 (to enjoy)
doit beaucoup (devoir): owes a lot to
 (to owe)
personnages: characters
qui expriment (exprimer): who convey
 (to convey)
allant de: ranging from
la colère: anger
la plus virulente: the fiercest
née (naître): born (be born)
a remporté (remporter): has won (to win)
de nombreux: many
prix littéraires: literary prizes

elle met ... en scène (mettre): she introduces
 (to introduce)
Acadie : the name given to lands in northeastern
 North America that included parts of Canada
 and the area she was from.
inlassablement: tirelessly
dans la plupart: in most
ses ouvrages: her works
un déracinement: an uprooting
été déportée (déporter): were deported
 (to deport)
vers: toward
éparpillée par (éparpiller): scattered by
 (to scatter)
le conquérant: the winner

art connaît (connaître): her art meets with
 (to meet with)
apothéose: climax
elle parvient à(parvenir): she manages to
 (to manage to)
imprimer: to leave an imprint
forte: strong
jouant (jouer): playing (to play)
les riches sonorités: playful sounds
les mots anciens: old words
qui ponctuent (ponctuer): which punctuate
 (to punctuate)
langue natale: native language
transmettre: to convey
un lecteur: reader
épique: epic
qui l'a vu naître: where she was born

a reçu (recevoir): has received (to receive)
une vingtaine: about twenty
elle a enseigné (enseigner): she has taught
 (to teach)
elle réside (résider): she lives (to live)
la plupart du temps: most of the time

Écrivaine acadienne

C'est **grâce à ses romans** *La Sagouine* et *Pélagie-la–Charrette,* tous deux **publiés** en 1979, qu'Antonine Maillet s'est **fait connaître comme une écrivaine** canadienne française de premier plan. **Le rayonnement** international dont **elle bénéficie doit beaucoup** à son style authentique et à la complexité de ses **personnages**, majoritairement féminins, **qui expriment** une vaste gamme d'émotions **allant de** l'humour à **la colère la plus virulente**. **Née** à Bouctouche en 1929, dans la province canadienne du Nouveau-Brunswick, la romancière **a remporté de nombreux prix littéraires**, dont le Prix Goncourt pour son roman *Pélagie-la-Charrette*.

C'est toute l'histoire de l'**Acadie** qu'**elle met inlassablement** en **scène dans la plupart** de **ses ouvrages** ; une histoire marquée par les joies et les souffrances de ce peuple au destin particulier. Le peuple acadien issu de de la colonisation française de 1604, a connu **un déracinement** majeur en 1755, lorsque la presque totalité de ses dix mille habitants a **été déportée vers** les États-Unis et **éparpillée par le conquérant** britannique.

C'est donc avec *Pélagie-la-Charrette* que son **art connaît** son **apothéose**, puisqu'**elle parvient à** y **imprimer** la conscience collective d'une nation à l'identité incertaine, mais pourtant **forte** et déterminée. **Jouant** avec **les riches sonorités** et **les mots anciens qui ponctuent** sa **langue natale**, elle parvient avec originalité et habileté à **transmettre** au **lecteur**, dans une vision symbolique et **épique**, la mémoire de la nation **qui l'a vu naître**.

Antonine Maillet, qui a publié plus de quarante romans, **a reçu une vingtaine** de distinctions honorifiques dont l'Ordre du Canada et l'Ordre de la Légion d'honneur française. **Elle a enseigné** la littérature et le folklore à l'Université Laval de Québec ainsi qu'à Montréal, où **elle réside la plupart du temps**.

À la découverte de Matisse

Le tableau *Les coucous, tapis bleu et rose* a été vendu cette année à Paris pour 32 millions d'euros, une somme historique. S'il ne fallait qu'une preuve que Matisse est encore et toujours apprécié, ce serait celle-ci.

Henri Matisse, un des artistes les plus connus du XXème siècle, était un peintre, un dessinateur et un sculpteur français. Considéré comme le chef de file du fauvisme, Matisse était célèbre pour ses larges aplats de couleurs vives et violentes. Son influence était telle que Picasso lui-même l'a reconnu comme son rival… mais aussi comme son ami.

Grand voyageur, Matisse s'inspirait des lumières et des couleurs de Sud. Ses sujets de prédilection restent, comme pour Picasso, les femmes et les natures mortes. Cependant, contrairement à son rival, Matisse préférait peindre à partir de modèles réels, qu'il plaçait généralement dans un décor détaillé.

À partir de 1917, le peintre a quitté Paris et s'est installé à Nice. C'est là-bas qu'il est mort d'une crise cardiaque en 1954, après une carrière prolifique et parfois teintée de scandales.

Moins de dix ans plus tard, en 1963, c'est donc logiquement que la ville de Nice lui a consacré un musée. Situé sur la colline de Cimiez, le musée Matisse est tout proche de l'ancienne résidence du peintre, l'Hotel Regina. On y trouve une collection permanente, composée en majorité de peintures, dessins, gravures et sculptures. Chaque année, des expositions temporaires, ainsi que des conférences et projections, sont organisées à l'intention des visiteurs.

le tableau: painting
(il) a été vendu (vendre): (it) has been sold (to sell)
une année: year
une somme: sum
s'il ne fallait qu' (falloir): if it were only necessary (to be necessary)
une preuve: proof
encore: still
toujours: always
apprécié: appreciated
ce serait (être): it would be (to be)
celle-ci: that one

les plus connus: the most famous
le siècle: century
(il) était (être): (he) was (to be)
un peintre: painter
un dessinateur: draftsman
considéré: considered
le chef de file: leader
le fauvisme: Fauvism
célèbre: famous
des aplats (un aplat): painted surfaces
vives (vif): bright
lui-même: himself
(il) l'a reconnu (reconnaître): (he) recognized him (to recognize)
mais aussi: but also
un ami: friend

un voyageur: traveler
(il) s'inspirait (s'inspirer): drew inspiration from (to be inspired)
des lumières (une lumière): lights
le Sud: the South (of France)
sujets de prédilection: favorite subjects
restent (rester): remain (to remain)
les femmes (la femme): women
les natures mortes: still lifes
cependant: nevertheless
peindre: to paint
à partir de: from
qu'il plaçait (placer): that he placed (to place)
un décor: setting
détaillé: detailed

a quitté (quitter): left (to leave)
(il) s'est installé (s'installer): (he) settled (to settle)
il est mort (mourir): he died (to die)
une crise cardiaque: heart attack
après: after
parfois: sometimes
teintée de: touched by

moins de: less than
plus tard: later
logiquement: logically
consacré: devoted
un musée: museum
la colline: hill
tout proche: very close
on y trouve (trouver): you can find (to find)
composé: made of, composed of
des dessins (un dessin): drawings
chaque année: each year
ainsi que: as well as

Une personnalité fondamentale

L'**homme** est l'une des figures contemporaines les plus importantes des Antilles françaises. **D'ailleurs** dans son **île natale**, la Martinique, **il est quasiment vénéré** comme **un dieu**. Pourtant **le nom** d'Aimé Césaire **a dépassé les frontières** des Antilles et a atteint une notoriété **mondiale** au cours du **vingtième siècle**.

Aime Césaire **est né** en 1913, **soixante-cinq ans** après l'abolition de l'esclavage et un an avant la Première Guerre mondiale, dans une Martinique alors colonie française. **Il est dote depuis son plus jeune âge** de dispositions intellectuelles remarquables, **qui vont le conduire** à 18 ans dans **un lycée parisien de renom**. **Très peu** de **jeunes noirs** issus des colonies **l'avaient fait avant lui**. Sa scolarité supérieure **sera couronnée** par l'obtention de la prestigieuse Agrégation de lettres, qui a fait de lui un professeur au lycée Schoelcher en Martinique.

Ce jeune homme **qui était destiné** à **devenir un fonctionnaire fidèle** au système colonial français a, **au fil des années** à Paris, de ses expériences et de ses échanges intellectuels, **commencé à réfléchir** au système dans lequel **il avait grandi** et dans lequel son **île** et toutes les autres colonies **se trouvaient encore**. Cette réflexion a **trouvé un écho** lors de ses échanges avec d'autres jeunes étudiants noirs **venus** d'autres colonies françaises, caribéennes.

De ces échanges intellectuels et littéraires est né le concept de négritude **qui représentait** un rejet de la politique coloniale, **accusée d'aliéner** et d'acculturer les populations locales puisqu'**il s'agissait** alors de **les assimiler plutôt que** de développer leur **identité propre**.

Aimé Césaire **marquera** cette réflexion par **une œuvre parue** en 1939, intitulée *Cahier d'un retour au pays natal*, dans laquelle **il dénonce** les conséquences du colonialisme sur la population martiniquaise mais aussi sur les populations africaines dont **il a entendu parler par** son **ami** Léopold Senghor. Ce texte **parle de douleur** et de révolte **contre** un système dont il a évalué les effets lorsqu'**il vivait** en Europe.

Cahier d'un retour au pays natal **a été suivi** en 1950 **par** le *Discours sur le colonialisme*. Ce pamphlet qui comme son nom l'**indique** est une attaque claire contre le colonialisme **a été réédité** en 1955, après le début de la Guerre d'indépendance d'Algérie. **L'auteur** a alors **pris position** pour **le pays** du Maghreb et contre l'oppression coloniale. Et c'est d'ailleurs, à cette période **des guerres** de décolonisation, que le nom d'Aimé Césaire **a commencé à traverser les frontières grâce à ses écrits**, dont la dimension universelle **dépassait** la Martinique et **même** la France.

À la fin de la Seconde Guerre mondiale, **qui a vu l'implication** de nombreux jeunes Martiniquais dans les armées de libération américaines ou françaises en exil et **malgré** ses positions idéologiques, Aimé Césaire **choisit** de **s'engager** en politique **en devenant maire** de Fort-de-France (capitale de la Martinique) de 1945 à 2001 et aussi député de l'île de 1958 à 1993.

C'est **la mort** d'Aimé Césaire en avril 2008 **qui a prouvé**, si c'était **vraiment nécessaire**, à quel point **il était devenu** une figure incontournable de la littérature francophone, de **la pensée** universelle et du combat des peuples **opprimés** dans **le monde**. **En effet**, **les hommages rendus à l'annonce de son décès ont été** nombreux et **ont réunis** des intellectuels de tous pays et de tous horizons. C'est avec **tristesse** mais aussi beaucoup de **fierté** que **des milliers** de Martiniquais l'**ont accompagné** jusqu'à **sa dernière demeure**, comme des membres de sa propre famille.

Les débuts de Coco Chanel

Née en 1883, Gabrielle Bonheur Chanel est **placée** à l'**orphelinat à l'âge de** 12 ans après **le décès** de **sa mère**. À 18 ans, elle débute **le dur apprentissage** du **métier** de **couseuse**. En 1903, **elle commence** à **travailler** en tant que telle dans une maison **spécialisée en** trousseaux et **layettes**.

Mais Gabrielle a de l'ambition et **surtout** une **forte** personnalité. Étienne Balsan, riche **homme d'affaires**, la **remarque**. Une **idylle** commence rapidement. **Par son biais**, Gabrielle Chanel **apprend** le fonctionnement de **la haute société** et surtout **étoffe** ses relations. C'est ainsi qu'**elle va rencontrer** Arthur Capel, **dit** « Boy », **l'amour de sa vie**. **Il jouera un rôle clef** dans la création des premières boutiques Chanel, **notamment en apportant** son **soutien financier**.

Gabrielle Chanel, dite « Coco », commence par **créer ses propres chapeaux** et **vêtements** qu'**elle porte** à l'occasion de **soirées mondaines**. **Elle teste** ainsi ses modèles et en assure la promotion **au sein de** la haute société de l'**époque**. Son style est **décalé**, **sobre**, **épuré**, **bref à contre-courant** de la mode du début du XXème **siècle**. Ses modèles **plaisent**, si bien qu'**elle ouvre** sa première boutique en 1913 au 21 **rue** Cambon à Paris, **sa deuxième** à Deauville la **même année** et **sa troisième** en 1915 à Biarritz. Elle créera sa maison de haute couture en 1918, rue Cambon, où **elle se trouve encore aujourd'hui**.

Le style Chanel est en **rupture** avec la mode de l'époque. Gabrielle Chanel crée une nouvelle **allure**. **Elle libère le corps** des femmes en créant des modèles **novateurs**, confortables mais élégants: **les jupes** sont **raccourcies**, **la taille des robes** est **supprimée**. **Elle utilise** aussi **des matières** plus fluides comme le jersey qui **jusque-là n'était pas** du tout utilisé dans la confection féminine.

Mais Coco Chanel est surtout une avant-gardiste car **elle perçoit avec une grande justesse** l'évolution de la société française et notamment la place qu'**occupent les femmes au sein de celle-ci**. Pendant et après **la Première Guerre mondiale**, les femmes **sont devenues** une **vraie force de travail**. Elle crée donc des modèles **qui correspondent** aux nouveaux **besoins quotidiens** des femmes de l'époque. Ses vêtements sont simples, pratiques mais chics. **Sa mode** s'inspire largement **des tenues masculines** et sportives **des stations balnéaires** qu'**elle côtoie**. Elle introduit **le pantalon**, **la jupe plissée courte** et le polo comme autant de modèles qui constituent aujourd'hui les basiques de **nos garde-robes**. Parmi ces classiques, **la petite robe noire** (**fourreau droit sans col** à **manches** trois quart) est une idée de **génie** qui sera **très souvent copiée** et recopiée. Quant aux couleurs, Mademoiselle Chanel **ne jurait que par le noir**, le blanc et le beige.

Mais Coco est aussi une icône, un modèle pour les femmes de l'époque. Extrêmement **mince**, les cheveux courts, **bronzée**, elle impose sa silhouette androgyne. Elle crée de nouveaux **canons de beauté qui vont marquer** ses contemporaines mais aussi les générations **suivantes**.

Depuis 1983, le styliste Karl Lagerfeld **perpétue** l'esprit et assure la continuité du style Chanel **en retravaillant** les codes fondamentaux de **la fondatrice**, **à savoir** le blanc, le noir, les perles, le jersey et le tweed ... Ainsi **pour chacune** de ses nouvelles collections, il utilise comme source d'inspiration les archives de Chanel renouvelant ainsi **à sa manière** le style **indémodable** de Coco.

une rupture: a break
une allure: style
elle libère (libérer): she frees (to free)
le corps: the bodies
novateurs (novateur): innovative
les jupes (la jupe): skirts
raccourcies (raccourci): shortened
la taille: waist
des robes (une robe): dresses
supprimée (supprimer): removed (to remove)
elle utilise (utiliser): she uses (to use)
des matières (une matière): materials
jusque-là: until then, until that point
il n'était pas utilisé (utiliser): it was not used (to use)

elle perçoit (percevoir): she feels (to feel)
avec une grande justesse: in all fairness
(elles) occupent (occuper): they hold (to hold)
les femmes (une femme): women
au sein de celle-ci: within this one
la Première Guerre mondiale: the First World War
sont devenues (devenir): became (to become)
vraie (vrai): real
une force de travail: a labor force
qui correspondent (correspondre): that match, correspond (to correspond)
besoins quotidiens: daily needs
sa mode (une mode): her fashion
des tenues masculines: menswear
des stations balnéaires: seaside resorts
elle côtoie: she moves in, rubs shoulders with
le pantalon: pants
la jupe plissée courte: short pleated skirt
des garde-robes (une garde-robe): wardrobes
la petite robe noire: the little black dress
un fourreau: a sheath dress
droit: straight
sans col: collarless
des manches (une manche): sleeves
le génie: genius
très souvent: very often
copiée (copier): copied (to copy)
ne jurait que par (jurer): she only swore by (to swear)
le noir: black

mince: slim
bronzée (bronzer): tanned (to tan)
les canons de beauté: beauty rules
qui vont marquer: that are going to leave a mark
suivantes (suivant): next

perpétue (perpétuer): perpetuates (to perpetuate)
en retravaillant: by working again
la fondatrice: founder
à savoir: that is to say
pour chacune: for each
à sa manière: his way
indémodable: that will never go out of fashion

Évaluez votre compréhension

Ingénieur français célèbre, page 88

1. Who inspired the course of Gustave Eiffel's professional career?

2. After the Eiffel Tower, what famous project did he undertake?

3. What other types of projects did Eiffel engineer?

Écrivain et philosophe français, page 94

1. Jean-Paul Sartre's childhood was marked by what tragedy?

2. How did he defy the social norms of his times?

3. What happened during his first year at *École normale supérieure de Paris*?

Cinéaste français, page 92

1. What is the style or technique of *la Nouvelle Vague*?

2. What is the result of filming this way?

3. When watching a Truffaut film, he seems to be telling us what?

Prix Nobel de médecine, page 95

1. Frederick Grant Banting is famous for what invention?

2. When Banting started attending university, what was his major?

3. After being injured at war, what did he go on to study?

Test your comprehension

La Môme, page 96

1. Édith Piaf is compared to what American singer?

2. At seven years old what happened to Édith?

3. Why was she given the nickname *la môme piaf*?

Une personnalité fondamentale, page 100

1. What did Aimé Césaire accuse the local goverment of doing to its people?

2. What did he do for the country of Maghreb, and how did this affect his popularity?

3. After The Second World War, what did he do to get further involved in politics?

Écrivaine acadienne, page 98

1. Describe the characters in Maillet's novels.

2. What does she introduce in most of her works?

3. How many novels has she published?

Les débuts de Coco Chanel, page 102

1. Who was the love of Coco Chanel's life? What was his nickname?

2. What fabric did she introduce into fashion?

3. Describe the dress style she was known for creating.

Coutumes

Bises ou pas bises ?

La façon de dire bonjour à une personne dépend généralement du type de relations que l'on a avec elle mais également de la situation (l'âge, les rapports hiérarchiques, etc.) Ce seront les rapports plus ou moins intimes que l'on entretient qui détermineront si l'on utilise la poignée de main ou si l'on se fait la bise.

Avec des personnes que vous connaissez peu ou que vous rencontrez pour la première fois et avec lesquelles vous souhaitez marquer une « certaine distance », la poignée de main peut être utilisée. Elle sera le signe de votre volonté de ne pas faire la bise, ou de marquer un certain respect envers la personne mais tout en faisant preuve de politesse. Ensuite quand on connait un peu mieux la personne, il est de coutume de se faire la bise.

Dans les relations professionnelles pour lesquelles il est nécessaire de conserver une certaine distance entre les personnes, il est donc mal vu de se saluer en se faisant la bise. Il est donc préférable de serrer la main, que vous soyez entre hommes ou femmes.

Dans le contexte personnel, avec des amis ou la famille la bise se fait presque systématiquement en France, mais c'est selon le sexe de la personne a qui vous dites bonjour. Les femmes se font automatiquement la bise entre elles, et un homme embrassera également systématiquement une femme (et vice-versa). Cela est moins courant pour les hommes entre eux qui ne le font que s'ils ont un certain degré d'intimité (s'ils sont d'une même famille par exemple ou s'ils sont amis depuis un certain nombre d'années).

Le **nombre** de bises à faire est une question à laquelle les français **eux-mêmes ne savent pas toujours répondre**. Dans la grande majorité des cas, on se fait deux bises, mais dans certaines régions de France, comme dans **le Sud**, ou **le Nord**, **on peut en faire** 3, voire 4, … mais même les Français **ne sauraient déterminer** « la norme » du nombre de bises a faire quand on se dit bonjour…. On reste donc beaucoup dans l'improvisation et l'adaptation pour le nombre de bises à faire et **par quelle joue commencer**.

Dans le doute, pour **être sûr** de faire preuve de politesse, **la meilleure** des solutions est de **tendre** la main, et de « **suivre** » ce que la personne **en face de** vous **va vous proposer**. Elle vous tend la main, faites une poignée de main **ferme** et **franche**, **qui montrera** que vous êtes sûr(e) de vous. Si la personne **vous tend** la joue pour vous faire la bise tout **en** vous **tenant** la main, **suivez-la** et **lancez-vous** en faisant la bise également ! C'est la preuve que cette personne **souhaite établir** un contact **chaleureux** avec vous.

Mais quel que soit **le mode** de salutations **choisi**, une fois que l'on a fait la bise a **quelqu'un**, **ne plus la faire** à **la rencontre suivante** peut être considéré comme le fait qu'il y a un problème ou comme un signe d'impolitesse.

nombre: number
eux-mêmes: themselves
(ils) ne savent pas (savoir): they don't know (to know)
toujours: still
répondre: to answer
le Sud: the South
le Nord: the North
on peut en faire (pouvoir): people can do (can, to be able to)
(ils) ne sauraient déterminer: they wouldn't be able to tell
par quelle: which
une joue: cheek
commencer: to start

être sûr: to be sure
la meilleure: the best
tendre: to hold out
suivre: to follow
en face de: in front of
va vous proposer (aller): is going to suggest to you (to go)
ferme: strong
franche: sincere
qui montrera (montrer): which will show (to show)
la personne tend (tendre): this person reaches out (to reach)
en tenant (tenir): holding (to hold)
suivez-la (suivre): follow it (to follow)
lancez-vous (se lancer): put yourself out there (to get involved)
souhaite établir (souhaiter): wishes to set up (to wish)
chaleureux: warm

le mode: the way
choisi: selected, chosen
quelqu'un: someone
ne plus la faire: not do it anymore
la rencontre: meeting
suivante: following

Ne pas avoir l'air d'un touriste

des pays (un pays): countries
visités (visiter): visited (to visit)
un monde: world
très courant: very common
rencontrer: to meet
surtout: above all
un été: summer
si vous souhaitez (souhaiter): if you wish (to wish)
éviter: to avoid
être pris pour (prendre): being considered as (to consider)

La France est un **des pays** les plus **visités** au **monde**. Il est donc **très courant** d'y **rencontrer** des touristes, **surtout** en période d'**été**. **Si vous souhaitez éviter** d'**être pris pour** le touriste typique, il y a certains stéréotypes à éviter.

un habillement: clothing
vous permettra (permettre): will help you (to help)
vous confondre: you to mix up with
vous promenez (promener): you walk around (to walk around)
les rues (la rue): the streets
des chaussettes blanches: white socks
une casquette: a cap
un appareil photo: a camera
en bandoulière: over the shoulder
il y a fort à parier que: it is most likely that
adoptez (adopter): go for (to go)
une tenue vestimentaire: outfit
vous pourrez (pouvoir): you will be able to (can, to be able to)
passer inaperçu: to go unnoticed

L'**habillement vous permettra** tout d'abord de **vous confondre** un peu avec la population locale. Si vous **vous promenez** dans **les rues** de Paris en Bermuda, avec des baskets, **des chaussettes blanches, une casquette** (imprimée « I Love Paris ») et **un appareil photo en bandoulière, il y a fort à parier que** les Français vous considèrent comme un touriste. **Adoptez** donc **une tenue vestimentaire** plus classique de type jeans, t-shirt. C'est classique, mais cela reste très commun en France et **vous pourrez passer inaperçu** si vous le souhaitez.

vous ne parlez pas (parler): you don't speak (to speak)
vous pouvez (pouvoir): you can (can, to be able to)
toutefois: nevertheless
prendre la peine: take the time to
apprendre: to learn
quelques mots (un mot): some words
vous aurez (avoir): you will have (to have)
montrer: to show
vous rencontrerez (rencontrer): you will meet (to meet)
vous avez (avoir): you have (to have)
très fiers: very proud
aborder: to approach
assez: quite
mal vu: frowned upon
très impoli: very rude

Vous ne parlez pas français ? **Vous pouvez toutefois prendre la peine** d'**apprendre quelques mots** ou phrases dont **vous aurez** l'utilité pour **montrer** aux personnes que **vous rencontrerez** que **vous avez** le respect de la langue. Les Français sont **très fiers** de leur langue et de leur culture. **Aborder** des Français en langue anglaise en considérant que c'est la langue que tout le monde parle est **assez mal vu** et **très impoli**.

Si vous avez des difficultés avec l'**apprentissage** de la langue, prenez donc juste la peine d'apprendre une phrase vous permettant de leur **demander**, en Français, s'ils parlent anglais et si **cela** leur **pose un souci** de vous **renseigner** dans cette langue. **Il est quasiment sûr que la plupart** des Français **seront ravis** de vous montrer qu'ils sont capables de communiquer en anglais et de vous **tirer une épine du pied**.

En France, **les horaires sont assez** structurés et **si vous voulez vivre** « à la sauce française », calez-vous sur les horaires types. **Il vous suffira de savoir** que **le dimanche** la plupart des boutiques sont **fermées**, que **entre midi et deux** de nombreux **endroits** sont également fermés **pour faire la pause déjeuner** et que les plats « to go » **ne font absolument pas partie** de la culture française. Les Français **aiment s'asseoir** à une table, en terrasse ou au **comptoir** d'un café pour **boire un coup. Ils prennent le temps de** déjeuner le midi et **ne mangent pas** « **sur le pouce** ». **Ne cherchez donc pas** à stresser les serveurs **pour qu'ils vous servent** plus rapidement… Après tout, n'êtes-vous pas en vacances ?

Enfin, dans les bars et restaurants, il y a une grande différence avec les pays anglo-saxons: **le service** est **inclus** dans l'addition ! Si vous souhaitez **laisser un** peu de **pourboire**, vous pouvez le faire quand vous êtes content de **la façon** dont **vous avez été servi**. Cette coutume **se fait en général** sur **le rendu de monnaie** quand vous payez l'addition.

Le meilleur moyen de **se confondre** avec la population est donc d'**essayer** de **se mettre à la place** de la personne avec laquelle vous souhaitez communiquer. Vous n'aurez ainsi **sans nul doute** aucune difficulté à **comprendre** quelle est la meilleure attitude à adopter, et à **être accueilli chaleureusement**.

---

apprentissage: learning
demander: to ask
cela pose un souci (poser): it causes any trouble (to cause)
renseigner: to inform
il est quasiment sûr: it is almost sure, obvious
la plupart: most of
seront ravis (être): will be happy (to be)
tirer une épine du pied: to get someone out of a hard spot

les horaires: hours
sont assez (être): are quite (to be)
si vous voulez vivre (vouloir): if you want to live (to want to)
il vous suffira de savoir: you need to know
le dimanche: on Sunday
fermées (fermer): closed (to close)
entre midi et deux: lunch break
endroits: places
pour faire la pause déjeuner: to have their lunch break
(ils) ne font absolument pas partie de: they absolutely don't belong to
aiment s'asseoir (aimer): love sitting (to love)
un comptoir: bar counter
boire un coup: to have a drink
ils prennent le temps de (prendre): they take the time to (to take)
(ils) ne mangent pas (manger): they don't eat (to eat)
sur le pouce: on the run
ne cherchez donc pas (chercher): so don't try to (to try to find)
pour qu'ils vous servent (servir): so that they serve (to serve)

le service: service (tip)
inclus (inclure): included (to include)
laisser un pourboire: to leave a tip
la façon: the way
vous avez été servi (servir): you were served (to serve)
se fait en général (faire): is generally done (to do)
le rendu de monnaie (rendre): given change (to give back, to return)

le meilleur moyen: the best way
se confondre: to mix up
essayer: to try
se mettre à la place: to walk in someone else's shoes
sans nul doute: without any doubt
comprendre: to understand
être accueilli chaleureusement: to receive a warm welcome

L'étiquette professionnelle

Les Français **travaillent en moyenne** 35 heures par **semaine**. Les heures **habituelles** de travail **se situent** de 8h30 à 12h00/12h30 et de 13h30/14h00 à 18h30/19h00. **Les pauses déjeuner** sont quasi systématiques en France, et il est très difficile de **joindre** des personnes par téléphone **entre midi et 14h00**. **Il est courant** pour **les cadres** d'effectuer des heures supplémentaires et de travailler **plus tard le soir**.

En général, **on vouvoie** les personnes que l'**on rencontre** pour **la première fois**, le supérieur hiérarchique ou une personne **plus âgée** que soi. En **affaires**, **le tutoiement spontané** est **ressenti** comme **un manque** de respect. Par la **suite**, si une relation de confiance s'installe **entre** deux personnes, **ils conviendront** de **se tutoyer** ou de s'appeler par leur **prénom**. Mais dans tous les cas, lors d'une première rencontre, l'usage du « vous » est obligatoire en affaires, et la personne **doit être appelée par** son nom de famille (Monsieur X) et non par son prénom.

Pour **les femmes**, **si vous ne savez pas** si vous avez à faire à une personne **mariée** ou non, l'usage de « Madame » **reste la valeur sûre**, car le terme de Mademoiselle peut être perçu péjorativement **selon** le statut de la femme que vous saluez.

Les Français sont plutôt formels dans la rencontre. S'il s'agit d'une première rencontre, **on pourra dire** : « Enchanté », « **Ravi de vous rencontrer** », ou tout simplement **annoncer** son nom : « Bonjour, Nicolas Martin ».

La **poignée de main** reste **le geste** le plus adéquat pour toute personne que vous rencontrez pour la première fois, homme ou femme. **Serrer** la main est en France un rituel d'**ouverture** et de **fermeture** de la rencontre ; l'acte de **se saluer** et de **se quitter** est obligatoirement **marqué** par ce geste. Une rencontre, **même de moins de cinq minutes** peut être introduite par une poignée de main et terminée par une autre.

Les Français considèrent **impoli** d'**arriver en retard** à un rendez-vous d'affaires. L'idéal étant de **se présenter** avec 5 minutes d'avance **par rapport** à l'**heure prévu** de rendez-vous. **Vous ne serez pas considéré** comme arrivant trop en retard jusqu'à 10 mn **dépassant** l'horaire prévue.

Les rendez-vous d'affaires autour d'**un repas** sont **monnaie courante** en France. S'il s'agit d'**un déjeuner**, il commencera habituellement **vers** 13h00 et **pourra durer jusqu'**à 15h00. **S'il a lieu** le soir, les invitations sont généralement **lancées** autour de 20h00 et la soirée **se terminera** aux alentours de 23h00.

Faire des cadeaux n'est pas une coutume dans les affaires en France, **sauf pour** les occasions particulières de type **fin d'année** ou **pour sceller** la négociation d'un contrat important. Si vous venez de l'**étranger** et **désirez** faire un cadeau à une personne avec qui **vous souhaitez établir** une relation à long terme, optez pour un cadeau représentatif de votre **pays** qui sera certainement apprécié.

Enfin, **sachez** qu'il est très impoli de demander à un Français que vous **ne connaissez pas** quelles sont ses opinions politiques ou **ce qu'il a voté aux dernières élections**. **C'est perçu comme** une agression dans **la vie privée** et c'est un sujet **qui n'est abordé** qu'entre personnes **ayant déjà** une certaine complicité dans la relation.

---

la poignée de main: the handshake
le geste: the gesture, act
serrer: to shake
une ouverture: opening
la fermeture: closing
se saluer: to greet
se quitter: to leave
marqué: marked
même de moins de cinq minutes: even less than five minutes

impoli: rude, impolite
arriver: to arrive
en retard: late
se présenter: to arrive
par rapport: in relation to
une heure prévu: scheduled hour
vous ne serez pas considéré (considérer): you won't be considerated (to consider)
dépassant: exceding

un repas: meal
monnaie courante: common practice
un déjeuner: lunch
vers: around, about
(il) pourra durer jusqu' (pouvoir): it can last until (can, to be able to)
s'il a lieu (avoir lieu): if it occurs (to occur)
(elles) sont lancées (lancer): they are launched (to launch)
(elle) se terminera (terminer): it will end (to end)

faire des cadeaux: to give gifts
sauf pour: except for
la fin d'année: end of the year
pour sceller: to seal
étranger: abroad
vous désirez (désirer): you wish (to wish)
vous souhaitez (souhaiter): you wish (to wish)
établir: to establish
le pays: country

(vous) sachez (savoir): you must know (to know)
vous ne connaissez pas (connaître): you do not know (to know)
ce qu'il a voté aux dernières élections: what he voted for at the last elections
c'est perçu comme (percevoir): it is seen as (to be seen as)
la vie privée: private life
qui n'est abordé (aborder): which is only addressed (to address)
ayant déjà (avoir): already having (to have)

La bienséance autour d'une table

Les Français **attachent beaucoup** d'importance à la qualité de **leurs repas** ; qualité dans l'**assiette mais également** en terme de **comportement.** C'est un moment de convivialité **pendant** lequel **les amis** et/ou membres de la famille **partagent** et **échangent autour** des assiettes. Les repas en France **sont quotidiennement pris assis**, à table, **ensemble** et **en même temps. Que ce soit entre** amis, en famille ou avec **des invités de marque,** il y a certaines **règles** de **savoir-vivre** et de politesse à respecter autour d'une table en France.

Tout d'abord, c'est généralement l'hôtesse **qui place** ses invités à table. **À moins** qu'**elle n'ait précisé** que **chacun** se place **à sa guise**, il faut généralement **attendre** qu'**elle vous indique** votre place. Quand cela est possible, **par rapport à** la diversité des personnes présentes, il est de coutume d'**alterner homme/femme** sur **les sièges.**

Il est d'usage que **le maître** et la maîtresse de **maison** président le repas et **se fassent face en bout de table.** D'un point de vue **plus protocolaire,** avec des invités, les personnes les plus importantes, ou **les plus âgées** ou encore **celles qui viennent** pour **la première fois seront placées** à la **droite** et à la **gauche** des maîtres de maison. **Enfin**, si le dîner ou repas est organisé en l'honneur d'une personne en particulier, ce sera cette personne qui sera placée en bout de table. Par exemple, pour **des fiançailles** ou un mariage, **les amoureux** président la table.

Une fois à table, les règles de savoir-vivre sont nombreuses et certains gestes simples **peuvent devenir** une marque de grande impolitesse. Les plus basiques consistent à ne pas parler **la bouche pleine**, et surtout à **fermer** la bouche **en mangeant**. Il est très impoli de **mâcher** la bouche **ouverte en faisant du bruit.**

La **serviette se pose** sur **les genoux** et **ne s'accroche pas autour du cou**, ceci étant réservé aux plus **jeunes enfants** uniquement. À une table française, il est par ailleurs impoli de **laisser sa main** sous la table sur **la cuisse** ; les deux mains et **bras doivent** être placés sur la table, **de chaque coté** de l'assiette et **il ne faut pas s'appuyer sur ses coudes.** Tenir son **visage** dans ses mains en s'appuyant sur la table avec les coudes **relève** de la **pire** impolitesse en termes de **tenue à table** !

Si vous avez besoin d'utiliser vos mains pendant le repas, les couverts **doivent** être **posés** dans l'assiette une fois utilisés et non sur **la nappe**, ou la table directement, **cela évite** de la **tacher.** Quand **vous avez terminé** le repas, les couverts doivent être placés sur votre assiette verticalement, **les dents** de **la fourchette vers le bas.** Ceci est le signe que vous avez terminé votre repas.

Dans les repas **plus formels**, il n'est pas rare de **trouver plusieurs** paires de **couverts** (entrée, plat, fromage, dessert). **Si vous ne savez pas** quel couvert correspond à quel plat, **il suffit de** les utiliser dans l'ordre de l'extérieur vers l'intérieur de l'assiette, et de les **poser** à **chaque fois** dans l'assiette (et non pas sur **le rebord** uniquement) **pour marquer le fait** que vous avez terminé le plat en question.

Ces règles sont les usages basiques du savoir-vivre à table en France. En famille ou avec des invités, elles sont inculquées aux enfants dès leur plus **jeune** âge comme la base d'une **tenue respectable** pendant les repas.

Il y a ensuite d'autres règles à respecter **selon les mets** que vous mangez (par exemple de ne jamais **couper les feuilles de salade** ou ne pas **introduire toute la cuillère** à soupe dans la bouche), ainsi que des usages **plus minutieux** pour les repas protocolaires. Mais respecter ces premières règles sont les bases minimum pour **se forger** une **bonne** image **autour d'**une table en France. **Nous espérons** que **ces quelques conseils vous permettent** d'adopter la « French attitude » à table. Bon appétit !

la serviette: the napkin
se pose (poser): is put (to put)
les genoux (le genou): knees
elle ne s'accroche pas (s'accrocher): it is not hung (to hang)
autour du: around
le cou: neck
les jeunes enfants: young children
laisser: to let
sa main (une main): his/her hand
la cuisse: thigh
le bras: arm
(ils) doivent (devoir): they must (to have to)
de chaque coté: on each side
il ne faut pas: you must not
s'appuyer sur: to lean on
ses coudes (le coude): their elbows
tenir: to hold
un visage: face
cela relève de (relever): it comes under (to come under)
pire: worse
la tenue à table: table manners

si vous avez besoin: if you need
(ils) doivent (devoir): they must (must, to have to)
posés (poser): put (to put)
la nappe: tablecloth
cela évite (éviter): it avoids (to avoid)
tacher: to stain
vous avez terminé (terminer): you have finished (to finish)
les dents (la dent): teeth
la fourchette: fork
vers le bas: face down

plus formels: more formal
trouver: to find
plusieurs: several
couverts: cutlery
si vous ne savez pas (savoir): if you do not know (to know)
il suffit de (suffir): you just need (to need)
poser: to put down
chaque fois: each time
le rebord: edge
pour marquer le fait: to indicate

jeune: young
une tenue respectable: good manners

selon: according to
les mets (le mets): dishes
couper: cut
les feuilles de salade: salad leaves
introduire: introduce
la cuillère: a spoon
plus minutieux: more meticulous
se forger: to forge
bonne (bon): good
autour de: around
nous espérons (espérer): we hope (to hope)
ces quelques conseils: this bit of advice
vous permettent (permettre): will allow you

La signification des gestes

Lorsque l'**on voyage** dans **les pays** où la culture est à prédominance méditerranéenne, comme la France par son **côté sud**, on est souvent **étonné par la façon imagée** dont **les autochtones illustrent** leurs **propos**. Non seulement **il leur arrive de faire des simagrées**, mais **ils utilisent** aussi abondamment **leurs mains** pour **accompagner** leur discours, **aussi ténu soit-il**.

Il est important de **connaître ces gestes**, car **ils permettent** de **mieux comprendre** certaines expressions qui, autrement, **pourraient paraître nébuleuses** ou **porter à confusion**.

Voici la signification de quelques-uns des gestes les plus **souvent utilisés**, accompagnés de l'expression parfois idiomatique **qu'elle cherche** à illustrer.

Je ne veux pas me prendre la tête avec ça. Cette expression **qui signifie** qu'**on ne veut pas se faire du souci** est souvent accompagnée d'un geste des deux mains que l'**on place de chaque côté** de **la tête**.

Oh la la ! Cette expression est utilisée pour **marquer** l'**étonnement** ou l'impatience **face à** une situation, ou à **un comportement** bizarre ou inapproprié de la part quelqu'un. Il est accompagné d'**un mordillement** de **la lèvre inférieure** et d'un mouvement de la main que l'**on secoue de gauche à droite**.

À peu près, est une expression qui indique l'approximation. **On l'utilise** avec un geste **qui ressemble** au précédent, **c'est-à-dire** que **le poignet**, **plutôt que** d'être secoué, **effectue** une **ample** rotation.

---

on voyage (voyager): people travel (to travel)
les pays (le pays): countries
côté sud: Southern part
étonné par: amazed by
la façon imagée: the colorful way
les autochtones illustrent (illustrer): the locals embellish (to embellish)
propos: words
il leur arrive (arriver): it happens to them (to happen)
de faire des simagrées: to play-act
ils utilisent (utiliser): they use (to use)
leurs mains (une main): their hands
accompagner: to illustrate
aussi ténu soit-il: as limited as it may be

connaître: to know
ces gestes (un geste): these gestures
ils permettent (permettre): they enable (to enable)
mieux comprendre: to better understand
pourraient paraître: could sound
nébuleuses: vague
porter à confusion: be confusing

souvent: often
utilisés: used
qu'elle cherche (chercher): which look for (to look for, to try to find)

qui signifie (signifier): which means (to mean)
on ne veut pas (vouloir): one does not want to (to want)
se faire du souci: to worry
on place de (placer): to put (to put)
chaque: each
côté: side
la tête: head

marquer: to show
étonnement: amazement
face à: in front of
un comportement: a behavior
un mordillement: biting
la lèvre inférieure: the lower lip
on secoue (secouer): one shakes (to shake)
de gauche à droite: from left to right

on l'utilise (utiliser): it is used (to use)
qui ressemble (ressembler): which resembles (to resemble)
c'est-à-dire: that is to say
le poignet: the fist
plutôt que: instead of
être secoué (secouer): being shaken (to shake)
effectue (effectuer): does (to do)
ample: large

C'est foutu. Cette expression, qui indique que **quelque chose est raté** et **qu'il n'y a plus vraiment** de raison légitime d'**espérer** est utilisée en plaçant une main sur **le front**, comme pour **indiquer** que la catastrophe est imminente.

C'est juré, craché. Cette expression est utilisée pour signifier que l'**on va accomplir** la chose promise. Il y a deux gestes **qui sont adaptés** à cette affirmation **quasi solennelle**, **on crache par terre** ou on peut, en plus, **croiser** l'index et **le majeur**. Le fait de cracher est **bien entendu tout à fait optionnel**.

Il est barjot ou il est cinglé. On emploie cette expression à la limite de l'impolitesse lorsque l'**on veut indiquer** que quelqu'un est **fou** ou **qu'il n'a pas toute sa tête**. Pour accompagner cette affirmation, on place **le bout** de **l'index** sur sa **tempe** et **on le fait tourner**.

J'ai sommeil ou je suis fatigué. Cette expression simple et **limpide** indique que l'**on est épuisé** et qu'**on aimerait aller dormir**. C'est en plaçant ses deux mains **paume contre paume** sur un **des côtés** du **visage** que l'on illustre cette phrase universelle.

C'est parfait ! C'est **en faisant** un cercle avec **le pouce** et l'index que l'on indique que la situation ou **le travail** accompli est **sans défaut** et mérite **les applaudissements**.

C'est délicieux ! Cette expression, **partagée par** tout le pourtour méditerranéen, **incluant** l'Italie, **laisse entendre** que **la nourriture qu'on nous sert possède** toutes les qualités. On l'utilise en **embrassant le bout** de ses **doigts fermés puis en ouvrant** rapidement la main.

Ces quelques gestes placés à **bon escient permettront** à l'**étranger** non seulement de **se faire comprendre**, mais peut-être, **qui sait**, de **passer pour un natif** du pays.

quelque chose est raté (rater): something has gone wrong (to spoil, to fail)
qu'il n'y a plus vraiment: there is no more
espérer: to hope
le front: forhead
indiquer: to point out, to show

on va accomplir: one is going to fulfill
qui sont adaptés: which are appropriate
quasi solennelle: almost solemn
on crache par terre (cracher): one spits on the ground (to spit)
croiser: to cross
le majeur: the middle finger
le fait: the fact
bien entendu: no need to say
tout à fait optionnel: completely optional

on veut indiquer (vouloir): one wants to show (to want)
fou: crazy
qu'il n'a pas toute sa tête: someone has lost their mind
le bout: the tip
l'index: the forefinger
tempe: temple (side of forehead)
on le fait tourner (faire): one makes it turn (to make)

limpide: clear
on est épuisé: someone is exhausted
on aimerait: would like
aller: to go
dormir: to sleep
paume contre paume: palms together
des côtés (un côté): sides
un visage: face

en faisant (faire): doing (to do)
le pouce: thumb
le travail: the job
sans défaut: flawless
les applaudissements: applause

partagée par: shared by
incluant (inlure): including (to include)
laisse entendre (laisser): implies (to imply)
la nourriture: food
qu'on nous sert (servir): we are served (to serve)
possède (posséder): has (to have)
embrassant: kissing
le bout: the top
doigts (un doigt): fingers
fermés: closed
puis en ouvrant (ouvrir): then opening (to open)

bon escient: accurately
permettront (permettre): will enable (to enable)
étranger: foreigner
se faire comprendre: to be understood
qui sait (savoir): who knows (to know)
passer pour: to pass for
un natif: native

Les expressions usuelles

Il existe de **nombreux** proverbes et expressions **usuelles** dans **la langue** française. **Ils ne sont pas réservés** à l'usage de **l'écriture** et **il n'est pas** rare d'en **utiliser** dans le langage **parlé** pour **imager ses propos** ou pour **apporter** une touche d'ironie tout en **apportant** un **peu** de morale.

Voici quelques expressions utilisées **couramment** au cours de discussions sur le thème de l'action et des relations :

« Avoir plus d'une corde à son arc »

Un arc ne possède qu'**une seule corde**. Considérer que cet arc a **plusieurs** cordes **permet de pouvoir tirer ses flèches** de différentes **façons**, et dans différentes directions. « Elle a plusieurs cordes à son arc » **veut dire** que cette personne a différentes types de ressources ou différentes possibilités d'action pour **arriver** à un **même** résultat.

« Avoir le bras long »

Signifie qu'une personne a **un bon carnet d'adresses et donc**, qu'elle est **influente**. **Cela peut parfois avoir** une connotation **péjorative** pour **préciser** que la personne peut **se permettre** beaucoup de

choses car **elle sera toujours** « **sauvée** » par **ses connaissances** qui sont influentes, **grâce à** son « **bras long** » qui peut **atteindre** plus de choses qu'un bras **de taille** « normale ».

« Avoir une idée derrière la tête »

Cette expression **désigne** une idée qui **n'a pas encore été exprimée clairement**. **Dire** de quelqu'un qu'il « a une idée **derrière la tête** » signifie que la personne **agit de façon à réaliser** ce à quoi **elle pense**, mais que **cette pensée** n'a pas encore été exprimée **ouvertement**.

---

il existe (exister): there are/exist (to exist)
nombreux: many, numerous
usuelles (usuel): common, everyday
la langue: the language
ils ne sont pas réservés (réserver): they are not kept (to keep, to set aside)
l'écriture: writing
il n'est pas (être): it is not (to be)
utiliser: to use
parlé (parler): spoken (to speak)
imager: to illustrate
ses propos (un propos): his/her intentions
apporter: to bring
apportant (apporter): bringing (to bring)
un peu: a bit

voici: here are
quelques: a few
couramment: commonly

un arc: a bow
il ne possède que (posséder): it only has (to have)
une seule (seul): a single
une corde: string
plusieurs: several
permet de pouvoir: it enables
tirer: to shoot
ses flèches (une flèche): one's arrows
façons (une façon): ways
(il) veut dire (vouloir dire): it means (to mean)
arriver: to get to
même: same

il signifie (signifier): it means (to mean)
un bon carnet d'adresses: a good address book
et donc: and therefore
influente (influent): of influence
cela peut (pouvoir): that can (can, to be able to)
parfois: sometimes
avoir: have
pejorative (péjoratif): pejorative, derogatory
préciser: to make clear
se permettre: to allow oneself
choses (une chose): things
toujours: always
elle sera sauvée (sauver): she will be saved (to save)
ses connaissances (une connaissance): her acquaintances
grâce à: thanks to
bras long: long arm
atteindre: to reach
de taille (une taille): sized, of a size

elle désigne (désigner): it refers to (to refer to)
elle n'a pas été exprimée (exprimer): it has not been expressed (to express)
clairement: clearly
dire: to say
derrière: behind
la tête: head
agit (agir): she acts (to act)
de façon à: so that
réaliser: to carry out, make happen
elle pense (penser): she thinks (to think)
cette pensée: this thought, this idea
ouvertement: openly

« Faire des ronds de jambe »

Faire des ronds de jambe signifie **se montrer extrêmement poli** pour **plaire** à quelqu'un. **Cette politesse** est souvent excessive et parfois **déplacée**. Ce terme **fait référence au** rond de jambe, ressemblant à des figures de **danse**, utilisés **lors des** révérences qui **se faisaient** en signe de respect au XIXème **siècle**.

« Faire cavalier seul »

Agir seul, sans demander **ni accepter** l'aide de personne. Ce terme **vient** également d'une figure de danse du XIXème siècle. Dans cette danse, **nommée** quadrille, les figures **étaient exécutées** à plusieurs, **sauf pour** « **le cavalier seul** » pour qui les pas de danse étaient exécutés par **un homme** tout seul. **De nos jours**, on utilise l'expression « faire cavalier seul » pour une personne qui agit seule **de façon volontaire**. Cette expression a souvent une connotation négative, pour **insister** sur le fait que la personne **soit ne veut pas** être **aidée, soit** ne veut pas **partager**.

« En avril **ne te découvre pas d'un fil**, en mai **fais ce qu'il te plaît !** »

Le climat en France en avril est très **capricieux**. Le mois d'avril **marque la fin** de **l'hiver** mais **les écarts** de températures sont importants. **Ainsi, il peut faire** quelques degrés **le matin** et **jusqu'à** 15 ou 20 **l'après-midi**. Il faut donc **s'habiller** de façon adéquate. **Quand bien même** le climat peut **prendre des allures de printemps** l'après-midi, il est très **courant** d'**attraper froid** pendant cette période car **la fraîcheur** arrive **très vite le soir** et le **moindre coup de vent** reste très frais à cette période. En mai **par contre**, les températures sont plus **clémentes** et on peut **porter des vêtements** d'été dès que le thermomètre **monte** dans les degrès, **sans risquer** de **tomber malade**. Ce proverbe est **couramment utilisé** avec **les enfants, pour leur faire comprendre** qu'il faut **rester couvert** en avril **malgré** qu'**ils aient envie** de **se découvrir**.

---

faire des ronds de jambe: to bow and scrape
se montrer: to appear
extrêmement poli: extremely polite
plaire: to please
cette politesse: this politeness
déplacée (déplacé): inappropriate
fait référence au: refers to
la danse: dance
lors des: at the time of
se faisaient (se faire): they were done (to do)
un siècle: century

agir seul: to act alone, solo
ni accepter: nor to accept
(il) vient (venir): it comes (to come)
nommée (nommer): called (to be called)
étaient exécutées (exécuter): were performed (to perform, to execute)
sauf pour: except for
le cavalier seul: single gentleman
un homme: a man
de nos jours: nowadays
de façon: in a manner
volontaire: headstrong, determined
insister: to insist
soit... soit: either ... or
ne veut pas (vouloir): does not want (to want)
aidée (aider): helped (to help)
partager: to share

ne te découvre pas un fil: don't take even a thread (of clothing) off
fais (faire): do (to do)
ce qui te plaît (plaire): what pleases you (to please)
capricieux: unreliable, fickle
marque (marquer): marks (to mark)
la fin: the end
l'hiver (un hiver): winter
les écarts: differences
ainsi, il peut faire: so, it can be
le matin: in the morning
jusqu'à: until
l'après-midi: the afternoon
s'habiller: to get dressed
quand bien même: even if
prendre: to take
des allures (une allure): looks
de printemps: of spring, springtime
courant: common
attraper froid: to catch a cold
la fraîcheur: coolness
très vite le soir: very quickly in the evening
moindre coup de vent: slightest gust of wind
par contre: on the other hand
clémentes (clément): mild
porter: to wear
des vêtements (un vêtement): clothes
monte (monter): rises (to rise)
sans risquer: without any risk
tomber malade: to fall ill
couramment: frequently
utilisé (utiliser): used (to use)
les enfants (l'enfant): children
pour leur faire comprendre: to make them understand
rester: to stay
couvert: warmly dressed
malgré: despite, even though
ils aient envie: they may want
se découvrir: to take some clothes off

Évaluez votre compréhension

Bises ou pas bises ?, page 108

1. When you meet someone for the first time, how should you greet him or her?

2. When you know the person a little better, what greeting is customary?

3. If in doubt, what is the best greeting to use?

Ne pas avoir l'air d'un touriste, page 110

1. Before going to France what should you try to learn?

2. What do French people frown upon, in regard to tourists visiting their country?

3. What is the custom for leaving a tip?

L'étiquette professionnelle, page 112

1. What is *les pauses déjeuner*, and when does this take place?

2. What is considered a lack of respect when meeting someone for the first time?

3. If you meet a woman and you don't know if she is married, how should you address her?

4. When should you arrive to a meeting? When does an evening meeting usually take place?

Test your comprehension

La bienséance autour d'une table, page 114

1. Why are mealtimes so important to the French?

2. What is the custom for seating guests at the dinner table?

3. Name three of the basic table manners you should follow.

4. At a formal dinner, if you don't know what cutlery to use, what should you do?

La signification des gestes, page 116

1. What does the expression *Oh la la !* indicate? Describe the accompanying gesture.

2. What does the gesture that goes with *C'est foutu* indicate? What does it look like?

3. If someone is tired, what gesture would you see?

4. What expression is popular in other Mediterranean countries as well? Describe this gesture.

Les Arts

Les humoristes québécois

L'humour étant la caractéristique la plus évidente de l'évolution d'un peuple, **il n'est pas surprenant** qu'**une vague** d'humoristes **en tous genres ait déferlé sur** le continent nord-américain et l'Europe **depuis quelques décennies**.

Le Québec, **qui doit naviguer entre rigueur** du climat, **querelles** linguistiques et impasses constitutionnelles **n'y a pas échappé**. Cette province francophone **se targue** de **posséder** le plus grand nombre d'humoristes au **kilomètre carré**, dont certains tels que Louis-Philippe Gagnon ou Stéphane Rousseau, **mènent également** une carrière lucrative en Europe ou aux États-Unis.

Organisatrice du Festival « **Juste pour rire** », Montréal **se veut** à l'avant-garde dans **le domaine** de **la farce**, puisqu'elle est **l'une des seules villes au monde** à **offrir**, depuis plus de **vingt ans**, un cursus des **plus sérieux** dans le domaine de l'humour. Ainsi, l'École nationale de l'humour a produit plus de 325 **joviaux diplômés** depuis son **ouverture**.

Des précurseurs tels les monologuistes Yvon Deschamps ou Michel Barrette et des pièces de théâtre **hilarantes** comme « Broue » **ont montré la voie suivie** par plus d'une centaine de **jeunes** humoristes comme Mario Jean, Claudine Mercier, Martin Matte, Patrick Huard et François Morency.

Les fêtes de fin d'année **ont aussi longtemps donné lieu** au fameux « Bye Bye » **animé par la diminutive** Dominique Michel, et **au cours duquel** les humoristes du moment **s'en donnaient à cœur joie en se moquant parfois férocement des travers** de **leurs semblables**, **révélés** au cours de l'année précédente.

Mais ce sont les années quarante à soixante **qui ont vu défiler un florilège** de comédiens, alors obscurs, **se donnant la réplique** dans les cabarets **enfumés** de la « Main » ou du bas de la ville. **C'est alors que** les Juliette Pétrie, Olivier Guimond, « Ti-Gus et Ti-Mousse », Dominique et Denise **ont fait rire aux larmes** de nombreuses générations de Québécois.

Les Petits Rats

Non, **il n'est pas** question ici de ces **désagréables rongeurs qui hantent les ruelles la nuit venue**. **Il s'agit plutôt** de l'**appellation imagée** et **ludique donnée à** ces petites danseuses et danseurs de **huit ans à peine** qui ont le privilège de **faire partie** de l'**école** de ballet de cette prestigieuse institution.

Leur nom **vient du bruit** de **trottinement** de leurs **chaussons** de danse dans les couloirs de l'Opéra Garnier **qui abritait les** premiers **élèves**. **Aujourd'hui**, c'est généralement par le biais de l'École de danse de l'Opéra national de Paris, située à Nanterre, que ces **aspirants** danseurs et danseuses débutent leur rigoureuse formation.

Car la danse à **haut niveau exige** non seulement une discipline **draconienne** mais le développement **harmonieux** de l'instrument qu'est **le corps**, incluant ses muscles, ses tendons et ses articulations. C'est ce qui motive leur enrôlement si **précoce**. **Chaque année, en moyenne** quatre cents enfants **se présentent** aux auditions dans l'**espoir** de faire partie de cette institution **renommée**. **Des critères** très précis comme **la taille**, **le poid**s et la conformation physique **permettent** de **réduire à** une vingtaine le nombre des privilégiés.

En fin de parcours, après des années de **douleurs** et de sélections **impitoyables**, **seuls** quatre ou cinq danseurs **pourront prétendre faire carrière** dans la danse classique. **Toutefois**, les enfants **ont régulièrement** l'occasion de **se produire** dans **des représentations** telles que « La Bayadère » ou « Casse-Noisette ».

Créée sous le règne de Louis XIV, il y a donc près de trois cents ans, l'École de danse de Nanterre a la prétention **légitime** de **former** les futurs danseurs et danseuses « étoiles » **qui illumineront** de leur grâce **éthérée** les ballets parisiens et internationaux, tout comme leurs modèles ont autrefois illuminé **les toiles** du **peintre** Degas.

L'art public à Montréal

Montréal est **une ville** unique qui **se distingue** tant par son histoire où **s'entremêlent** deux cultures distinctes, que par la beauté de son architecture et la qualité indéniable de sa **vie** culturelle, **attirant** de **nombreux** visiteurs enthousiastes.

Mais pour **les citadins**, l'une de ses particularités est de **posséder** une vaste collection publique d'**œuvres d'art qui est exposée** et **livrée** à leur appréciation admirative dans les squares, les parcs, **les bibliothèques**, certains quartiers cosmopolites, **aux abords de** quelques **édifices** gouvernementaux ou **intégrée** directement à l'architecture. Ces **trois cents** œuvres, inhérentes au caractère de la ville et **faisant partie** intégrante du **paysage** urbain, **adoptent souvent** la forme de monuments commémoratifs, de sculptures monumentales ou de murales.

Le métro de Montréal, **construit vers le milieu des années soixante** pour l'Exposition Universelle, en **compte à lui seul** des dizaines dont quelques-unes de dimensions spectaculaires ou **provenant** d'artistes québécois ou internationaux **célèbres** comme Frédéric Back.

Symbole de la ville, la Croix du Mont-Royal, **édifiée** en 1924, est l'une des premières œuvres d'art **ayant pavé la voie** de la vocation artistique publique de la municipalité. **Il faut dire** qu'une directive ministérielle encourage les villes à développer leur patrimoine extérieur d'œuvres d'art.

Le Palais des Congrès, **quant à lui**, propose la monumentale fontaine « La Joute » **conçue par** l'artiste Jean-Paul Riopelle, tandis que le musée McCord offre à la vue **des passants** une imposante sculpture Inuit de deux-cents tonnes alors qu'**une vache** en bronze **se repose** sur **la rue** Sherbrooke.

Dans le Vieux Montréal, au square de la Place d'Armes, ce sont quatre statues de personnages historiques, dont un Iroquois, **qui rappellent** aux **promeneurs les événements parfois** tragiques **qui se sont déroulés** au moment de la colonisation.

Qu'il s'agisse des immenses **pôles ornés** de **drapeaux coniques** multicolores **flottant au vent** à l'entrée du Parc Lafontaine, de l'espace extérieur d'exposition de photographies d'art Expo-Photos de la rue McGill ou des nombreuses sculptures agrémentant les rues du Centre-ville, Montréal **demeure une cité** à l'**âme** profondément artiste.

Il ne faut surtout **pas oublier** les Mosaïcultures, qui se déroulent **chaque année** dans le Vieux-Port et **qui proposent** une série de sculptures végétales monumentales et **féériques créées à partir d'arbres,** de plantes et de **fleurs**.

Enfin, l'un des plus grands artistes asiatiques contemporains, le sculpteur Ju Ming, a **été choisi** pour **enrichir** temporairement le patrimoine culturel de la ville **grâce à** plusieurs de ses œuvres plus imposantes que nature et aux qualités indéniables.

Faisant partie de la série *Taichi*, **dix-neuf** œuvres sont disséminées **à travers** la ville et plus particulièrement sur trois sites : les Quais du Vieux-Port, quartier historique possédant un riche patrimoine architectural propice aux explorations à vocation culturelle, le Mont-Royal, **montagne au cœur de** la ville et **lieu de rencontre** et de **convivialité estivale**, et le Quartier international, où les œuvres artistiques **servent** souvent de **repère** urbain.

Une nouvelle série de sculptures en bronze a également été installée à l'Arboretum et au Pavillon d'**accueil** du Jardin botanique de Montréal où la technique de l'artiste **fait non seulement jaillir de la matière** force et énergie, **mais établit le lien entre le corps humain** et les mouvements cosmiques.

---

qui rappellent: which remind (to remind)
promeneurs: strollers, walkers
les événements: episodes
parfois: sometimes
qui se sont déroulés: that happened (to happen)

qu'il s'agisse: whether it is about
des pôles ornés: decorated poles
drapeaux (un drapeau): flags
coniques: cone-shaped
flottant au vent: fluttering in the air
demeure (demeurer): remains (to remain)
une cité: a metropolis
une âme: spirit

il ne faut pas: one must not
oublier: forget
chaque: every
une année: year
qui proposent (proposer): which offer (to offer)
féériques: magical, enchanting
créées (créer): created (to create)
à partir d': with (here)
arbres (un arbre): trees
fleurs (une fleur): flowers

a été choisi (choisir): was chosen (to choose)
enrichir: to enhance
grâce à: thanks to

faisant partie de: belonging to
dix-neuf: nineteen
à travers: across
une montagne: mountain
au cœur de: in the middle of, in the heart of
un lieu de rencontre: a forum
convivialité estivale: summer friendliness
servent (servir): are used as (to be used)
un repère: landmark

accueil: welcome
fait... jaillir de la matière (faire): makes material spring out of (to make)
non seulement: not only
mais établit (établir): but also sets up (to establish)
le lien entre: the link between
le corps humain: the human body

La musique guadeloupéenne

Si l'on dit que « la musique est universelle », en Guadeloupe, c'est un élément essentiel. **Ceci se vérifie** au **quotidien** car la musique est omniprésente dans **la vie** de la population et évidemment, **chaque** genre musical est **indissociable** d'**une danse**. Pour **comprendre** cette importance, **voyons** les principaux types de musique que l'**on peut entendre** en Guadeloupe **aujourd'hui**, **en commençant** par la musique **dite traditionnelle**.

Tout d'abord, **parlons** du quadrille. Cette musique **est jouée** par un orchestre qui est **composé** d'un accordéon, d'un violon, de maracas, d'**un tambour** et d'un triangle. Il s'agit d'un accompagnement instrumental, **sur lequel dansent** quatre couples, d'où **le nom** de quadrille. Ce genre **qui est arrivé** aux Antilles avec **les riches colons** européens **a été repris** par les esclaves africains et **surtout interprété** et modifié à l'aide d'instruments **tels que** les maracas ou le tambour **pour devenir** ce qu'il est aujourd'hui.

Puis, du côté des traditions **venues** d'Afrique, **on trouve** le Gwo-Ka. Il s'agit d'un des types de musique **les plus joués** en Guadeloupe, mais **ceci n'a pas toujours été vrai**. C'est la musique d'une percussion **appelée** « ka », un tambour fait d'**un tonneau de rhum** et d'**une peau de cabri tendue**. **Pourtant interdite** par **les maîtres** d'esclaves pendant longtemps, cette musique **s'est perpétuée** parce qu'**elle permettait** une communication secrète entre les esclaves. Le Gwo-ka **se joue** sur sept rythmes, **chacun** ayant **un sens très précis** et qui correspond à un moment donné de la vie des esclaves. **Elle a gardé pendant longtemps ce goût** de fruit **défendu malgré le travail** des « met-ka » (maîtres du ka) comme Vélo ou Robert Loyson.

Aujourd'hui, le Gwo-Ka **a retrouvé** sa place dans **les veillées mortuaires**, le carnaval, les événements officiels et les soirées **en tout genre**. Le Gwo-Ka est indissociable du créole, **langue** régionale de la Guadeloupe.

À la fin des années 1970, un groupe de **jeunes** Guadeloupéens et Martiniquais **réunis autour** de l'**amour** de la musique et de leurs cultures **a lancé un nouveau courant** musical **qui a marqué** la vie des Antilles françaises: le Zouk. Ce groupe du nom de Kassav' (nom **emprunté** à **une galette sucrée faite de farine** de manioc, **aliment répandu** aux Antilles), **voulait** révolutionner à cette **époque** les genres musicaux **à la mode** tels que la biguine ou le kompa haïtien.

Tout en s'en inspirant, Kassav' a produit une musique nouvelle, **basée sur** un rythme du Gwo-Ka, **mêlée à** des instruments modernes comme la guitare ou **la batterie**. **Ce mélange** des cultures a **tout de suite** trouvé sa place dans **les mœurs** guadeloupéennes. Dans les années 1980, le groupe **a conquis** les Antilles françaises, l'Afrique, et puis **devient** populaire **mondialement grâce à** ses rythmes **novateurs** mais **qui rappelaient** malgré tout la culture antillaise.

Si Kassav', le pionnier du Zouk, **a choisi de toujours chanter** créole, la nouvelle génération de chanteurs antillais **obéit** à de nouvelles **règles**, notamment celle de **se faire connaître** en France hexagonale. Bien sûr cet impératif économique **les oblige** à chanter en français pour être compris par tout le monde et on entend maintenant **des tubes** dans les **hit-parades** français chantés par des jeunes artistes antillais de zouk comme Médhy Custos, Warren ou Fanny.

Ces dix dernières années, la Guadeloupe et la Martinique ont beaucoup dansé aux rythmes de musiques **venues d'ailleurs** grâce au développement d'Internet et **des réseaux** télévisés câblés. **On y retrouve** le dancehall jamaïcain, le rap américain, la salsa cubaine... Cette diversité venue d'ailleurs **n'empêche pas** les Guadeloupéens d'être encore **créatifs** car un nouveau genre qu'on appelle l'acoustique **a fait son apparition**. Il s'agit d'une musique consciente qui parle de la société, de **ses maux** ou de **ses bonheur**s, tout cela sur une musique acoustique, **plus naturelle à l'oreille**.

Les splendeurs de Versailles

Résidence de quatre générations de **rois** de France, dont Louis XIV le Roi Soleil, le *Château de Versailles,* à l'origine simple **pavillon de chasse ayant pris** une considérable expansion, est **sans nul doute** la plus grandiose résidence royale de France.

Le domaine **couvre** une superficie de 67 000 mètres **carrés** et le château **compte plus de** deux mille pièces. **Situé** dans la commune de Versailles, au **sud-ouest** de Paris, c'est sur plus de 815 hectares, dont 93 hectares de **jardins**, que **s'étend** le parc du château.

On y retrouve de nombreuses constructions annexes, dont le Petit et le Grand Trianon, le Hameau de la Reine, la pièce d'**eau dite** « des Suisses », une ménagerie, une orangerie **ainsi que** le grand et le petit canal. Le château est **également le siège** du *musée de l'Histoire de France.*

Un projet titanesque de rénovation du château et du parc, **débuté** en 2003 et financé en partie par l'État et en partie par **des mécènes**, **devrait s'étaler** sur plus de dix-sept **ans**. Le premier **volet** de ce projet d'**envergure** s'est achevé en 2007 et **visait entre autres** la réfection de la Galerie des Glaces.

Cette **célèbre** galerie, **longue** de soixante-treize mètres, compte trois cent cinquante-sept miroirs, d'où **elle tire son nom**. Cette salle, **qui était un lieu de passage** et de rassemblement de dignitaires, **exalte par** sa magnificence, **à la fois le pouvoir** royal et **la puissance** de la France de l'**époque**.

La **somptuosité** de sa décoration évoque autant les victoires politiques et diplomatiques que la prospérité de la France, **par le biais** de nombreuses **peintures allégoriques.** Elle compte en outre dix-sept **arcades** et pilastres de bronze **faisant face aux fenêtres.**

Les visiteurs **ont le loisir** d'admirer également les appartements royaux et **les** divers **bâtiments,** dont le Hameau de la Reine, **demeure** plus intimiste où Marie-Antoinette **avait choisi de fuir la rigueur** de l'étiquette de **la Cour.**

De nombreuses activités, **colloques**, **expositions**, **spectacles**, concerts de musique baroque et classique **prennent place** tout au long de l'année **selon** un calendrier riche et éclectique.

Ainsi, la Grande Écurie du château **accueille**, depuis 2003, *l'Académie du spectacle équestre* tandis que le *Centre de Musique baroque* **propose** une programmation complète allant de l'opéra aux récitals instrumentaux.

Des expositions d'art contemporain, de photographies ou d'objets représentant **le faste de la Cour** sont aussi organisées régulièrement. Pour **la première fois**, en 2009, une exposition fort attendue intitulée « Louis XIV, l'**homme** et le roi » **rappelle** aux visiteurs la grandeur et la gloire du Roi Soleil.

De nombreuses ressources scientifiques et documentaires, incluant de précieuses informations sur l'architecture du château, son iconographie ou sur ses jardins, **dessinés il y a près de** quatre cents ans par André Le Nôtre, sont **disponibles** à la consultation sur les sites Internet qui leur sont **dédiés.**

Plusieurs activités pédagogiques leur **permettant de mieux connaître** l'histoire et les particularités du Château de Versailles ont également été développées à l'intention **des enfants** ou de leurs **enseignants, afin de perpétuer** l'admiration due à ce sompteux palace, **inscrit depuis** trente ans au Patrimoine de l'Humanité.

Le théâtre français

Le mot théâtre **signifie à la fois le bâtiment** et les représentations **qui y ont lieu**. On peut donc **aller** au théâtre pour **se divertir**, **faire du théâtre** si l'on est comédien ou **concevoir** un théâtre si l'on est architecte. Le théâtre comme **art de**

la scène, prend toutefois naissance en Grèce, dans l'Antiquité, **vers** le VIème siècle av. J.-C. **Il fait partie intégrante des jeux**, précurseurs des Jeux olympiques. L'**on s'accorde** généralement pour **situer** au **Moyen Âge** l'avènement des premières représentations théâtrales en France.

Les scènes sont habituellement **liées** aux tableaux les plus populaires de **la vie** liturgique comme **Noël** et **Pâques**. Elles sont présentées dans les couvents ou monastères sous forme de dramatisations (ou *tropes*) des épisodes religieux **qui ponctuent l'année**.

Le théâtre **profane** fait son apparition en France vers le 12ème ou le 13ème siècle avec **des auteurs** tel Ruteboeuf, **mais il conserve toutefois** des composantes religieuses ou morales. **Il s'agit la plupart du temps** de pièces **écrites** en **vers rythmés** et en latin. **Par la suite**, les représentations **se font en plein air** et l'**on délaisse** le latin pour **adopter la langue** vernaculaire.

À **partir** du 13ème siècle, le théâtre **se décline** en **plusieurs** genres tels que *la farce*, qui est une pièce humoristique sur les défaillances humaines, *la pastourelle*, que l'**on situe** dans **un décor champêtre** et *la sottise* **qui dépeint** les interactions **remplies de quipropos entre des personnages jouant les sots** ou les idiots.

Il existe également d'autres types de représentations **abordant** les thèmes du mystère, de la moralité, du miracle ou de la passion. Mais c'est à la Renaissance que l'**on voit apparaître** la tragédie sous toutes ses formes, *les ballets de cour*, présentés devant les monarques, dont le plus **célèbre** est le *Ballet comique de la Reine,* et la comédie.

Ce n'est que vers 1680 que la Comédie-Française fait son apparition en France à l'instigation de Louis XIV pour **fusionner** les deux troupes de théâtre existantes. **Les principaux auteurs** de l'**époque** sont Molière, Jean Racine et Corneille. Par la suite, outre le théâtre antique et baroque, **se développent** le théâtre classique, le théâtre romantique, puis le vaudeville, **qui s'apparente** à *la farce*, et le théâtre contemporain.

Avant la Révolution française, **on voit apparaître** des auteurs tels que Voltaire, Marivaux et Beaumarchais, **suivis par** Feydeau et Mirabeau au 19ème siècle, alors que les batailles épiques entre le romantisme et la comédie **se jouent** sur les scènes des théâtres!

Le 20ème siècle **laisse place à** des auteurs de **la trempe** d'Alfred Jarry, Guillaume Apollinaire et Antonin Artaud. Le *théâtre d'avant-garde*, *le nouveau théâtre*, et *le théâtre expérimental*, **qui s'éloignent des sentiers battus**, permettent à Jean-Paul Sartre, Jean Genet et Eugène Ionesco d'**avoir** une influence prépondérante sur la société de leur époque.

De nos jours, le célèbre Festival d'Avignon, **qui a lieu chaque année** au **mois** de juillet en France, regroupe une pléthore d'auteurs, de comédiens et de **metteurs en scène venus** du **monde entier célébrer** cet art **plus que millénaire**.

à partir: from
se décline (décliner): is proposed (to propose)
plusieurs: many
on situe (situer): we situate (to situate)
un décor champêtre: a rustic decor
qui dépeint (dépeindre): that depicts (to depict)
remplies de: full of
quipropos: misunderstandings
entre: between
des personnages: characters
jouant (jouer): playing (to play)
les sots (un sot): silly people

il existe (exister): there exists (to exist)
abordant (aborder): addressing (to address)
on voit apparaître (apparaître): one sees (to see)
célèbre (célèbres): famous

fusionner (fusionner): merge (to merge)
principaux: principal
les auteurs (un auteur): author
époque: time
se développent (développer): progress (to progress)
qui s'apparente (apparenter): which resemble (to resemble)

avant: Before
on voit apparaître (voir, apparaître): one sees (to see)
suivis par (suivre): followed by (to follow)

se jouent (jouer): are played (to play)
laisse place à (laisser): give place to (to give)
la trempe: caliber
qui s'éloignent (éloigner): that distance from (to distance)
des sentiers battus: beaten paths
avoir (avoir): have (to have)

de nos jours: these days
qui a lieu (avoir): that takes place (to take)
chaque: each
année: year
mois: month
metteurs en scène: directors
venus (venir): who come (to come)
monde entier: worldwide
célébrer: to celebrate
plus que millénaire: for thousands of years

la plupart: most
des chanteurs (un chanteur): singers
qui se tiennent (se tenir): who keep
  themselves (to keep oneself)
les auteurs-compositeurs: songwriters
les interprètes: singers
(ils) ont des prétentions (avoir): (they) have
  ambitions (to have)
à la fois: at the same time
les pousse (pousser): moves them (to move)
écrire: to write
dépouillés (dépouillé): simple
intimistes (intimiste): intime
qui véhiculent (véhiculer): which promote
  (to promote)
lié à: linked to
la langue: the language

qui s'est déroulée (se dérouler): that took
  place (to take place)
entre: between
s'est fait sentir (se faire resssentir): it made
  known (to make known, to cause to be felt)
le besoin: the need
un carcan: constraint
des valeurs (une valeur): values
qui perdure (perdurer): that last (to last)
encore: still
aujourd'hui: today

(elle) est apparue (apparaître): (it) appeared
  (to appear)
les années soixante: the Sixties
chanteurs engagés: protest singers
qui ont su apporter: who knew how to bring
faisant (faire): making (to make, do)
ainsi: thereby, thus
ses racines (une racine): its roots

un engouement: passion
solitaire: lonely
(il) ne s'est jamais démenti (démentir): (it)
  has never been disclaimed (to disclaim)
perpétuer: to perpetuate
en représentant: by representing
chères (cher): near and dear
attachant: engaging

souvent: often
situés (situé): located
des sous-sols (un sous-sol): basements
enfumés (enfumé): smoky
la bière: beer
coule à flots (couler): flows (to flow)
la convivialité: conviviality
(ils) se sont fait entendre (se faire entendre):
  (they) made themselves heard (to make heard)

il y a eu: there were
avant tout: first and foremost
éponyme: eponymous, of the same name
qui accueillaient (accueillir): who welcomed
  (to welcome)
les têtes d'affiche (la tête): headliners
de nos jours: nowadays
faire honneur: to honor

Chansonniers québécois

Contrairement à **la plupart des chanteurs** français **qui se tiennent** habituellement loin des préoccupations sociales, **les auteurs-compositeurs** et **interprètes** francophones du Québec **ont des prétentions à la fois** musicales, esthétiques et politiques. Cette orientation spécifique **les pousse** à **écrire** des textes poétiques **dépouillés** et **intimistes qui véhiculent** généralement un message **lié à** leur identité nationale ou à la préservation de **la langue** française en Amérique.

Issue de la « Révolution tranquille » **qui s'est déroulée entre** 1960 et 1966 – une période de l'histoire québécoise où **s'est fait ressentir le besoin** de se libérer du **carcan des valeurs** traditionnelles dépassées – cette tendance musicale a vu l'éclosion d'un mouvement artistique **qui perdure encore aujourd'hui.**

Cette tendance **est apparue** dans **les années soixante** suite à la popularité de **chanteurs engagés** tels Félix Leclerc, Gilles Vigneault, Raymond Lévesque ou Claude Léveillé **qui ont su apporter** une couleur nationaliste à leurs écrits, **faisant ainsi** écho au grand attachement du peuple à **ses racines.**

Cet **engouement** patriotique du Québec pour le chanteur et poète **solitaire** s'accompagnant à la guitare **ne s'est jamais démenti.** Ainsi, de nombreux chanteurs continuent de **perpétuer** cette tendance **en représentant** dans leurs textes les valeurs **chères** au cœur de ce peuple sensible et **attachant.**

C'est principalement dans des « boîtes à chansons », qui sont des cabarets **souvent situés** dans **des sous-sols enfumés** où **la bière coule à flots,** favorisant ainsi l'expression poétique et **la convivialité,** que les premiers chansonniers **se sont fait entendre.**

À Montréal, **il y a eu avant tout** chez Bozo, en référence à la chanson **éponyme** de Raymond Lévesque, puis le Patriote, le Chat Noir et la Butte-à-Mathieu **qui accueillaient les têtes d'affiche. De nos jours,** Richard Desjardins, Daniel Bélanger ou Kevin Parent continuent de **faire honneur,** en chanson, à leurs origines.

Les troubadours au Moyen Âge

Au **Moyen Âge**, le troubadour est avant tout un poète **qui a compris** la nécessité d'**ajouter** l'argument irréfutable de l'art lyrique à la beauté **des strophes qu'il compose**.

Se produisant habituellement dans **les cours seigneuriales des châteaux** de l'**époque médiévale**, surtout dans les régions de l'Aquitaine, du Périgord, du Limousin et de la Provence françaises, ainsi qu'en Italie, **il a pour but** non dissimulé la séduction d'**une belle dame** souvent inaccessible, car d'un rang social plus **élevé**.

À cet égard, le « fin'amor » l'équivalent de l'amour délicat, incorpore l'idéalisation de la personne **convoité**e, la courtoisie et la **fine fleur** des **valeurs** chevaleresques, **sans toutefois** condamner systématiquement l'adultère. C'est principalement en *langue d'oc* ou ancien occitan, que des poètes comme Cercamon, Marcabru, Jaufré Rudel **traduisent** poétiquement et en musique, entre l'an 1100 et 1150, **les émois** de leur **âme** et les tribulations de leur **cœur éprouvé**.

La plupart des linguistes **s'entendent** pour **trouver** l'origine étymologique du **mot** troubadour soit dans le mot « trobar » dont la signification la plus probable en langue romane est « **composer** », soit dans le mot latin « tropus » **qui signifie** inventer une « trope » ou **une poésie**.

Le troubadour développe plusieurs genres comme **la chanson** en cinq ou six couplets, la sérénade du **chevalier amoureux**, **la pastourelle destinée** à une belle **bergère** ou la ballade **dansée** s'accompagnant du **luth**, de **la flûte à bec**, de **la lyre** et **plus tard** du **cistre**.

Fait intéressant, à Los Angeles, la légendaire **boîte de nuit** *Troubadour* **ayant pignon sur rue** à West Hollywood et **qui a adopté** ce nom évocateur avec beaucoup **d'à-propos**, **possède** la particularité d'**avoir découvert** ou **aidé à mousser** la popularité de **chanteurs** comme Elton John, Bob Dylan, James Taylor ou Bruce Springsteen.

Moyen Âge: Middle Ages
qui a compris (comprendre): who has understood (to understand)
ajouter: to add
des strophes (une strophe): stanzas
qu'il compose (composer): that he writes (to write)

se produisant (produire): playing (to play)
les cours seigneuriales: lordly courts
des châteaux (château): of castles
époque médiévale: medieval era
il a pour but: he aims
une belle dame: a beautiful lady
élevé (élevés): higher

à cet égard: in this regard
convoitée (convoiter): coveted (to covet)
fine fleur: finest
des valeurs (une valeur): values
sans toutefois: without however
traduisent (traduire): translated (to translate)
les émois (le émoi): emotions
une âme: soul
un cœur: heart
éprouvé (éprouver): put to the test (to put)

plupart: most
s'entendent (entendre): agree (to agree)
trouver (trouver): to find (to find)
un mot: word
composer (composer): write, compose (to write, to compose)
qui signifie (signifier): which means (to mean)
une poésie: a poem

la chanson: the song
chevalier amoureux: amorous knight
la pastourelle: shepherdess song
destinée (destiner): destined (to destine)
une bergère: shepherdess
dansée (danser): danced (to dance)
un luth: lute
la flûte à bec: recorder
plus tard: later
cistre (cistres): old mandolin

fait intéressant: interesting fact
boîte de nuit: nightclub
ayant pignon sur rue: well-established
qui a adopté (adopter): which has adopted (to adopt)
d'à-propos: relevance
possède (posséder): possesses (to possess)
avoir découvert: have discovered
aidé à mousser: helped to promote
chanteurs (une chanteur): singers

tout le monde: everyone	
entendu parler: heard about	
célèbre: famous	
un musée: museum	
il existe (exister): there exists (to exist)	
mais tout aussi: but also	
captivants (captivant): captivating	
qui valent vraiment le détour: that are truly worth (a visit)	

tout le monde: everyone

entendu parler: heard about

célèbre: famous

un musée: museum

il existe (exister): there exists (to exist)

mais tout aussi: but also

captivants (captivant): captivating

qui valent vraiment le détour: that are
 truly worth (a visit)

compte (compter): has (to have)

qui proposent (proposer): offer
 (to offer)

célébrant (célébrant): celebrating

la rive gauche: the left bank

un jardin: garden

le bâtiment: the building

qu'il occupe (occuper): it occupies
 (to occupy)

constitue (constituer): is (to be)

une œuvre: work

il s'agit (s'agir): it is (to be)

une gare: train station

construite pour: built for

l'Exposition universelle: The World Fair

qui incluent (inclure): which include
 (to include)

le mobilier: furniture

couvrant (couvrir): covering (to cover)

entre: between

on peut y admirer: we can admire there

mondialement connues: known worlwide

on y retrouve (retrouver): one can find
 (to find)

qui comble (combler): that fills (to fill)

mérite que (mériter): deserves that
 (to deserve)

l'on y flâne (flâner): we spend some time
 strolling or exploring (to stroll)

selon certains: according to some people

raffinerie de pétrole: oil refinery

huit niveaux (un niveau): eight levels

Les musées parisiens

Tout le monde a entendu parler du **célèbre musée** du Louvre de Paris, mais **il existe** dans la capitale française de nombreux autres musées de dimensions plus modestes, **mais tout aussi captivants,** et **qui valent vraiment le détour** !

La Ville Lumière **compte** plus de 136 musées et sites culturels **qui proposent** aux visiteurs la richesse de leurs collections permanentes et temporaires **célébrant** la création artistique sous toutes ses formes.

Le musée d'Orsay est situé dans le VIIème arrondissement de Paris, sur **la rive gauche** de la Seine, face au **jardin** des Tuileries. **Le bâtiment qu'il occupe constitue** la première **œuvre** d'art offerte aux regards des visiteurs. **Il s'agit** de l'ancienne **gare** d'Orsay à l'architecture audacieuse, **construite pour l'Exposition universelle** de 1900.

Ce musée présente des collections variées et éclectiques **qui incluent** la peinture, la sculpture, l'architecture, les objets d'art, **le mobilier**, le cinéma, la photographie, la musique et le décor d'opéra, et **couvrant** exclusivement la période située **entre** 1848 et 1914. **On peut y admirer**, entre autres, des œuvres **mondialement connues** de peintres tels que Renoir, Degas, Cézanne, Monet, Delacroix, Ingres et Van Gogh. **On y retrouve** également certaines œuvres de sculpteurs tels Rodin ou Claudel, de l'Art décoratif et de l'Art nouveau. Le musée d'Orsay, **qui comble** un espace chronologique entre le musée du Louvre et le Centre Pompidou, **mérite que l'on y flâne** lorsque l'on a la chance de visiter Paris.

Le Centre national d'art et de culture Georges-Pompidou situé dans le IVème arrondissement de Paris, dans le quartier Beaubourg, le Centre Pompidou a, **selon certains**, l'apparence caractéristique d'une « **raffinerie de pétrole** » sur **huit niveaux.**

On décrit également son architecture comme une « parodie technologique » avec ses **poutres** métalliques et ses **tuyaux apparents** peints en **vert** et **bleu**. Ce **qui ne l'empêche pas** d'**accueillir** près de 6,6 millions de visiteurs **chaque année**.

Créé en 1977 par le président Georges Pompidou, c'est un centre multidisciplinaire **qui comprend** le Musée national d'art moderne, **une bibliothèque** publique d'information, un institut de **recherche** et de coordination acoustique, **des salles de cinéma** et de **spectacles**, des espaces éducatifs, un restaurant et un café. **Il abrite** une imposante collection d'œuvres d'art moderne et contemporain et propose, entre autres, des tableaux de Picasso, Matisse, Mondrian, Balthus, Giacometti et Braque, **pour ne nommer** que ceux-là.

Le musée Rodin est **dédié** exclusivement à la conservation des œuvres du sculpteur Auguste Rodin. La collection est **partagée** entre deux sites, l'un situé dans le VIIème arrondissement de Paris, sur **la rue** de Varenne, **occupe** l'Hôtel Biron. Le second est situé à Meudon dans la Villa des Brillants, en Hauts-de-Seine. Plus de 6600 sculptures, **des dizaines** de **milliers** de dessins, photographies et objets d'art **conçus** et **réunis** par cet artiste prolifique et également collectionneur sont offerts à l'admiration des visiteurs.

On y retrouve également des œuvres de Camille Claudel, **qui a été** sentimentalement **liée à** Rodin et **à qui on a consacré** une salle. Des œuvres célèbres du sculpteur telles *Le Penseur* ou *La Porte de l'enfer* **nous rappellent** le caractère universel de son **génie**.

les arts 137

Un symbole de la culture

La marionnette « Guignol » **fait partie des souvenirs** d'enfance de tous les petits lyonnais. Mais Guignol est bien plus qu'une simple marionnette **qui les amuse** et **les fait rire**. Ce **personnage** est le symbole de Lyon et **incarne** l'identité lyonnaise.

Le personnage et la marionnette de Guignol **a été crée** par Laurent Mourguet en 1808. Laurent Mourguet était **un ouvrier tisserand** lyonnais, **autrement dit un canut**. Au **chômage**, **il décide** de **se reconvertir en marchand forain**, puis en **arracheur de dents**, pour **subvenir** aux **besoins de sa famille**. **Afin d'attirer** de potentiels clients, **il organisait des petits spectacles** avec des marionnettes en **reprenant** le répertoire italien (Polichinelle, Arlequin). Progressivement, **il crée ses propres** personnages : Gnafron puis **celui qui deviendra** le plus **célèbre**, Guignol, qui incarne un canut lyonnais.

Une version moderne de Guignol est par exemple l'émission de télévision française de Canal + « Les Guignols de l'info », **parfois appelée** tout simplement « Les Guignols ». Cette émission satirique de marionnettes est une parodie du journal télévisée **qui caricature le monde politique**, les medias, et la société française contemporaine. **On y retrouve** la même tradition satirique et théâtrale que dans le guignol traditionnel. **Cela a d'ailleurs permis à** l'émission d'**obtenir** une grande notoriété en France et à l'**étranger** … tout comme Guignol en son temps. Mais le Guignol satirique **d'antan** est toujours **vivant**. Une compagnie de théâtre lyonnaise, la Compagnie des Zonzons, **renoue** avec la tradition guignolesque, c'est-à-dire satirique, **tout en continuant** à faire des spectacles plus classiques pour les enfants.

Mais **que signifie le mot** « guignol » ? Et à quoi ressemble ce personnage lyonnais si célèbre ? **Vous connaissez** sûrement l'expression « faire le guignol » qui signifie s'amuser et amuser les autres en faisant **des plaisanteries**, **des pitreries** ou **des mimiques** ou encore plus simplement faire l'idiot. L'expression **tire donc son origine** du théâtre de Guignol. En revanche, l'origine du **nom** de Guignol est controversée. Certains **pensent** qu'il est issu de l'expression ancienne « c'est guignolant » qui signifie « **très drôle** ». D'autres pensent qu'il s'agit d'**un clin d'œil** à un des amis de Laurent Mourguet qui se serait appelé Jean Guignol. Enfin, **il s'agirait** d'une référence **au titre** d'une comédie **à succès de l'époque** « Nitouche et Guignolet ». Si l'on n'est donc pas certain de l'origine de ce nom, **cela ne l'a** toutefois **pas empêché** de passer dans les coutumes de la langue française.

Vous l'aurez bien compris, Guignol est une marionnette, mais une marionnette **à gaine**. **Elle n'est pas dirigée** par **des fils qui permettent** ses mouvements mais directement par **la main** du marionnettiste **qui l'enfile** en quelque sorte comme un gant. **Sa tête** est **en bois**. **Son visage** est **fendu** d'**un sourire** en accent circonflexe. **Ses yeux** sont **noirs** et il a **des fossettes**. Son costume consiste en une jaquette et **un nœud papillon rouge**. **Il porte** sur la tête **un bicorne** aux **bords rabattus**. **Ses cheveux** sont coiffés en **catogan**.

Guignol a un fort accent lyonnais. C'est un canut mais il est **un peu fainéant** et **travaille** le moins possible. Il est malicieux et **farceur** mais **il dénonce** les injustices. Bref, c'est un personnage attachant. Il est en général toujours **entouré** des mêmes personnages. **On peut citer** notamment Gnafron, l'ami de Guignol qui est **cordonnier**. Son visage **montre** qu'il aime bien **le vin** et le beaujolais en particulier. **Il a le nez rouge** et est toujours **mal rasé**. Madelon est l'épouse de Guignol. C'est une grande **bavarde** mais elle a **bon cœur**. Et puis, il y a aussi **le gendarme qui bat** Gnafron avec sa **matraque**.

En 2008, Guignol a eu **200 ans**. **Il n'a pas pris une seule ride** et continue de faire rire grands et petits !

La tradition du théâtre d'été

L'été, alors que le climat de la « *Belle Province* » s'**est adouci** au point où un bon **nombre** de **citadins trouve** refuge dans la **fraîcheur campagnarde**, le théâtre d'été offre une alternative de choix aux **étouffantes soirées estivales** à **arpenter les trottoirs de la ville en quête** de distractions.

Phénomène unique en genre, le théâtre d'été au Québec trouve son origine au début **des années soixante-dix,** alors que les vaudevilles et les comédies de boulevard sont à leur **apogée.** C'est donc plus de 25 spectacles, **auxquels assistent** environ 600,000 spectateurs, **qui sont présentés** tout au long de l'été dans un grand nombre de petites villes ou villages de **banlieue.**

Prenant place généralement dans **un bâtiment reconverti, une grange** ou **un corps de ferme réaménagé** pour l'occasion, la représentation est **la plupart du temps** une comédie **légère** ou romantique. **Elle donne lieu à des malentendus** et des **quiropos** et **met en scène des personnages tentant de se sortir** de situations **loufoques** ou inextricables, pour le plus grand plaisir ou l'hilarité des spectateurs.

Des acteurs comme France Castel, Claude Michaud et Gilles Latulipe sont **des habitués** de ces intermèdes estivaux présentés soit dans les Laurentides, soit dans les villes **environnantes** ou dans de nombreuses petites municipalités du Québec.

Trouvant en partie sa source dans le théâtre de Molière ou de Marivaux, **qui savait mêler** la dérision et **le rire** en excluant **un moralisme trop rigoureux,** le théâtre d'été du Québec **se veut le digne** successeur d'une tradition **qui remonte** à la commedia dell'arte en Italie, où les acteurs **jouaient en plein air** ou dans **des salles rudimentaires en laissant toutefois** une plus grande place à l'improvisation.

La Cinémathèque française

Haut lieu culturel dédié à la préservation, la restauration et **la diffusion** du patrimoine cinématographique français et **mondial**, la Cinémathèque française, **qui existe depuis le milieu des années trente**, a **été créée** à l'instigation de Henri Langlois et Georges Franju.

La vigilance de ces deux passionnés de cinéma **a permis de soustraire des milliers** de films à la destruction **ordonnée par** l'autorité **allemande**, **qui occupait** la France depuis le début de la Deuxième Guerre mondiale.

Ayant entrepris leur mission de préservation avec **seulement** dix films, la Cinémathèque française, **qui s'appelait** à l'origine le Cercle du cinéma, **compte désormais plus de** 40,000 **titres** ainsi que des milliers d'objets et de documents **liés au** monde du « septième art ». Bénéficiant au départ d'**appuis** et de **subsides privés**, c'est **dorénavant** un organisme subventionné en grande partie par **l'État** et dont la vocation première consiste **à protéger** et **mettre en valeur** la richesse du patrimoine audiovisuel **passé** et contemporain.

Le premier **musée** du cinéma ainsi qu'**une salle de projection** de 60 places s'**installe** à l'origine au 7, avenue de Messine, dans le 8ème arrondissement de Paris. **On y voit défiler** des grands **noms** du cinéma français tels François Truffaut, Éric Rohmer et Jean-Luc Godard.

Après avoir successivement **déménagé au fil des années** sur **la rue** de l'Ulm et dans la salle du Palais de Chaillot, **détruite subséquemment par un incendie**, la Cinémathèque prend finalement ses quartiers **définitifs** sur la rue de Bercy à Paris, dans l'ancien **bâtiment** de l'American Center.

Sous la présidence de Costa Gavras depuis 2005, la Cinémathèque a **fusionné** en 2007 avec la BiFi – Bibliothèque du film. **Nul doute** que la Cinémathèque française a su **rallier** depuis plus de quatre-vingts ans non seulement tous **les intervenants**, mais également tous **les inconditionnels** et **amoureux** du cinéma.

haut lieu culturel: top cultural space
dédié à (dédier): dedicated to (to dedicate)
la diffusion (une diffusion): the broadcasting
mondial: worldwide
qui existe (exister): that exists (to exist)
depuis: since
le milieu: the middle
des années trente: of the Thirties
été créée (créer): was created (to create)

a permis (permettre): permitted (to permit)
de soustraire: to withdraw
des milliers (un millier): thousands
ordonnée par (ordonner): ordered by (to order)
allemande: German
qui occupait (occuper): that occupied (to occupy)

ayant (avoir): having (to have)
entrepris (entreprendre): undertaken (to undertake)
seulement: only
qui s'appelait (s'appeler): that was named (to name)
compte (comper): includes (to include)
désormais: from now on
plus de: more than
titres (un titre): titles
liés au (lier): linked to (to link)
appuis (un appui): support
subsides privés: private subsidies
dorénavant: henceforth
l'État: The State
à protéger (protéger): to protect (to protect)
mettre en valeur (mettre): highlight (to highlight)
passé: past

un musée: museum
une salle de projection: a projection room
s'installe (installer): settle (to settle)
on y voit (voir): we can see (to see)
défiler (defiler): parading (to parade)
des noms (un nom): names

après avoir (avoir): after having (to have)
déménagé (déménager): moved (to move)
au fil des années: over the years
la rue: the street
détruite (détruire): destroyed (to destroy)
subséquemment: subsequently
par un incendie: by a fire
définitifs: final
un bâtiment: building

fusionné (fusionner): merged (to merge)
nul doute: no doubt
rallier (rallier): rejoins (to rejoin)
les intervenants: persons involved
les inconditionnels: ardent supporters
amoureux (un amoureux): lovers

Évaluez votre compréhension

Les Petits Rats, page 125

1. What are *Les Petits Rats*? Where does the name come from?

2. What are some of the strict criteria used to choose students?

3. How many students will go on to make a career in dance?

La musique guadeloupéenne, page 128

1. List the instruments that are used to produce quadrille.

2. *Gwo-Ka* music originates from what tradition?

3. A new trend in music began in the Seventies. What was it? Who was its pioneer?

L'art public à Montréal, page 126

1. How many public works of art can be found throughout Montreal?

2. What is the symbol of the city?

3. What will you find at *Le Palais des Congrès*?

Les splendeurs de Versailles, page 130

1. How did *La Galerie des Glaces* receive its name?

2. Who lived in *le Hameau de la Reine*? Why did she live there?

3. What important exhibit opened in 2009?

Test your comprehension

Le théâtre français, page 132

1. The performing arts were born in what country?

2. The early plays were often religious and linked to what holidays?

3. Comedies began in the 13th century. What were some of the early scenes?

Les musées parisiens, page 136

1. *Le musée d'Orsay* occupies a building said by some to be a work of art. What was this building and when was it built?

2. What is *Le Centre Pompidou* said to resemble?

3. What other artists' work will you find at *Le musée Rodin*?

Les troubadours au Moyen Âge, page 135

1. Where did the troubadours usually play?

2. What romantic themes did the poems express?

3. What are three types of songs the troubadours developed?

Un symbole de la culture, page 138

1. Who is the most famous marionette?

2. Guignol is a marionette worked with a glove or strings?

3. Describe Guignol's appearance.

Histoire

La fleur de lys

La fleur de lys, en **motif**, **se trouve** sur des documents archéologiques **très anciens** et de civilisations diverses. **Elle est apparue** dès le troisième millénaire **avant notre ère**, en Assyrie.

De nombreux passages de la Bible présentent **le lys blanc** comme symbole de virginité et de pureté, ce qui explique **le parallèle dressé** avec **Marie**. Des représentations de Marie avec des fleurs de lys **existent** sur **des monnaies** et **des sceaux émis** par **des évêques à partir du** XIème siècle.

Pourtant, à cette **époque**, cette **fleur n'a pas encore de lien privilégié** avec la monarchie française. C'est sous **les règnes** de Louis VI et Louis VII **que sera introduite** la fleur de lys dans la symbolique du **pouvoir royal**, **le roi étant considéré**, tout comme Marie, comme un protecteur et un médiateur **entre Dieu** et **les hommes**.

La fleur de lys **prend petit à petit place dans** les armoiries royales représentant le caractère sacré, divin, et céleste de la mission de la monarchie française. **L'écu est frappé** de trois fleurs de lys **sous le règne de** Philippe Auguste et la fleur **devient** l'emblème des rois de France au XIIème siècle puis emblème de **l'Etat à partir** du XVème siècle, emblème des Bourbons, de l'état français et de la nation française.

Une légende **raconte que** Clovis, premier roi Franc **chrétien** (466-511) **se serait caché derrière** des lys (**qui seraient en fait** une fleur d'iris stylisée avec 3 pétales **vers le haut** et le dernier vers le bas) **pour échapper** aux Wisigoths et en mémoire de cet épisode, **en aurait orné** son **blason**.

On dit également que de par **sa fonction génératrice**, le lys **fut choisi** comme emblème par les rois de France, **soucieux** de leur succession et de la multiplication de leur peuple. La fleur **aurait des pouvoirs** de **guérisons attribués** aux rois de France.

Historique du drapeau français

Le drapeau français tel que **nous le connaissons aujourd'hui a été adopté** en 1794. Ses trois couleurs représentent **le Roi** (le blanc) et **la ville** de Paris (le bleu et le rouge).

Les origines de ce drapeau **datent de** la période de la Révolution française. **Au début de** juillet 1789, **juste avant** la prise de la Bastille, alors qu'**une milice se constitue**, **celle-ci porte** en signe distinctif **une cocarde** bicolore **composée** des couleurs de Paris, le bleu et le rouge. Le 17 juillet, Louis XVI **se rend** à Paris **pour reconnaître** la nouvelle Garde Nationale. **Pour montrer** son accord avec la ville de Paris, **il porte** la cocarde bleu et rouge à laquelle Lafayette, commandant de la Garde, **a ajouté** le blanc, couleur royale.

Les trois couleurs **sont** donc d'abord **réunies** sous la forme d'une cocarde tricolore puis **agencées** par **le peintre** Louis David en bandes verticales, **qui symbolisent la foi** en la liberté. Au XIXème siècle, le blanc des royalistes légitimistes et les trois couleurs **héritées de** la Révolution s'affrontent. Le drapeau blanc **est remis à l'honneur** sous la Restauration mais Louis-Philippe **reprend** le drapeau tricolore **auquel il fait ajouter** l'emblème du **coq gaulois**.

Pendant la Révolution de 1848, si le drapeau tricolore est adopté par le gouvernement provisoire, c'est le drapeau rouge qui **est brandi par** le peuple en signe de révolte. Sous la IIIème République, un consensus **est établi** progressivement autour des trois couleurs. Les royalistes **finissent par l'accepter** pendant **la Première Guerre mondiale**. Les constitutions de 1946 et de 1958 **ont définitivement fait** du drapeau tricolore l'emblème national de la République.

le drapeau: the flag
nous le connaissons (connaître): we know it (to know)
aujourd'hui: today
(il) a été adopté: (it) was adopted (to adopt)
le Roi: king
la ville: city

datent de (dater de): date from (to date from)
au début de: at the beginning of
juste avant: just before
une milice: militia
se constitue: is set up (to set up)
celle-ci porte (porter): this latter wears (to wear)
une cocarde: official badge
composée: composed of
se rend (se rendre): goes to (to go to)
pour reconnaître: to recognize
pour montrer: to show
il porte (porter): he wears (to wear)
(il) a ajouté (ajouter): (he) has added (to add)

(elles) sont réunies (réunir): (they) are gathered (to gather)
agencées (agencer): layed out (to lay out)
le peintre: painter
qui symbolisent (symboliser): that symbolize (to symbolize)
la foi: faith
héritées de: inherited by
est remis à l'honneur (remettre): is honored again (to honor)
reprend (reprendre): retakes (to retake)
auquel: which
il fait ajouter: he added
le coq gaulois: the Gallic rooster

pendant: during
est brandi par (brandir): is brandished by (to brandish)
est établi (établir): is established (to establish)
finissent par l'accepter: finally accept it
la Première Guerre mondiale: The First World War
(elles) ont définitivement fait (faire de): they made definite (to make)

À la découverte de la Martinique

porte le surnom de (porter): carries the
  nickname of (to carry)
île aux fleurs: island of flowers
grâce à: thanks to
la tradition veut que: tradition says that
fût nommée (nommer): was named
  (to name)
qui poussaient (pousser): that grew
  (to grow)
alors: then, at that time

un siècle: century
le sud: south
(elle) a connu (connaître): it has known
  (to know)
deux puissances (une puissance): two powers
Angleterre: England
se disputaient (se disputer): argued
  (to argue)
situées (se situer): located (to be located)
des guerres (une guerre): wars
des accords historiques : historical agreements
qui ont décidé (décider): that have decided
  (to decide)
des destins (un destin): destinies
si proches (proche): so close
c'est ainsi: that is how
est devenue (devenir): has become
  (to become)
à la suite: after
un accord politique: a political agreement

une colonie sucrière: sugar colony
un jardin: garden
aujourd'hui: today
a fait (faire): it has made (to make, to do)
sa renommée (la renommée): its reputation
nombreuses (nombreux): numerous
datant de: dating from
telles que (tel que): such as
(elles) existent (exister): they exist (to exist)
encore: still
elles permettent (permettre): they allow
  (to allow)
découvrir: discover
célèbre: famous
qui présentent (présenter): that present
  (to present)
l'oiseau du paradis: bird of paradise

montagneux: montainous
des événements (un événement): events
ayant marqué (marquer): having left a mark
  (to leave a mark)
la montagne: mountain
dévasté: devastated
la ville: the city
furent tués (tuer): were killed (to kill)
trois rescapés (un rescapé): three survivors
sauvé: saved
les murs (le mur): walls

Si la Martinique **porte le surnom** d'**île aux fleurs**, c'est **grâce à** sa végétation luxuriante. **La tradition veut que** l'île **fût nommée** « Madinina » par ses premiers habitants, les Amérindiens, en l'honneur de la diversité et de la profusion de fleurs **qui** y **poussaient alors**.

Du XVIIème au XIXème **siècle**, cette île du **sud** des Antilles, d'une superficie totale de 1 100 km2, **a connu** une longue histoire de possession et dépossession de la part de **deux puissances** européennes : l'**Angleterre** et la France. Les deux pays **se disputaient** alors quatre îles **situées** dans cette zone de l'arc antillais : la Guadeloupe, la Dominique, la Martinique et Sainte-Lucie. Ce sont **des guerres** et **des accords historiques qui ont décidé des destins** de ces îles aux histoires **si proches**. **C'est ainsi** que la Martinique **est devenue** définitivement française en 1814, **à la suite** d'**un accord politique**.

Lors de sa longue histoire de **colonie sucrière** française, la Martinique a développé sa tradition de **jardin** créole qui la caractérise **aujourd'hui** et **a fait sa renommée**. En Martinique, de **nombreuses** résidences **datant de** la période coloniale, **telles que** l'Habitation Latouche ou l'Habitation Clément, **existent encore**. Elles **permettent** de **découvrir** des jardins dits créoles, comme le très **célèbre** jardin de Balata, **qui présentent** un panel de fleurs tropicales, tel que **l'oiseau du paradis** ou le Bougainvillier.

La végétation de l'île a beaucoup influencé son histoire, tout comme son relief très **montagneux** et volcanique. L'un **des événements** majeurs **ayant marqué** la mémoire collective martiniquaise est l'éruption du volcan, **la montagne** Pelée, qui a **dévasté** l'ancienne capitale, **la ville** de Saint-Pierre en 1902. Les 30 000 habitants **furent tués**. Il n'y eut que **trois rescapés**, dont un prisonnier **sauvé** par **les murs** de sa prison.

La population martiniquaise de **l'époque était composée** des colons européens et des descendants d'africains **venus en esclaves**, puis **s'est enrichie de travailleurs** venus d'Inde **mais aussi** d'immigrants **chinois, syriens** ou **libanais. Toutes les composantes de** cette population **désormais** multiculturelle ont en commun **une langue** : le créole.

Cette langue **liée** à **l'identité même** de l'île s'est construite depuis la période de la colonisation **jusqu'à** aujourd'hui. **Elle a** aussi **traversé les frontières grâce à** un genre musical, le zouk, **né** dans **les années** 1980 par le biais d'un groupe d'artistes martiniquais et guadeloupéens nommé Kassav'. Ce **groupe mythique a fait connaître** la culture antillaise et la langue créole au **monde entier.** Le zouk n'a pas été l'unique **fenêtre** de la Martinique sur le monde car l'île **fut** aussi **le berceau** d'une personnalité **mondialement connue** : Aimé Césaire.

Cet intellectuel et **homme politique**, connu dans le monde entier pour ses idées, **a beaucoup réfléchi** sur l'identité martiniquaise et française. **Décédé** en 2008, l'homme est **la fierté** d'un peuple **qui lui doit beaucoup**, notamment une idée positive de la littérature antillaise. **On peut d'ailleurs** nommer **des auteurs** martiniquais très connus tels que Patrick Chamoiseau ou Edouard Glissant. **Ils appartiennent tous deux** à un genre littéraire que l'on nomme la Créolité.

Si aujourd'hui, la Martinique **est connue** comme toutes les îles des Antilles pour **ses beaux paysages**, c'est surtout **un lieu** où la culture **se mêle** harmonieusement **à** la nature.

---

l'époque (une époque): the era
était composée de (se composer de): was made of (to be made of)
venus en esclaves (venir): arrived as slaves (to arrive)
(elle) s'est enrichie de: (it) was expanded, made richer by
des travailleurs (un travailleur): workers
mais aussi: but also
chinois: Chinese
syriens: Syrians
libanais: Libanese
toutes les composantes de: all the parts of
désormais: from now on
une langue: language

liée (lier): linked (to link)
l'identité même (une identité): identity itself
jusqu'à: until
elle a traversé (traverser): it has crossed (to cross)
les frontières (une frontière): borders
grâce à: thanks to
né (naître): born (to be born)
les années (une année): years
un groupe: band
mythique: mythical
il a fait connaître (faire connaître): it has made known (to make known)
le monde entier: entire world
la fenêtre: window
fut (être): was (to be)
le berceau: the birthplace
mondialement connue (connaître): known worldwide (to know)

un homme politique: politician
beaucoup: a lot
(il) a réfléchi (réfléchir): (he) reflected upon, thought about (to think)
décédé: deceased
la fierté: pride
qui lui doit beaucoup (devoir): who owe him a lot (to owe)
on peut (pouvoir): we can (can, to be able to)
d'ailleurs: besides
des auteurs (un auteur): authors
ils appartiennent à (appartenir à): they belong to (to belong to)
tous deux: both of them

est connue (être connu): is known (to be known)
ses beaux paysages (un paysage): its beautiful landscapes
un lieu: a place
se mêle à (se mêler à): mixes with (to mix with)

La Nouvelle-France

C'est au XVIème **siècle** que débute l'aventure française en Amérique du Nord. **Le récit** de l'implantation des premiers **colons** est **ponctué de nombreuses** difficultés d'adaptation **au climat**, à **la faim,** aux **raids amérindiens** et **plus tard**, à l'invasion britannique.

À l'époque, la France, **avide** de **richesses nouvelles**, **confie** l'exploration du continent nord-américain à Jacques Cartier. Celui-ci **débarque** à Gaspé en 1534, où **il revendique** le territoire **au nom du roi** de France **avant de poursuivre** sa route dans **les terres** de la vallée du Saint-Laurent. **Il découvre** les villages amérindiens de Stadaconé et d'Hochelaga, **aujourd'hui** Québec et Montréal, et **fait la connaissance** des tribus amérindiennes de la région.

Québec est la première **implantation** française en Amérique du Nord. **Elle est fondée** en 1608. D'abord une **colonie-comptoir destinée** à l'approvisionnement en ressources, la Nouvelle-France **devient** une colonie **de peuplement** sous les ordres du roi de France **qui désire** y **implanter** des familles de colons.

À **son apogée**, le territoire de la Nouvelle-France **s'étendait** de la vallée du Saint-Laurent jusqu'au golfe du Mexique, en passant par la vallée de l'Ohio et du Mississippi. Les colonies britanniques, **quant à elles**, se concentraient sur **la côte** est, en Nouvelle-Angleterre, à l'est des Appalaches. **À l'époque**, **on y dénombrait** environ 1,5 millions de colons contre **seulement** 60 000 du côté français. La progression **vers l'ouest** des colons anglais est donc **freinée** par la présence française dans la vallée de l'Ohio, zone particulièrement **convoitée** pour ses ressources naturelles et **le commerce des peaux**.

Les premiers **affrontements ont lieu** en 1756, alors que le conflit **semble** inévitable. **La lutte** pour le territoire nord-américain est une des causes **qui précipite** l'entrée **en guerre** de la France et de la Grande-Bretagne dans la guerre de Sept Ans, **laquelle se joue** également sur le continent européen.

Durant **les** premières **années**, les Français résistent bien aux attaques des Britanniques, mais **le vent finit** par **tourner** et **ces derniers s'emparent** des principaux forts de la vallée du Mississippi et de l'Ohio. En s'emparant du fort de Louisbourg (aujourd'hui situé dans la province de Terre-Neuve), **ils disposent** d'une formidable base pour commencer l'invasion des terres de la vallée du Saint-Laurent.

Une des batailles les plus légendaires est celle des Plaines d'Abraham qui opposa les forces britanniques, **sous le commandement** du général Wolfe, aux forces du général Montcalm. En 1759 les forces britanniques, **ayant remonté le fleuve** Saint-Laurent, **encerclent la ville** de Québec. **Ils l'assiègent** et la bombardent **pendant plusieurs mois**. Le 13 septembre, **ils débarquent** à terre en **profitant** d'une **habile** diversion, et **livrent** une courte mais **sanglante bataille** aux Français sur les plaines d'Abraham. La bataille **ne dure que** quinze minutes, mais les deux commandants y trouvent **la mort**. Bien qu'**inférieure** en **nombre**, l'armée britannique mieux disciplinée **inflige** une **cuisante défaite** aux armées françaises, et Québec **tombe** ainsi sous domination anglaise.

Quelques mois **plus tard**, les Français **rappliquent** à la bataille de Ste-Foy, une victoire qui sera de courte durée, car les renforts britanniques arrivent en grand nombre et **remontent** le fleuve jusqu'à Montréal qui capitule en 1760 **sans offrir de résistance**.

Le traité de Paris de 1763 **met fin à** la guerre de Sept Ans et **cède** officiellement les colonies françaises d'Amérique du Nord à la Grande-Bretagne. La France **ne conserve que** quelques **îles** dans les Antilles qu'elle juge plus profitables, à cause du **sucre** qu'**on y produit**.

On dit parfois que **la conquête** de la Nouvelle-France **aura précipité** la Révolution américaine de 1776. Les colonies d'Amérique **ayant enrayé** la menace française **pourront plus aisément se passer** de l'aide de **leur métropole** : la Grande-Bretagne.

les années (une année): years
le vent: the wind
finit (finir): ends up (to end up)
tourner: to turn
ces derniers (un dernier): the latter
(ils) s'emparent (s'emparer): they take over, they seize (to seize)
ils disposent (disposer): they have available (to have available)

sous le commandement: under the command
ayant remonté (remonter): having sailed up (to sail up)
le fleuve: the river
(elles) encerclent (encercler): encircled (to encircle)
la ville: the town
ils l'assiègent (assiéger): they lay siege to it (to lay siege to)
pendant: during
plusieurs: several
mois (un mois): months
ils débarquent (débarquer): they land (to land, to disembark)
profitant (profiter): taking advantage (to take advantage)
habile: clever
(ils) livrent (livrer): they wage (battle) (to wage)
sanglante bataille: bloody battle
ne dure que (durer): only lasts (to last)
la mort: death
inférieure (inférieur): lower, smaller
nombre (un nombre): number
inflige (infliger): inflicts (to inflict)
cuisante (cuisant): stinging
une défaite: defeat
tombe (tomber): falls (to fall)

plus tard: later
rappliquent (rappliquer): turn up (to turn up)
(ils) remontent (remonter): they sail up (to sail up)
sans offrir de résistance: without putting up any resistance

le traité: the treaty
met fin à: puts an end to
(il) cède (céder): it gives up (to give up)
ne conserve que (conserver): only keeps (to keep)
îles (une île): islands
le sucre: sugar
on y produit (produire): they produce (to produce)

on dit (dire): it is said, people say (to say)
parfois: sometimes
la conquête: the conquest
aura précipité (précipiter): hastened (to hasten)
ayant enrayé (enrayer): having halted (to halt)
(elles) pourront (pouvoir): they will be able (can, to be able to)
plus aisément: more easily
se passer: to do without
leur métropole: their mother country

Les sans-culottes

Les sans-culottes sont **des personnages** emblématiques de la Révolution française (1789). Révolutionnaire, parisien **le plus souvent**, et **issu des milieux populaires** et du **petit artisanat**, le sans-culotte **se définit** comme celui **qui s'habille** simplement, avec **un pantalon**, et **qui ne porte donc pas** « la culotte » comme **le font** les nobles et les Aristocrates. Ce terme **ne définit pourtant pas** une classe sociale ou économique en tant que telle. Le sans-culotte est donc l'**homme libre** révolutionnaire **qui revendique** sa liberté, **mais également** la nécessaire égalité de **droits entre les citoyens**. Des personnages tels que Robespierre et Danton **firent partie de** ce mouvement.

La tenue vestimentaire du sans culotte **se composait** d'un simple pantalon, d'**une chemise**, du **bonnet phrygien** et d'**une veste courte appelée** carmagnole (**qui donna** son **nom à une chanson créée** en 1792 et **qui montre** leur **haine** et leur **mépris** de la famille royale).

Le bonnet phrygien, **souvent rouge**, symbolise la liberté (ce bonnet **était porté par les esclaves affranchis** sous l'Empire romain)**, la cocarde** et **les trois couleurs** symbolisent l'union et l'unité des sans-culottes ainsi que son attachement à la patrie.

À cette tenue **se rajoutait** généralement **le sabre** et **la pique** révolutionnaire.

Outre l'égalité et la fraternité, les principales revendications des sans-culottes étaient généralement **liées** aux problèmes de **pénuries alimentaires** et à l'augmentation des produits de consommation. Les sans-culottes **ont joué** un rôle primordial lors de la Révolution française en organisant **plusieurs** insurrections très importantes comme celle du 10 août 1792.

Ils mirent en place des comités de surveillance, **ce qui leur apporta un moyen de pression** sur la politique ; **cela engendra des dénonciations** de traîtres et conspirateurs **supposés par milliers**.

Les sans-culottes ont eu une implication très importante lors de « La Terreur », un des éléments du gouvernement révolutionnaire **mis en place** en France en 1793 et 1794 **pour lutter contre** les opposants et les ennemis de la Révolution. La Terreur **fit** plusieurs dizaines de milliers de **morts** et **entraîna des centaines** de milliers d'**arrestations**.

En 1794, avec **la chute** de Robespierre, les sans-culottes **perdirent** leurs **pouvoirs** ainsi que leur rôle politique et culturel.

se rajoutait (se rajouter): would add up (to add up)
le sabre: the saber
la pique: the pike

liées (lier): related (to relate)
pénuries alimentaires: food shortages
ont joué (jouer): played (to play)
plusieurs: several

ils mirent en place (mettre en place): they set up (to set up)
des comités (un comité): comittees
ce qui leur apporta (apporter): which gave them (to give)
un moyen de pression: pressure tactics
cela engendra (engendrer): it caused (to cause)
des dénonciations: denunciation acts
supposés: par alleged by
milliers: thousands

mis en place (mettre): was installed (to install)
pour lutter: to fight
contre: against
fit (faire): made (to make)
morts: dead
entraîna (entraîner): caused (to cause)
des centaines: hundreds
arrestations: arrests

la chute: the fall
perdirent (perdre): lost (to lose)
pouvoirs: powers

CULTURE NOTE The Three Musketeers–fact or fiction? While Alexander Dumas's novel *The Three Musketeers* was a great balance of fact and fiction, the Musketeers of France were indeed factual and an important part of French history. A *mousquetaire* was an early modern type of infantry soldier equipped with a musket. The Musketeer first came into fame under King Louis XIII of France. He kept a company as his personal guard, and Musketeers were an important part of early modern armies. True to their name, Musketeers were excellent shots. Unfortunately the musket had to be reloaded each time it was fired. This made the musket a limited weapon if ranks were overrun and combat turned hand-to-hand. Due to this, survival for the Musketeer depended on being an excellent swordsman as well. Today, those who don the traditional outfit of the Musketeer invoke an image of the finest qualities in all men: gallant, brave, chivalrous, and debonair.

L'Arc de Triomphe

Qui n'a jamais vu, **ne serait-ce qu'une seule fois**, dans des atlas géographiques ou des manuels d'histoire, l'imposante majesté de l'Arc de Triomphe de Paris, sur **lequel débouche** la magnifique avenue des Champs Élysées, et dont l'allure caractéristique **représente si bien** la France ?

Situé sur le rond-point de **la place** de l'Étoile et s'ouvrant sur une douzaine d'avenues **qui rayonnent** dans toutes les directions, ce **célèbre** monument **se trouve** à **un peu plus de** deux kilomètres au nord-est de la place de la Concorde. Certaines des rues **qui y prennent leur point de départ commémorent** des victoires napoléoniennes telles que Wagram, Iéna ou Friedland, ou rappellent la grandeur de quelques généraux **qui ont œuvré pour** l'Empire.

Napoléon 1er, **qui voulait célébrer** ses victoires avec **faste**, **commanda** l'Arc à l'architecte Chalgrin en 1806. **S'inspirant** de l'Antiquité, **ce dernier a conçu** un monument de cinquante-cinq mètres de **hauteur** et de quarante-cinq mètres de **largeur** présentant de nombreux bas-reliefs impressionnants.

De plus, quatre sculptures **ornant ses piliers** et **intitulées** Le Départ, Le Triomphe, La Résistance et la Paix illustrent de manière évocatrice différentes **étapes** de **la guerre**. Son **nom**, intrinsèquement **lié** à l'idée de victoire, **rappelle** la vocation première de l'avenue des Champs Élysées **qui devait être** une avenue triomphale **allant du** Louvre **à** la place de la Nation, **en passant par** la place de la Bastille.

Les fondations, **à elles seules, exigeront deux années** de travaux **qui seront interrompus** suite aux **défaites** et abandonnés temporairement sous la Restauration. Ce n'est que sous Louis-Philippe que les travaux **seront achevés** entre 1832 et 1836. Monument à **forte** connotation historique, **il n'est pas dénué** d'une **forte** charge émotionnelle pour **ceux qui ont perdu des proches** lors de batailles antérieures, puisque l'**on retrouve à ses pieds** la tombe du **soldat inconnu** de la Première Guerre mondiale.

---

qui n'a jamais vu (voir): who has never seen (to see)
ne serait-ce qu'une seule fois: at least once
lequel débouche (déboucher): which opens onto (to open onto)
représente si bien (représenter): represents well (to represent)

la place: square, plaza
qui rayonnent (rayonner): that radiate (to radiate)
célèbre: famous
se trouve (trouver): is found (to find)
un peu plus de: a little more than
qui y prennent leur point de départ: that have their starting point
(elles) commémorent (commémorer): they commemorate (to commemorate)
qui ont œuvré pour (œuvrer): who worked for (to work)

qui voulait célébrer (vouloir): who wanted to celebrate (to want)
faste: pomp, splendor
(il) commanda (commander): (he) ordered (to order)
s'inspirant de (s'inspirer): drawing his inspiration from (to draw one's inspiration)
ce dernier: the latter
(il) a conçu (concevoir): (he) designed (to design)
la hauteur: height
la largeur: width

ornant (orner): decorating
ses piliers (un pilier): its pillars
intitulées (intitulé): entitled
étapes (une étape): steps
la guerre: the war
un nom: name
lié: linked
(il) rappelle (rappeler): (it) reminds (to remind)
qui devait être (devoir): that must have been (must, to have to)
allant du… à (aller): going from … to (to go)
en passant par (passer): passing through (to pass)

à elles seules: alone, just them
elles exigeront (exiger): they will require (to require)
deux années (une année): two years
les travaux (un travail): work
qui seront interrompus (interrompre): that will be interrupted (to interrupt)
défaites (une défaite): defeats
(ils) seront achevés (achever): (they) will be finished (to finish)
forte (fort): strong
il n'est pas dénué de: it is not without
ceux qui ont perdu (perdre): those who have lost (to lose)
des proches (un proche): loved ones
on retrouve (retrouver): we find (to find)
à ses pieds (un pied): at its base
le soldat inconnu: unknown soldier

La Cité médiévale

La cité de Carcassonne, **posée sur un piton rocheux** dans le département de l'Aude, en Languedoc-Roussillon, est, avec ses doubles **remparts**, ses cinquante-deux tours, son château **comtal**, ses **quatre portes** monumentales et la basilique de St-Nazaire **qu'elle accueille**, la plus grande **ville fortifiée** d'Europe. Son histoire mouvementée l'a **conduite à subir** des transformations architecturales continues et **parfois hétéroclite**s **qui s'étendent** sur une période de plus de **deux mille cinq cents ans**. **Occupée** dès le Vème siècle avant J.C, elle a été successivement une ville romaine, une ville fortifiée puis une cité médiévale.

Sa **double enceinte**, **qui s'étire** sur plus de trois kilomètres, **constitue** l'une des magnifiques et **étonnantes** particularités **qui lui ont permis** d'être **inscrite**, depuis 1996, au patrimoine mondial de l'Unesco. Soumise à de nombreuses attaques, dominations et abandons, la ville a **été modifiée, agrandie** et **restaurée** à de multiples **reprises**.

Située dans l'**axe** où **le rejet** de la doctrine de l'**église** catholique **a fait** le plus d'**adeptes**, la ville de Carcassonne a rapidement été **considérée comme le chef-lieu** des Cathares. Le catharisme est un mouvement **chrétien** médiéval **dissident qui comptait**, à l'époque, **plus de huit cents** églises en France.

Confronté à la montée du catharisme, **le pape** Innocent III initie la croisade des Albigeois dont **le but** est de **soumettre** les hérétiques. La Cité est **assiégée par** les croisés le 1er août 1209 et les principaux instigateurs de la rébellion, le comte de Toulouse et **le vicomte** de Trencavel **se rendent** rapidement en échange de **la vie sauve** des habitants de la ville.

La Cité, **qui a retrouvé** depuis **fort longtemps** l'ambiance **paisible des lieux** dont la riche histoire **appartient au passé**, **reçoit** plus de quatre millions de visiteurs annuellement et se classe parmi les sites historiques bénéficiant de l'un des plus **hauts taux** d'affluence en France.

posée sur (poser): located on top (to locate)
un piton rocheux: a rocky peak
remparts: fortified walls
comtal: of earl
quatre portes (une porte): four doors
qu'elle accueille (accueillir): it shelters (to shelter)
la ville fortifiée: fortified city
l'a conduite à (conduire): has led it to (to lead)
subir: to undergo
parfois: sometimes
hétéroclites: mismatched
qui s'étendent (étendre): which extended (to extend)
deux mille cinq cents ans (un an): two thousand five hundred years
occupée: inhabited

double enceinte: double wall
qui s'étire (s'étirer): which stretches (to stretch)
constitue (constituer): represents (to represent)
étonnantes: amazing
qui lui ont permis (permettre): which have contributed (to contribute)
inscrite: registered
été modifiée (modifier): was transformed (to transform)
agrandie (agrandir): expanded (to expand)
restaurée (restaurer): renovated (to renovate)
reprises: times

un axe: major area
le rejet: refusal
une église: church
a fait... adeptes: recruited ... followers
considérée comme (considérer): considered as (to consider)
le chef-lieu: capital city
chrétien: Christian
dissident: opponent
qui comptait (compter): which was composed (to be composed)
à l'époque: at the time
plus de: more than
huit cents: eight hundred

confronté à: facing
la montée: the rise
le pape: pope
le but: goal
soumettre: to subdue
assiégée par (assiéger): invaded by (to invade)
le vicomte: viscount
se rendent (se rendre): surrender (to surrender)
la vie sauve: the sound life

qui a retrouvé (retrouver): which recovered (to recover)
fort longtemps: for a long time
paisible: peaceful
des lieux: the place
appartient (appartenir): belongs to
au passé: the past
reçoit (recevoir): welcomes (to welcome)
hauts taux: highest rates

Histoire de France

Au cœur de Paris, sur l'île de la Cité où **se dresse** la **célèbre** Cathédrale Notre Dame et qui est aussi le premier Lutèce (ancien **nom** de Paris), **autour duquel** s'est **petit à petit construite** la capitale, **on peut aujourd'hui** visiter la Conciergerie. Lieu

où la **dernière reine** de France **a vécu** ses **ultimes** moments, avant d'être guillotinée suite à un long et **pénible procès**. Cette exécution et celle de **son époux signa la fin** de la monarchie et **ouvrit** un **nouvel avenir** politique pour **le pays** : la république démocratique de France.

Marie-Antoinette, **jeune** et **jolie autrichienne fut mariée** à 15 ans **au futur roi** de France Louis XVI. Elle vécut de 1755 à 1793 et **fut de tout son règne** – jusqu'à la Révolution française **qui éclata** en 1789 – très impopulaire **auprès** du peuple **qui ne pouvait souffrir**, en ces temps de misère, **le faste** dans lequel la reine **aimait** à **vivre**. Elle organisait de grandes **fêtes** pour toute **la cour** du Roi, **brillait** par le luxe de **ses toilettes**, son **amour** de la musique, de la danse et du **jeu** et **ne tolérait pas** qu'on lui refusât le moindre caprice.

À quelques trente kilomètres de Paris, **elle fit bâtir** dans les jardins du Château de Versailles, **construit** par le célèbre Louis XIV, dit le Roi Soleil, le Petit Trianon où **elle se plaisait** à s'**occuper** d'animaux de **ferme** et cultivait **des fleurs**, **revêtant avec** ses compagnes de **légères robes** de **campagne**. La reine **vivait ainsi**, **sans qu'il semble** qu'**elle n'accepte jamais** de **prendre** les responsabilités politiques **qui étaient les siennes vis-à-vis** du peuple dont elle était la souveraine. **Il est** aussi **rapporté** que lorsqu'**on vint lui dire que** les Français subissaient une grave famine et qu'ils n'avaient plus de **pain** pour **se nourrir** elle répondit frivolement : « **S'ils n'ont plus de** pain, qu'**ils mangent** de la brioche ».

Ainsi, alors que Paris commençait à **brûler**, elle continua à refuser tout compromis avec l'Assemblée et **poussa le placide** et faible roi Louis XVI, son époux, à leur résister également et finalement **à fuir** avec la famille royale, **ce qui provoqua** l'intervention militaire **étrangère**. Tout cela contribua à **attiser la colère** du peuple français, colère **qui aboutira** à la Révolution française, à son **propre** emprisonnement et finalement, à son exécution. **On dit que** tout au cours de son procès, la Reine **resta** courageuse et **digne**, **malgré** son jeune âge, et **qu'il ne lui fut cependant pas pardonné** d'**avoir fait appel** aux Autrichiens **pour venir** à son **secours**. Elle fut guillotinée le 16 octobre 1793.

elle fit bâtir: she had ... built
construit (construire): built (to build)
elle se plaisait (plaire): she enjoyed (to enjoy)
occuper: to take care
une ferme: farm
des fleurs (une fleur): flowers
revêtant avec (revêtir): covered with, dressed with (to cover)
légères robes: light dresses
la campagne: countryside
vivait ainsi (vivre): lived thus
sans qu'il semble (sembler): without seeming (to seem)
elle n'accepte (accepter) jamais: she never accepted (to accept)
prendre: to take
qui étaient (être): which were (to be)
les siennes: hers
vis-à-vis: toward
il est rapporté (rapporter): it is said (to say)
on vint lui dire que (venir): people came to tell her that (to come)
un pain: bread
se nourrir: to feed
s'ils n'ont plus de (avoir): if they don't have ... anymore
ils mangent (manger): they eat (to eat)

commençait (commencer): started (to start)
brûler: to burn
poussa (pousser): pressured (to pressure)
le placide: the quiet
à fuir: to escape
ce qui provoqua (provoquer): which triggered (to trigger)
étrangère: foreign
attiser: to light up
la colère: anger
qui aboutira (aboutir): which will come to (to come to)
propre: own
on dit que (dire): it is said that (to say)
resta (rester): remained (to remain)
digne: dignified
malgré: in spite of
qu'il ne lui fut pas pardonné: she was not forgiven for...
cependant: however
avoir fait appel: to have called
pour venir: to come
secours: help, aid

Jeanne d'Arc

Jeanne d'Arc, **surnommée également** « **la Pucelle** d'Orléans », **a conduit son pays** à la victoire **contre** les Anglais lors de **la Guerre de Cent Ans**. Elle est l'une des trois saintes patronnes de la France.

Née au sein d'une famille de cinq **enfants**, dans le village de Domrémy en Lorraine, de parents notables **qui seront par la suite ennoblis**, Jeanne est **une jeune fille pieuse** au **caractère bien trempé**. Son franc-parler, son courage, sa sensibilité et sa pureté **laisseront une empreinte** indélébile sur tous ceux **qui la côtoieront**.

La Guerre de Cent Ans **couvre** en réalité une période de 116 **ans s'étendant entre** les années 1337 à 1453 et **mettant en scène** deux dynasties en conflit, les Plantagenêts et les Capétiens, **qui revendiquent** la possession du territoire français **au nom de** leur **roi** respectif, d'Angleterre ou de France.

C'est au cours du siège d'Orléans que l'action **intrépide** de Jeanne **permettra d'éviter** que les Anglais **ne s'emparent** de la ville et **aient** ainsi un **libre** accès au **sud** de la France. Jeanne **affirme avoir entendu**, à treize ans **à peine**, la voix de l'archange St-Michel et de deux saintes **lui demandant** de **libérer le royaume** de France de **la main** des Anglais, afin que **le dauphin**, **fils** du roi Charles 1er, dont la légitimité **est mise en doute**, **puisse monter sur le trône**. Mais ce n'est qu'à seize ans qu'**elle accède** finalement **à leur demande**.

Elle tente par deux fois de s'**enrôler** dans les troupes qui combattent pour le dauphin, mais sans succès. **Ce n'est que l'année suivante** qu'une escorte **lui est accordée afin qu'elle puisse se rendre** à Chinon **où se trouve** l'**héritier** du trône.

À **partir de** ce moment, la jeune fille **ne portera** que **des vêtements** masculins **qui lui permettront** de **traverser** incognito les villes bourguignonnes **qui la séparent** du **but ultime** de son voyage. **Ayant enfin pu s'entretenir** avec le dauphin, elle l'informe de quatre **événements** futurs **qui conduiront** la France à la victoire, et pour lesquels elle a été mandatée par **la puissance** divine.

Après avoir été interrogée et **examinée à deux reprises** par **des matrones** pour **constater** sa virginité et confirmer l'origine surnaturelle de ses affirmations, **elle est équipée** d'une armure et d'**une bannière blanche**, et part pour Orléans accompagnée de **ses frères** et de troupes de soldats qu'on lui a accordés.

C'est **sa foi** et son enthousiasme qui lui permettront d'encourager les soldats **à poursuivre** les combats jusqu'à forcer les Anglais à **quitter** la ville d'Orléans assiégée, dans **la nuit** du 7 au 8 mai 1429. **Malgré** ses victoires **qui conduisent** le dauphin à être sacré roi de France le 17 juillet 1429 dans la cathédrale de Reims, **elle finit** par être capturée et **rachetée par** les Anglais **au prix de dix mille livres**.

Elle est accusée d'hérésie par l'Église lors d'un procès **entaché** d'irrégularités et de **mensonges**, **pour avoir porté des vêtements d'homme** et s'en **être remise à la voix de Dieu** plutôt qu'à l'autorité ecclésiastique.

Elle sera brûlée vive, le 30 mai 1431 sur **un bûcher**, mais, **comble de l'ironie**, sera canonisée cinq cents ans **plus tard** par ses persécuteurs.

à partir de: from
ne portera que (porter): will only wear (to wear)
des vêtements: clothing
qui lui permettront (permettre): that will allow her (to allow)
traverser: to cross
qui la séparent de (séparer): that separate her from (to separate)
le but ultime: final goal
ayant enfin pu s'entretenir: having finally been able to discuss
des événements (un événement): events
qui conduiront (conduire): that will lead (to lead)
la puissance: power, strength

après avoir été interrogée et examinée: after being questioned and examined
à deux reprises: twice, two times
des matrones (une matrone): matrons
constater: to observe
elle est équipée (équiper): she was equipped (to fit out)
une bannière blanche: white banner
ses frères (un frère): her brothers

sa foi: her faith
poursuivre: to keep going
quitter: to leave
la nuit: the night
malgré: despite
qui conduisent (conduire): that lead to (to lead)
elle finit par (finir par): she ended up (to end up)
rachetée par: bought by
au prix de: at the price of
dix mille livres: ten thousand pounds

elle est accusée (accuser): she is accused (to accuse)
entaché de: tainted by
mensonges (un mensonge): lies
pour avoir porté (porter): for having worn (to wear)
des vêtements d'homme: men's clothes
s'en être remise à la voix de Dieu: having left (her fate) in God's hands

elle sera brûlée (brûler): she was burned (to burn)
vive: alive
un bûcher: stake
le comble de l'ironie: the height of irony
plus tard: later

La Révolution française

La Révolution française **correspond** en France au passage de la royauté (ou monarchie absolue) à la première République : le peuple français **s'est révolté** en 1789 pour protester **contre** les privilèges de la noblesse et du clergé **afin de**

proclamer pour la première fois l'égalité de tous **les hommes face aux lois** et la souveraineté de la Nation. Cet événement a eu et continue d'**avoir une portée** internationale **puisqu'il a donné naissance** aux Droits de l'Homme et du Citoyen **qui restent jusqu'à aujourd'hui** la base de toutes les républiques démocratiques constitutionnelles.

À la fin du XVIIIème **siècle**, la France **sur laquelle règne le faible roi** Louis XVI et **sa fastueuse épouse** Marie-Antoinette, est **couverte de dettes** et le peuple **périt dans** la misère et la famine. **Les goûts** extravagants de **la reine** vont **favoriser la montée** de **la haine** et de **la rancœur** du peuple **envers ses souverains** jusqu'à **devenir** une **vraie** révolution. Le 14 juillet 1789 – date **devenue** depuis lors **le jour** de **la fête** nationale française – le peuple **va prendre** d'assaut la prison parisienne royale de la Bastille, symbole de l'arbitraire de la monarchie. Cette date signe la capitulation de l'armée royale et **donne** victoire pour la première fois au peuple. La Révolution française **durera** jusqu'en 1799, **décennie au cours de** laquelle **seront jugées** et exécutées les figures principales de l'ancien régime.

À **la mort** du Roi, c'est Robespierre, un avocat originaire d'Arras, **qui prit le pouvoir**. **Sa place au sein du** Comité de Salut Public est toujours controversée. **Il fut guillotiné** en 1794 et on continue de questionner son rôle dans la Grande Terreur **qui coûta la vie** à des milliers d'hommes. Son procès **donna néanmoins** lieu à la Nouvelle Constitution **qui proclamait enfin le droit** inaliénable du peuple à **disposer** de **lui-même**. De nombreuses réformes **virent le jour** tout au long **des années qui suivirent**, jusqu'à l'obtention d'une Constitution viable et suffisamment solide **qui protège** les droits **des citoyens** et donne toute la souveraineté à la Nation. De la révolution du peuple français **est né** l'Etat de France **tel que nous le connaissons** aujourd'hui.

Du côté des idées, **on retient** souvent que la Révolution française correspond à l'accomplissement des idées véhiculées par le mouvement intellectuel, scientifique et artistique **appelé** « Les Lumières » caractérisé par la place centrale qu'il donne à la Raison et la Liberté. Les figures du mouvement **s'engagèrent contre** la relativité, l'irrationalisme et la superstition de **la croyance** et de **la foi qui maintenaient**, comme **un organe** politique, le peuple dans **la peur** et dans l'obéissance : en d'**autres termes**, **qui le privaient** de sa liberté.

Les Lumières **font ainsi** la promotion du progrès scientifique et de la liberté individuelle et c'est le modèle de l'encyclopédie universelle (**qui s'emploie à faire** une classification rigoureuse de la totalité des connaissances humaines) **qui va prendre** le premier plan dans le projet scientifique de l'homme **qui y reconnaît** ainsi sa vocation première. Les Lumières et la Révolution française ont ainsi contribué à **définir** et **peut-être** aussi à **créer** l'Homme Moderne de nos sociétés actuelles.

---

la mort: the death
qui prit (prendre): who seized (to seize)
le pouvoir: the power
sa place: his role
au sein du: inside
il fut guillotiné: he was decapitated
qui coûta la vie (coûter): that cost the life (to cost)
il donna néanmoins (donner): nevertheless, it gave (to give)
qui proclamait (proclamer): which proclaimed (to proclaim)
enfin: at last
le droit: the right
disposer: to enjoy
lui-même: themselves
virent le jour (voir): were born (to see)
des années (une année): years
qui suivirent (suivre): which followed (to follow)
qui protège (protéger): which protects (to protect)
des citoyens: the citizens
est né (naître): was born (to be born)
tel que: such as
nous le connaissons (connaître): we know it (to know)

du côté: as for
des idées (une idée): ideas
on retient (retenir): people remember (to remember)
appelé (appeler): called (to call)
s'engagèrent (engager): committed (to commit)
contre: against
la croyance: belief
la foi: faith
qui maintenaient (maintenir): which maintained (to maintain
un organe: institution
la peur: fear
autres termes: other words
qui le privaient (priver): which deprived (to deprive)

font ainsi (faire): thus did (to do)
qui s'emploie à (s'employer): which works to (to work)
faire: to make
qui va prendre: who will take
il reconnaît (reconnaître): that acknowledges (to acknowledge)
définir: to define
peut-être: maybe
créer: to create

Évaluez votre compréhension

La fleur de lys, page 146

1. In the bible the white lily is a symbol of what?

2. *La fleur de lys* represents what on the royal arms?

3. Which king designated this as the royal emblem of France?

Historique du drapeau français, page 147

1. What colors are the flag? Which color was added last?

2. What do the bands on the flag symbolize?

3. What did Louis-Philippe add to the flag?

À la découverte de la Martinique, page 148

1. What is Martinique's nickname?

2. What two countries fought over the islands? When did they become French territory?

3. What natural disaster left a major mark on Martinique?

La Nouvelle-France, page 150

1. Where was the first French settlement in North America?

2. *La vallée de l'Ohio* was coveted for what?

3. What was one of the most famous battles?

Test your comprehension

Les sans-culottes, page 152

1. Revolutionaries in Paris most often came from which social class?

2. What is the literal meaning of *sans-culotte*? What are they known for doing/believing?

3. *Le bonnet phrygien* was what color and what did it symbolize?

L'Arc de Triomphe, page 154

1. What do the monument's four engravings entail?

2. What lies at the base of the monument?

Histoire de France, page 156

1. The execution of Marie Antoinette's husband (the King) signaled what two significant events?

2. What country did Marie Antoinette come from?

3. What made her stand out?

Jeanne d'Arc, page 158

1. What is Jeanne d'Arc's nickname? How does she symbolize France?

2. Why did she wear men's clothing?

3. What happened following her capture in 1429?

Géographie

Les trois fleuves de France

Un fleuve se distingue d'une rivière en ce que **cette dernière se jette** dans **un autre cours d'eau tandis que** le fleuve se jette dans **une mer** ou dans un océan. La France **est traversée par** de nombreux fleuves dont **trois des plus connus** sont la Seine, la Loire et le Rhône.

La Seine **s'étend sur** 777 km du Plateau de Langres en Côte d'Or **jusqu'à** la Manche, **en passant par** la capitale française, Paris, et par l'un des plus grand ports fluviaux et maritimes, Rouen. **Elle a très souvent été**  **représentée par les peintres** (Monet) et dans la littérature (Balzac). Ses rives parisiennes ont **par ailleurs été classées** en 1991 au patrimoine mondial de l'UNESCO. **En empruntant** les **jolis** « bateaux mouches » pour une promenade fluviale dans Paris, les visiteurs **peuvent ainsi admirer tour à tour** la petite statue de la Liberté, le musée de l'ancienne Gare d'Orsay, le palais du Louvre, l'île de la Cité avec sa cathédrale Notre Dame, **passer sous** la statue de Sainte Geneviève **la protectrice** de Paris **et encore bien** d'autres monuments **célèbres** de la « ville lumière ».

Une autre histoire **raconte que la fille** du grand **écrivain** Victor Hugo, Léopoldine Hugo, **s'est noyée** dans la Seine le 4 septembre 1843 alors que son **embarcation à voile avait chaviré**. **On pense également** à l'« **inconnue** de la Seine », **belle jeune femme** qui a été **retrouvée** dans **les eaux** et dont **on a fait un masque très convoité** par les artistes parisiens du XXème **siècle** tant son **sourire** était mystérieux et beau.

---

un fleuve: a river

se distingue de (se distinguer): differs from (to differ)

cette dernière: the latter

se jette (se jeter): flows (to flow)

un autre: another

un cours d'eau: watercourse, river

tandis que: whereas

une mer: the sea

est traversée par (traverser): is crossed by (to cross)

trois des plus connus: three of the most well known

s'étend sur (s'étendre sur): stretches over (to stretch)

jusqu'à: to

en passant par: by going through

elle a été représentée par (représenter): it has been portrayed by (to portray, depict)

très souvent: very often

les peintres (le peintre): painters

par ailleurs: besides

(elles) ont été classées: (they) have been classified (to classify)

en empruntant: by taking

jolis (joli): nice, pretty

peuvent (pouvoir): can (can, to be able to)

ainsi: then

admirer: admire

tour à tour: one by one

passer sous: to go under

la protectrice: protector

et encore bien: and much more

célèbres (célèbre): famous

raconte que (raconter): says that (to say)

la fille: the daughter

un écrivain: writer

(elle) s'est noyée (se noyer): (she) drowned (to drown)

une embarcation à voile: small sailboat

(elle) avait chaviré (chavirer): (it) capsized (to capsize)

on pense (penser): we think (to think)

également: also

une inconnue: unknown female

belle: beautiful

jeune: young

une femme: woman

retrouvée (retrouver): found (to find)

les eaux: waters

on a fait (faire): (someone) made (to make)

un masque: a mask

très convoité: very sought-after

un siècle: century

un sourire: smile

Ce n'est que depuis la **dernière** glaciation de 12 000 avant J.-C. que la Seine **a obtenu** son aspect d'**aujourd'hui**. **Avant que**, la Seine et la Loire **formaient un seul et même fleuve**. La Loire est aujourd'hui le plus long fleuve de France. **Elle parcourt** 1 013 km depuis sa source dans le Massif Central en Ardèche et se jette dans l'océan Atlantique. Elle est **cependant mondialement connue pour** les très **nombreux** et **somptueux châteaux qui la bordent. On en compte environ** quarante-deux **dont la plupart ont été remaniés** à la Renaissance française. **Parmi eux, on peut citer** le château d'Amboise **qui a servi de** résidence à de nombreux **rois** de France ou encore le château de Chenonceau que le roi Henri II **offrit** à sa favorite Diane de Poitiers.

Le troisième fleuve **mentionné**, le Rhône, est un fleuve européen **qui prend sa source** à Gletsch en Suisse, qui traverse Genève en alimentant **le** magnifique **lac** Léman **pour finir** sa course en France, en Camargue, et se jeter dans la Méditerranée. Il est **le second débit** de tous les fleuves méditerranéens après le Nil. La particularité de ce fleuve **tient en** la diversité de son **bassin versant. En effet, il est alimenté entre** mai et juillet par **les apports alpins (fonte des neiges** et des glaciers), puis, en **hiver** par des apports océaniques (par la Saône) et finalement en **automne** et en **été** par des apports méditerranées **qui sont régulièrement la cause de très grandes crues.**

---

ce n'est que depuis: it is only since
la dernière (dernier): the last
a obtenu (obtenir): obtained (to obtain)
aujourd'hui: today
avant que: before that
formaient (former): formed (to form)
un seul et même fleuve: a single river
elle parcourt (parcourir): it covers (to cover)
cependant: nevertheless
mondialement: worldwide
connue pour (connu): famous for
nombreux: numerous
somptueux: somptuous
châteaux (un château): castles
qui la bordent (border): that border it (to border)
on en compte (compter): we can count (to count)
environ: around, about
dont la plupart: most of them
ont été remaniée (remanier): were remodeled (to remodel)
parmi eux: among them
on peut citer: we can mention
qui a servi de (servir): that was used as (to be used)
rois (un roi): kings
offrit (offrir): offered (to offer)

mentionné (mentionner): mentioned (to mention)
qui prend sa source: that begins flowing
le lac: lake
pour finir: to finish
le second débit: second hightest flow rate
tient en (tenir en): resides in (to reside in)
un bassin versant: watershed
en effet: indeed
il est alimenté (alimenter): it is fed (to feed)
entre: between
les apports alpins: Alpine contributions
fonte des neiges: snowmelt
un hiver: winter
un automne: fall
un été: summer
qui sont régulièrement la cause de: that are regularly the cause of
très grandes crues (une crue): very big floods

Les plages françaises

En France, **on peut distinguer** trois types de **plages** différents. **En effet**, la France est **entourée** de **deux mers** : **la Manche** au **nord** et la Méditerranée au **sud**, et **bordée par** l'Océan Atlantique. Ainsi, les Français ont le choix **entre** les plages du nord, du sud et de l'ouest.

La Méditerranée est une mer **plutôt** calme **qui n'a pas** de **marée étant donnée** sa position géographique. Dans le sud de la France, **les étés** sont **toujours** plus **chauds** et **les hivers** moins **froids**. **Le soleil** est souvent présent et sa **douce chaleur réjouit** les touristes lorsqu'en été, les plages sont **envahies** par les joyeux Français en **vacances**.

La plage de Nice, par exemple, **offre** en plus de sa beauté les avantages de **la ville** dans laquelle **elle est située**. À quelques pas **derrière** la plage de **galets se trouve** le Vieux Nice **qui séduit** les vacanciers par les odeurs et **les saveurs** délicieuses de son marché, ses nombreuses boutiques de **savons** et d'épices et ses restaurants typiques.

Les plages de Corse, **île** située au sud de la France, sont des plus magnifiques et **le plaisir** d'**enfoncer ses pieds** dans **le sable fin** s'allie **à celui de contempler un paysage** splendide. **L'eau**, agréablement **tiède**, y est presque transparente. C'est un lieu idéal **pour faire** de **la plongée sous-marine** et observer **la vie aquatique**.

Les plages de l'ouest, **donnant sur** l'Atlantique, **offrent** un panorama quelque peu différent. Les océans sont **toujours plus agités** que les mers, et les marées sont très importantes. L'eau y est également plus **froide**, mais offre des possibilités d'activités différentes. Par exemple, la ville de Biarritz, située dans la région des Pyrénées-Atlantiques, est **connue pour** ses surfeurs et ses **séjours** de **thalassothérapie**. La tradition gastronomique des régions du sud-ouest **ajoute au plaisir** de la plage **celui du goût**.

Toujours sur la côte ouest, mais un peu plus au nord, **se trouve** la Vendée. On y trouve de nombreuses plages aux paysages divers. Sur l'île d'Yeu, située à 17 kilomètres de la côte, on trouve **des côtes sauvages** où **des falaises altières entourent des criques** de **sable blond**. On peut **se promener** facilement sur **les chemins longeant les falaises**, observant la mer en **contrebas**.

Enfin, au nord de la France, on trouve les plages **bordant** la Manche. L'eau y est assez froide, mais **vivifiante**. Moins fréquentées que les plages du sud, l'été, **elles deviennent** une **aire de jeu** pour **les enfants**, et une zone de repos pour les adultes qui, **allongés au soleil**, **dévorent** leurs magazines et leurs **livres favoris**.

En Normandie, par exemple, on trouve des plages bordées de **falaises de craie**, qui, **grâce à la lumière** spécifique à cette région, offrent un panorama **étonnant**, comme **on peut voir** à Étretat.

L'existence de plages si différentes en France **permet à tout le monde** d'y trouver son **bonheur**.

---

donnant sur (donner): opening on (to open)
offrent (offrir): offer (to offer)
toujours: always
plus agités (agiter): more turbulent
froide: cold
connue pour (connaître): known for (to know)
séjours (un séjour): stays
thalassothérapie: mineral springs
ajoute au (ajouter): add to the (to add)
plaisir (des plaisirs): pleasure
celui du goût: of one's taste, liking

se trouve (se trouver): is found (to find)
des côtes sauvages: wild seacoasts
des falaises altières: high bluffs
entourent (entourer): encircle (to encircle)
des criques (une crique): creeks
sable blond: white sand
se promener: walk
les chemins longeant: a road running beside
les falaises (la falaise): the cliffs
contrebas: below

bordant (border): bordering (to border)
vivifiante: invigorating
elles deviennent (devenir): they become (to become)
aire de jeu: playing area
les enfants (un enfant): the children
repos: rest
allongés au (allonger): lying down under the (to lie down)
un soleil: sun
dévorent (dévorer): devour (to devour)
livres (un livre): books
favoris: favorite

falaises de craie: chalk cliffs
grâce à: thanks to
la lumière: the light
étonnant (étonner): surprising (to surprise)
on peut voir (pouvoir): one can see (can, to be able to)

permet (permettre): allows (to allow)
à tout le monde: everyone
bonheur: happiness

Les Alpes

montagnes (une montagne): mountains
qui se trouve (trouver): that you can find
 (to find)
limite: borders
huit pays (un pays) eight countries
en effet: in fact
il marque (marquer): it traces (to trace)
la frontière: the border
Suisse: Switzerland
Autriche: Austria
Allemagne: Germany
se trouve (trouver): is found (to find)
au cœur de: in the heart of
on distingue (distinguer): we distinguish
 (to distinguish)
occidentales (occidental): western
qui s'étendent (étendre): that stretch out
 (to stretch out)
on trouve (trouver): we find (to find)
entre: between
la val: the valley
se situent (situer): are situated (to situate)

les deux villes (la ville): the two cities
surnommée par: nicknamed by
le paysage: the landscape
incroyable: incredible
une fleur: the flower
qu'on appelle (appeler): that we call (to call)
étoile: star
conifères (un conifère): conifers
les épicéas (un épicéa): the spruce (trees)
lacs (un lac): lakes
parsèment (parsemer): sprinkle (to sprinkle)
surface miroitante: glassy surface
sans doute: without a doubt
qui offre (offrir): which offers (to offer)

on parle (parler): we talk (to talk)
on pense (penser): we think (to think)
un hiver: winter
pratiquer: practice
pistes (une piste): slopes
mises à la disposition (mettre): put at the
 disposal (to put)
le bonheur: the happiness
les plus petits: the smallest
faire: to make, to do
un printemps: spring
un automne: fall
ont beaucoup (avoir): have a lot (to have)
à offrir (offrir): to offer (to offer)
cueillant: picking
par-ci par-là: here and there
on laisse (laisser): we let (to let)
le vent: the wind
nous emporter vers: take us toward

Les Alpes sont une chaîne de **montagnes qui se trouve** à la **limite** d'une totalité de **huit pays**. **En effet**, **il marque** une partie de **la frontière** de l'Italie, de la France, de la **Suisse**, de Monaco, du Liechtenstein, de l'**Autriche**, de l'**Allemagne** et de la Slovénie. Le point culminant des Alpes **se trouve** au sommet du Mont Blanc, à 4 810, 45 mètres. **Au cœur** des Alpes, **on distingue** trois parties géographiques de ce terrain montagneux : les Alpes **occidentales**, **qui s'étendent** de la Méditerranée au Mont Blanc, les Alpes centrales, que l'**on trouve entre le Val** d'Aoste et le Brenner, ainsi que les Alpes orientales qui **se situent** entre le Brenner et la Slovénie.

Les deux villes les plus importantes situées dans les Alpes sont Innsbruck en Autriche, et Grenoble en France. La ville de Grenoble est **surnommée par** les Français « la capitale des Alpes ». **Le paysage incroyable** des Alpes offre une végétation diverse et luxuriante. On y trouve par exemple la fameuse Edelweiss, cette **fleur qu'on appelle** aussi l'**étoile** des glaciers, et ces grands **conifères** que sont **les épicéas**. De nombreux **lacs parsèment** les Alpes de leur **surface miroitante**. Le plus important est **sans doute** le Lac Léman, puis le Lac du Bourget **qui offre** un panorama inoubliable.

Mais quand **on parle** des Alpes, **on pense** surtout aux sports d'**hiver**. En France, il existe de très nombreuses stations de ski, dont Tignes, le Val d'Isère, ou Megève. On peut y **pratiquer** le ski ou le snowboard sur les différentes **pistes mises à la disposition** des vacanciers, ou encore, pour le bonheur **des plus petits** ou des plus grands, **faire** une descente en luge. Ainsi, été comme hiver, **printemps** comme **automne**, les Alpes **ont beaucoup à offrir** et c'est avec plaisir que, cueillant quelques fleurs **par-ci par-là**, **on laisse le vent nous emporter vers** d'autres horizons.

La Dune du Pyla

Surplombant le Bassin d'Arcachon et **située dans la commune** de Teste-de-Buch, en Gironde, dans le sud-ouest de la France, la plus **haute** dune d'Europe est **constituée** de soixante millions de mètres **cubes** de **sable qui s'étendent** sur cinq cents mètres en largeur et 2.7 kilomètres en longueur.

C'est une structure maritime mobile qui **avance vers** l'intérieur **des terres** situées à l'est, à cause **des vents** qui **altèrent** constamment sa surface et modifient sa position. **Sa hauteur**, également variable, **oscille entre** 100 et 117 mètres au-dessus du **niveau de la mer**. Le Bassin d'Arcachon, **qu'elle domine**, est une large **cuvette enclose s'ouvrant sur un estuaire étroit**. Il est, avec **le littoral** atlantique, **le lieu de prédilection des marins-pêcheurs**, **des ostréiculteurs** et des vacanciers.

Appelée à l'origine Pilat et **faisant écho** à de nombreuses dénominations similaires dans la région, **on a retrouvé** son **nom** sur **des cartes qui datent de** 1708. **Il a été modifié**, en 1910, **par la suite** en Pyla-sur-Mer par un promoteur immobilier, Daniel Meller, **qui souhaitait remplacer le vieux** nom de « Sabloneys » souvent attribué à la région et signifiant en Gascon « sables nouveaux ».

Le vacancier **qui s'aventure** dans cette belle région d'Aquitaine et qui souhaite **escalader** courageusement la dune ou visiter la ville, **sera étonné** de **constater** que **les panneaux indicateurs se contredisent parfois**, certains utilisant Pilat et d'autres Pyla, respectant ainsi l'esprit de l' **humour facétieux** typiquement français.

Un escalier en bois, conçu pour les touristes les moins intrépides, **permet d'atteindre** son sommet en quelques minutes où une vue **à couper le souffle** du Bassin d'Arcachon **les attend**. **Les promeneurs** les plus **sportifs**, qui souhaitent **attaquer** sa face la plus abrupte **devront** y **mettre**, **outre la sueur**, une bonne vingtaine de minutes en plus du **souvenir sablonneux qu'ils rapporteront** dans **leurs chaussures**.

Sur la route des baleines

Pour bien situer la ville de Tadoussac sur **une carte** du Québec, **on peut prendre le lac** Saint-Jean comme **point de repère.** Cet immense lac **se trouve** à **environ** 200 kilomètres au **nord** de la ville de Québec. C'est là que la rivière Saguenay prend sa source et **se jette un peu plus** à l'est dans **le fleuve** Saint-Laurent.

C'est à l'endroit où la rivière Saguenay **rencontre les eaux** du fleuve que se trouve la ville de Tadoussac, une destination **très prisée** par tous **ceux qui aiment échapper** aux **chaleurs estivales** du **sud** de la province pour **contempler** la beauté **des paysages taillés** par les glaciers et **surtout** sa remarquable **faune aquatique.**

Tadoussac est **d'abord reconnue pour** l'observation **des baleines,** mais ce qu'on ignore souvent c'est qu'**elle constitue également** un des tout premiers établissements de la colonie en Nouvelle-France. L'histoire de sa fondation **précède même celle de** la ville de Québec. C'est en 1600 qu'une première tentative d'établissement **a eu lieu. Une maison de poste en bois fut construite** et 16 **hommes furent laissés** sur place. **Comme ils ignoraient la rigueur des hivers** canadiens, **ils furent durement éprouvés par le froid,** en plus de **devoir affronter la faim** et **les maladies. Seulement cinq d'entre eux** réussirent à survivre, **en quittant leur poste de traite** et **en se réfugiant auprès** des Amérindiens.

Aujourd'hui elle ne compte environ que 1000 habitants mais elle est surtout renommée à cause de sa faune aquatique : **les phoques, les marsouins, les rorquals**, et les fameux bélugas du Saint-Laurent **qui viennent** s'y **alimenter**. C'est **le mélange** entre l'**eau douce** de la rivière Saguenay et l'**eau salée** du fleuve qui favorise l'abondance de krill et de plancton dont **se nourrissent** les baleines. Les bélugas sont d'adorables petites baleines **blanches surnommées** « canaris des **mers** » à cause des **nombreux sons** qu'ils utilisent pour communiquer **entre eux**.

Les bélugas **sont de loin** l'espèce **la plus connue** à habiter les eaux du fleuve. **Ils ont soulevé l'attention du** grand public à **plusieurs reprises au cours de** l'histoire. **Pendant longtemps, ils ont été l'objet d'une chasse** intensive mais dans **les années quarante, on leur déclare carrément la guerre**. **On les accusait** en effet de **nuire à la pêche** commerciale et on encourageait **tout pêcheur qui verrait** un béluga à l'**abattre sur-le-champ**. Aujourd'hui l'espèce est **protégée** et on s'assure également de maintenir la pollution du fleuve à **des niveaux** acceptables. Pendant plusieurs années, le fleuve était **tellement pollué** qu'on considérait les carcasses de bélugas **retrouvées** sur le rivage comme **des matières** toxiques.

Mais il existe aussi d'autres espèces de baleines à observer dans le Saint-Laurent, d'autres beaucoup plus gigantesques que les bélugas, comme **les rorquals à bosse** ou **les rorquals bleus**. À Tadoussac, plusieurs excursions en mer **offrent** un spectacle **saisissant** lorsqu'un de ces mammifères géants **vient reprendre son souffle** à quelques mètres de notre **embarcation**, avec ses **coups de queue** et ses immenses **nageoires**. Si l'on vient dans la région de Tadoussac, **il ne faut pas non plus oublier** de visiter les rives majestueuses du fjord du Saguenay ou les fameuses **dunes de sable** au nord de la ville qui sont **les plus hautes** au Canada.

Les pays de mer et de montagne

(elle) demeure (demeurer): (it) remains (to remain)
depuis toujours: has always been
le cœur: heart
située: located
nord-est: northeast
elle forme (former): it forms (to form)
juste au nord: just to the north

en longeant: by following
le fleuve: river
bien après: well beyond
on peut (pouvoir): we can (can, to be able to)
accéder: to reach
à mesure que: as
(il) défile (défiler): (it) unfolds (to unfold)
le paysage: landscape
(il) se change en (se changer en): (it) turns into (to turn into)
une mer: sea
air marin: sea air
ses petites vagues (une vague): its small waves
qui naissent (naître): that form (to be born)
(elles) se brisent (se briser): they break (to break)
au loin: in the distance
enclavée: impacted
entre: between
les falaises (une falaise): the cliffs
la côte: the coast
nous ouvre (ouvrir): opens us (to open)
des centaines de (une centaine): hundreds of
en ceinturant: surrounding
le long du littoral: along the shore

il nous fait d'abord: it makes us first
découvrir: discover
pêcheurs (un pêcheur): fishermen
embarcations (une embarcation): boats
la ville: the city
qui joue (jouer): that plays
la pêche: fishing
renommée (renommé): well-known
célèbre: famous
la crevette: shrimp
les mélanges (le mélange): combinations
eau douce: fresh water
eau salée: salt water
nombreuses (nombreux): numerous
oiseaux (un oiseau): birds
poissons (un poisson): fish

en s'aventurant: by venturing, by going
un peu plus loin: a little bit further
on pénètre dans (pénétrer dans): we get into (to get into)
qui abrite (abriter): that shelters (to shelter)
que l'on trouve (trouver): that we find (to find)
les plus hauts (haut): the highest
dépassant: rising above

La Gaspésie **demeure depuis toujours** une destination touristique privilégiée dans **le cœur** des Québécois. **Située** au **nord-est** de la province, **elle forme** une péninsule bien visible, **juste au nord** du Nouveau-Brunswick.

C'est **en longeant le fleuve** Saint-Laurent, **bien après** Québec, Rivière-du-Loup, Rimouski, qu'**on peut** y **accéder**. **À mesure que** défile le **paysage**, le fleuve **se change** graduellement en **une mer** ondulante, avec son **air marin** et **ses petites vagues qui naissent** et **se brisent au loin**. La route 132, **enclavée entre les falaises** et **la côte, nous ouvre des centaines de** kilomètres de paysages **en ceinturant** toute la péninsule, **le long du littoral**.

Cet itinéraire **nous fait d'abord découvrir** la région de la côte qui est riche en petits villages de **pêcheurs** à l'architecture typique et aux **embarcations** colorées. **La ville** de Matane, **qui joue** un rôle central dans le secteur de **la pêche**, est **renommée** pour sa **célèbre crevette**. **Les mélanges** entre **eau douce** et **eau salée** sont à l'origine d'un riche écosystème où prolifèrent de **nombreuses** espèces d'**oiseaux** et de **poissons**.

En s'aventurant un peu plus loin, **on pénètre dans** la Haute-Gaspésie **qui abrite** de nombreux parcs et réserves fauniques. C'est dans cette portion québécoise de la chaîne des Appalaches **que l'on trouve les plus hauts** sommets du Québec, **dépassant** les 1 000 mètres d'altitude.

Cette région **a gardé** son caractère **sauvage** et **on y vient surtout** pour les sports de **plein-air**, pour **chasser l'ours**, **l'orignal** et autres **petits gibiers;** ou pour ses rivières cristallines **qui regorgent** de **saumons**.

C'est à Gaspé, **aujourd'hui** la principale ville de Gaspésie, que Jacques Cartier a d'abord **planté sa croix** en 1534 **pour revendiquer** le territoire du Canada au **nom** du **roi** de France. Un des points **forts** de notre visite **est situé** à l'extrémité de la péninsule, dans la ville de Percé, **où se trouve le célèbre rocher** Percé, **véritable** ambassadeur de toute la région. Le rocher percé est un bloc massif aux **rebords escarpés** qui mesure environ 88 mètres de haut et 433 mètres de long et **qui se dresse** dans l'eau, à quelques mètres du **rivage** avec une arche naturelle en son centre.

Des excursions en **bateau** sont **disponibles** à Percé et **nous permettent** de **nous rapprocher** du fameux rocher. **On peut même** s'aventurer dans **son trou** lorsque **la marée** est **basse**. **Plus loin**, **on aperçoit** l'île Bonaventure qui abrite la plus importante colonie de **fous de Bassan au monde**.

En poursuivant notre chemin sur la route 132, on arrive dans la région de la Baie-des-Chaleurs qui doit son nom à son microclimat unique. Dans cette région, à **la frontière** entre la Gaspésie et le Nouveau-Brunswick **on trouve** d'**étonnants** dialectes comme le français-acadien et le chiac, **qui empruntent des mots** à l'ancien français et à l'anglais, et qui ont une prononciation singulière, parfois difficile à **comprendre** pour **les non-initiés**.

Outre ses paysages **qui frappent** l'imaginaire, sa faune, sa flore, ses festivals, sa culture, ses habitants, la péninsule gaspésienne **nous laisse**, à chaque visite, d'**heureux souvenirs** et **une envie** constante d'y **revenir**.

---

a gardé (garder): has kept (to keep)
sauvage: wild
on y vient (venir): we come here (to come)
surtout: in particular, especially
plein-air: outdoor
chasser: to hunt
l'ours (un ours): bear
l'orignal (un orignal): moose
petits gibiers (un gibier): small game
qui regorgent (regorger): that abound (to abound)
saumons (un saumon): salmon

aujourd'hui: today
(il) a planté (planter): he planted (to plant)
sa croix (une croix): his cross
pour revendiquer: to claim
le nom: name
le roi: king
forts (fort): strong
est situé (situer): is located (to be located)
où se trouve (se trouver): where is (to be)
célèbre: famous
le rocher: rock
véritable: real, true
des rebords (le rebord): edges
escarpés (escarpé): steep
environ: about
qui se dresse (se dresser): which stands (to stand)
le rivage: shore

le bateau: boat
disponibles (disponible): available
(elles) nous permettent de (permettre): (they) allow us (to allow)
nous rapprocher: to get closer
on peut même: you can even
son trou (un trou): its hole
la marée: the tide
basse: low
plus loin: further
on aperçoit (apercevoir): we can catch sight of (to catch sight of)
les fous de Bassans: gannets *(type of bird)*
au monde: in the world

en poursuivant: by continuing
notre chemin (un chemin): our path
la frontière: the border
on trouve (trouver): we find (to find)
étonnants (étonnant): surprising
qui empruntent (emprunter): that borrow (to borrow)
mots (un mot): words
parfois: sometimes
comprendre: to understand
les non-initiés: laymen, lay person

qui frappent (frapper): that strike (to strike)
elle nous laisse (laisser): it lets us (to let)
une envie: a desire
heureux souvenirs: happy memories
une envie: desire
revenir: to come back

la flore: the flora	
variées: varied	
un monde: world	
grâce à: thanks to	
des îles (une île): islands	
arc antillais: Antillean arch	
en effet: in fact	
situées: located	
arrosée par: showered by	
des pluies saisonnières: seasonal rains	
balayées par les vents: windswept	
des sols (un sol): grounds	
propices: auspicious	
à la croissance: to the growth	
la floraison: the blossoming	
pendant: during	
une année: year	

Des fleurs et encore des fleurs

La flore antillaise est l'une des plus **variées** au **monde**, essentiellement **grâce à** la situation inter-tropicale **des îles** de l'**arc antillais**. **En effet**, **situées** dans une région tropicale **arrosée par des pluies saisonnières** et **balayées par les vents** « alizés », les îles telles que la Guadeloupe et la Martinique sont **des sols propices à la croissance** et à **la floraison** de différents types de végétation et ce, **pendant** une grande partie de l'**année**.

pluie (une pluie): rains
sol: soil
d'ailleurs: incidentally
on compte (compter): one counts (to count)
environ: about
paysages (le paysage): landscapes

La diversité de la végétation est essentiellement due aux **pluies** et au relief des **sols**. **D'ailleurs**, **on compte** environ 3 ou 4 **paysages** naturels dans les îles.

on retrouve (retrouver): one finds (to find)
une forêt: a forest
il pleut (pleuvoir): it rains (to rain)
qui permet à (permettre): which allows (to allow)
verte: green
préservée: preserved
est devenue (devenir): has become (to become)
la fougère: the fern

En Guadeloupe, **on retrouve** dans la région de la Basse-Terre, **une forêt** humide ou tropicale où **il pleut** énormément durant toute l'année, ce **qui permet à** une végétation très **verte** et luxuriante de se développer. D'ailleurs, cette forêt encore **préservée est devenue** l'un des Parcs Nationaux français. La plante emblématique de cet environnement est **la fougère**.

entre: between
marécageuse: swampy
qui s'appelle (s'appeler): which is called (to call)
la mangrove: mangrove, coastal wetland
les eaux (une eau): waters
viennent (venir): come (to come)
se jeter: to run into
très utiles: very useful
un poisson: fish
un crustacé: shellfish
reproduire: to reproduce
le palétuvier: mangrove tree
un arbre: tree
racines (une racine): roots
épaisses: thick
vivre: to live
dépérissent (dépérir): decline (to decline)
on sait (savoir): people know
par conséquent: consequently

Entre les deux îles de Grande-Terre et de Basse-Terre, on trouve toute une zone **marécageuse qui s'appelle la mangrove**. C'est là que **les eaux** de rivière et de pluie **viennent se jeter** à la mer. Les mangroves sont des zones **très utiles** au développement de la faune aquatique puisque de nombreuses espèces de **poisson** et autre **crustacé** viennent s'y **reproduire**. La plante qui symbolise la mangrove est **le palétuvier**. **Arbre** aux **racines** très longues et très **épaisses** autour desquelles viennent **vivre** et se reproduire les poissons. Lorsque les palétuviers **dépérissent**, **on sait** que la mangrove est en danger et **par conséquent** la faune aquatique aussi.

les reliefs: relief
plats: flat
bas: low
sèche: dry
amour: love
des jardins (un jardin): gardens
colorées: colorful

En Grande-Terre, on retrouve dans **les reliefs** plus **plats** et plus **bas**, une végétation plus **basse** et plus **sèche**. Pourtant ce que l'on retrouve partout en Guadeloupe, c'est l'**amour des jardins**, dits tropicaux, aux fleurs et aux plantes variées et **colorées**.

Un pays aux contrastes

S'étendant en une mince bande de terre entre littoral, massifs montagneux, régions lacustres et plateaux, le Togo est un petit pays d'Afrique de l'Ouest bordé par le Ghana, le Bénin et le Burkina Faso et s'étirant sur près de 550 km du nord au sud.

Sa côte sablonneuse, qui s'ouvre à peine sur le golfe de Guinée, est plutôt inhospitalière et fréquentée principalement par les pirogues des pêcheurs qui connaissent bien cette zone de lagunes. On y retrouve également le lac Togo, dont le nom signifie « nous irons au-delà de la colline ».

Vivant surtout de pêche, d'agriculture et de commerce du coton, du café ou du cacao, la population locale se concentre principalement dans la région de la capitale Lomé, ou dans les petites villes environnantes. Cette région est traversée, le long du golfe de Gui, par une grande route d'une part et par une région surélevée de nature sédimentaire, d'autre part, qui culmine parfois jusqu'à 200 mètres.

Le massif montagneux qui traverse le pays dans le sens nord-est/sud-ouest, est d'une hauteur moyenne de 700 mètres. Avec le mont Agou, il atteint cependant 986 mètres. Les principales rivières qui arrosent le pays naissent de ces reliefs accidentés. C'est le fleuve Mono qui marque la frontière avec le Bénin et qui, avec ses affluents, constituent la ligne de partage des bassins de la Volta et de l'Oti.

Située à environ 167 km de Lomé, Atakpamé est la principale ville de la région des Plateaux. Contrairement à son nom, cette région, qui culmine à 500 mètres est caractérisée par ses maisons à flanc de colline. Le Togo, qui compte environ 4,5 millions d'habitants répartis en une quarantaine d'ethnies, a cependant la réputation d'être un pays dont le climat parfois subéquatorial parfois tropical se reflète jusque dans le cœur chaleureux et accueillant de ses habitants.

s'étendant (s'étendre): stretching (to stretch)
une mince bande: a thin strip
une terre: land
entre: between
un littoral: sea coast
montagneux: mountainous
lacustres: lake
un pays: country
bordé par: bordered by
s'étirant (s'étirer): stretching (to stretch)

côte sablonneuse: sandy coast
qui s'ouvre (s'ouvrir): which opens (to open)
à peine sur: barely on
les pirogues (une pirogue): canoes
des pêcheurs: fishermen
qui connaissent (connaître): who know (to know)
on y retrouve également: one also finds there
le lac: lake
le nom: the name
signifie (signifier): means (to mean)
nous irons (aller): we will go (to go)
au-delà de: over
la colline: the hill

vivant (vivre): living (to live)
pêche: fishing
se concentre (concentrer): concentrated (to be concentrated)
les villes environnantes: nearby cities
est traversée (traverser): is crossed (to cross)
le long: along
surélevée: above the level
qui culmine (culminer): which culminates (to culminate)
parfois: sometimes
jusqu'à: up to

le sens: the direction
une hauteur moyenne: an average height
il atteint cependant: however it tops
qui arrosent (arroser): which irrigate (to irrigate)
naissent de: spring from
reliefs accidentés: precipitous reliefs
le fleuve: river
qui marque (marquer): which marks (to mark)
la frontière: the border
affluents (un affluent): tributaries
la ligne de partage: the dividing line

située à (situer): located (to locate)
environ: approximately
ses maisons (une maison) its houses
à flanc: on the side
répartis (répartir): divided (to divide)
se reflète (se refléter): reflects (to reflect)
le cœur: heart
chaleureux: warm
accueillant: welcoming

Le Lac Léman

Le Lac Léman, qui est le plus grand lac d'origine glaciaire d'Europe occidentale, est **le quarantième** lac au **monde** pour le volume et le quarante-troisième pour **la profondeur, celle-ci culminant** à près de trois cents mètres sous **le niveau** de **la mer**.

Son **nom**, d'origine celtique **nous a été retransmis** par le latin. Il est si ancien que même Jules César, **qui traversait** la région en 58 avant J.C. en a fait mention.

Adoptant la forme d'**un croissant** ou d'**une virgule, il possède** une superficie de cinq cent quatre-vingt-deux kilomètres carrés, et est situé en partie en France du côté sud et en partie en Suisse du côté nord, **la frontière séparant** les **deux pays** de **part en part**.

On peut dire à la blague que cette configuration simplifiait considérablement **les tracasseries douanières** et administratives pour **les plaisanciers qui souhaitaient traverser** en Suisse **pour déguster le meilleur** chocolat d'Europe ou **acheter une montre**, avant son adjonction à l'espace Schengen.

Et avec raison, car la masse d'**eau douce qu'il contient permet de créer** un microclimat, plus particulièrement à Montreux, qui favorise **la croissance** de plantes exotiques comme les palmiers et les agaves, bien qu'il soit situé dans le nord de la France, région habituellement **froide dont le ciel est souvent grisâtre**.

Toutefois, il arrive que l'humidité chaude qui s'élève du lac en **hiver rencontre un mur** d'air froid et **sec** immobilisé dans l'atmosphère, ce qui peut parfois créer l'apparition d'**un brouillard tenace qui s'élève** souvent à plus de 1000 mètres d'altitude.

---

le quarantième: the fortieth
monde (un monde): world
la profondeur (les profondeurs): the depth
celle-ci culminant (culminer): this one culminating (to culminate)
le niveau: the level
la mer: the sea

nom: name
nous a été retransmis (retransmettre): has been transmitted to us (to transmit)
qui traversait (traverser): who crossed over (to cross over)

adoptant (adopter): adopting (to adopt)
un croissant: crescent
une virgule: comma
il possède (posséder): he possesses (to possess)
la frontière (des frontières): the border
séparant (séparer): separating (to separate)
les deux pays (un pays): the two countries
part en part: right through

on peut dire (pouvoir): one can say (can, to be able to)
à la blague: joking
les tracasseries douanières: the hassles of customs
les plaisanciers (un plaisancier): the amateur sailors
qui souhaitaient (souhaiter): who wished (to wish)
traverser: to cross
pour déguster: to taste
le meilleur: the best
acheter: to buy
une montre: a watch

eau douce: fresh water
qu'il contient (contenir): that it contains (to contain)
permet de créer: allows to create
la croissance: the growth
froide: cold
dont le ciel: so the sky
est souvent: is often
grisâtre: grayish

toutefois: however
un hiver: winter
rencontre (rencontrer): meets (to meet)
un mur: a wall
sec: dry
un brouillard tenace: a persistent fog
qui s'élève (élever): that rises (to rise)

Trouvant sa source dans **plusieurs** rivières environnantes, mais plus précisément du Rhône, situé en Haute-Savoie, **il reçoit également** le déversement de plusieurs **cours d'eau** du Vaud et du Valais suisse.

Bien que son **niveau** de pollution ait **été préoccupant** dans **les années** 80, une meilleure oxygénation due à la diminution **des algues** a **permis de maintenir** la situation à un niveau acceptable.

Abritant une faune et une flore riche et variée, **il permet** à de nombreux **pêcheurs riverains** d'**en tirer** leur subsistance grâce, **entre autres**, à l'abondance de **truites**, **perches**, **brochets** et écrevisses américaines **qui pullulent** dans ses eaux. Pour les amateurs d'**oiseaux recherchant** des sites d'observation, le Lac Léman, qui **se trouve** sur **un courant** migratoire entre le Jura et les Alpes, reçoit la visite de plus de cent cinquante- mille volatiles **qui viennent** y **prendre** leurs quartiers d'hiver chaque année.

Site touristique **extrêmement prisé** tout au long de l'année, il offre aux visiteurs de nombreuses occasions de **plaisir** et de **détente**, **ne serait-ce que** la traditionnelle **balade en bateau**, puisque vingt mille **embarcations** de tous types y sont **amarrées**.

Ses **abords** riches en végétation, avec une profusion d'**arbres** comme **l'érable**, **le charme**, **le hêtre**, **le peuplier** et **le frêne**, et la couleur changeante de ses eaux calmes **attirent de** nombreux vacanciers **qui veulent profiter** de sa situation exceptionnelle aux confins de deux pays limitrophes riches et **accueillants**.

trouvant (trouver): finding (to find)
plusieurs: several, many
il reçoit également (recevoir): it receives also (to receive)
un cours d'eau: water stream

un niveau: level
été préoccupant (préoccuper): has been alarming (to alarm)
les années (une année): the years
des algues (une algue): the seaweed
permis de (permettre): allowed to (to allow)
maintenir: maintain

abritant (abriter): sheltering (to shelter)
il permet (permettre): it allows (to allow)
pêcheurs riverains: lakeside fishermen
en tirer: to draw from it
entre autres: among other things
truites (une truite): trout
perches (une perche): sea bass
brochets (un brochet): pike
qui pullulent (pulluler): that multiply rapidly (to multiply)
oiseaux (un oiseau): birds
recherchant (rechercher): searching for (to search for)
qui se trouve (trouver): is located (to locate)
un courant: flow, path
qui viennent (venir): that come from (to come)
prendre (prendre): take (to take)

extrêmement prisé: extremely prized
plaisir: pleasure
détente: relaxation
ne serait-ce que (être): this would not be (to be)
balade en bateau: boat ride
embarcations (une embarcation): boats
amarrées (amarrer): moored (to moor)

abords: surroundings
arbres (un arbre): trees
l'érable: maple tree
le charme: charm tree
le hêtre: beech
le peuplier: poplar
le frêne: ash tree
attirent de (attirer): attract many (to attract)
qui veulent profiter (profiter): who want to take advantage of (to take advantage of)
situation: location
accueillants (accueillir): welcoming (to welcome)

Évaluez votre compréhension

Les trois fleuves de France, page 166

1. What are the three great rivers of France?

2. What lake does the Rhone river empty into?

3. What will you find on the banks of the Loire river?

Les Alpes, page 170

1. How many countries do the Alps run through?

2. Which city is called the "Capital of the Alps"?

3. What famous flower is found in the Alps? (List both names.)

Les plages françaises, page 168

1. France is surrounded by what seas and bordered by what ocean?

2. What is *Les plages de Corse* an ideal place for?

3. Describe Normandy's coastline.

Sur la route des baleines, page 172

1. What two rivers will you find in Tadoussac?

2. What are two notable things that Tadoussac is known for?

3. Why are beluga whales called "canaries of the sea"?

Test your comprehension

Les pays de mer et de montagne, page 174

1. What is the view you will find along Route 132?

2. What environmental feature promotes a great variety of fish and birds?

3. What is *Le rocher percé*?

Un pays aux contrastes, page 177

1. The sandy coast of Togo opens onto what body of water?

2. What is the main agriculture and commerce of Togo?

3. What geographical feature marks the border with Bénin?

Des fleurs et encore des fleurs, page 176

1. What helps the abundant growth of flowers and vegetation in Martinique?

2. What plant is symbolic of the tropical forest?

3. What plant symbolizes the coastal wetlands or swamps?

Le Lac Léman, page 178

1. What is the shape of the lake?

2. Pollution has caused what to grow too much?

3. What trees will you find around the lake?

Gastronomie

vous promenant (promener): walking
(to walk)
dans: in
les rues (une rue): the streets
une ville: town
vous serez parfois: you will be sometimes
étonné de (étonner): be surprised (to surprise)
voir: to see
manger (manger): eating (to eat)
un morceau (des morceaux): a piece
chaud: hot
que lui a tendu (tendre): given by (to give)
sa mère (une mère): his/her mother
au sortir de: while leaving
la boulangerie: the bakery

le pain: the bread
servi (servir): served (to serve)
un mets: a dish
un aliment: a food
à part entière: complete
dégusté (déguster): eaten (to eat)
un homme: man

amour entre: love between
on dit (dire): we say (to say)
les campagnes (une campagne): campaigns
on prétend (prétendre): we pretend
(to pretend)
allongée (allonger): stretched (to stretch)
se prêtait mieux (prêter): lent itself better
(to lend)
la poche (les poches): the pocket
un pantalon: pants
des soldats (un soldat): soldiers
ne soit pas avérée (avérer): is not proven true
(to prove)
tout de même: all the same
n'ont vu que (voir): have seen only (to see)

mesurant (mesurer): measuring (to measure)
largeur: width
épaisseur: thickness
elle serait (être): it would be (to be)
(de toute) manière: in any case
moins longue: less long
cuire (cuire): bake (to bake)
à la recherche (rechercher): looking for
(to look for)
un peu de temps: a little free time
pour rêver (rêver): to dream
se rendant (se rendre): going to (to return)
qu'ils peuvent exercer: they can exert
loisir: leisure, pastime
surcroît: additional
un commerce: store
entre eux: between themselves
achètent (acheter): buy
chaque jour: each day

demeure (demeurer): remains (to remain)
qu'il existe (exister): that exists (to exist)
levain: yeast
une noix: nuts
ménage: homemade
froment: wheat

Le pain français

Vous promenant dans les rues de Paris ou de toute autre **ville** française, **vous serez parfois étonné de voir** un enfant **manger** avec plaisir **un morceau** de baguette encore tout **chaud que lui a tendu sa mère au sortir de la boulangerie**.

Alors qu'en Amérique **le pain** est **servi** en accompagnement d'**un mets** ou **constitue** un élément essentiel du traditionnel sandwich ou hambourgeois, en France, il est **un aliment à part entière. Dégusté** souvent nature, sans beurre ni garniture, le pain y est apprécié pour ce qu'il est: l'un des principaux aliments de l'**homme**.

L'histoire d'**amour entre** la France et le pain, et plus particulièrement avec la traditionnelle baguette, débute à ce que l'**on dit** avec **les campagnes** napoléoniennes. **On prétend** en effet que leur forme **allongée se prêtait mieux** à son transport dans **la poche** du **pantalon des soldats**, qu'un pain rond. Bien que cette légende **ne soit pas avérée**, les Français, qui ont **tout de même** l'esprit pratique, **n'ont vu que** des avantages à cette forme oblongue.

Mesurant environ soixante-cinq centimètres de longueur sur cinq à six centimètres de **largeur**, par trois à quatre centimètres d'**épaisseur**, **elle serait** de toute **manière moins longue** à **cuire** que le pain rond. Ce qui, pour un Français, toujours **à la recherche** d'**un peu de temps pour rêver**, n'est pas du tout négligeable. C'est en **se rendant** à la boulangerie **qu'ils peuvent** exercer à **loisir** leur **surcroît** d'imagination, car c'est dans ce petit **commerce** de proximité que soixante-et-onze pour cent d'**entre eux achètent** leur pain **chaque jour**.

Pour soixante-quatorze pour cent de ces consommateurs, la baguette **demeure** leur variété de pain préférée, quoi **qu'il existe** en France quatre-vingts types de pains régionaux tels le pain au **levain**, le pain brioché, le pain aux **noix**, le pain de **ménage**, le pain de **froment** et tant d'autres, tout aussi délicieux les uns que les autres.

Beignes de nos grand-mères

Régalez-vous avec cette **recette** de **beignes**, **une pâtisserie** traditionnelle du Québec. **On peut se procurer** des beignes dans les pâtisseries, mais les **meilleurs** sont sans doute ceux **faits à la maison à partir de** recettes transmises de génération en génération par **les grand-mères** à **leurs filles** et **maintenant à vous** !

Ingrédients :
4 **œufs**
2 1/2 **tasses sucre blanc granulé**
2 tasses crème 15%
1 **c.à thé soda à pâte** et **poudre à pâte**
1 c.à thé **sel**
4 tasses **farine tout-usage**, pour **épaissir**
1 c.à thé essence de **citron**
Grains de **muscade**

Séparer les blancs d'œuf **des jaunes**. **Battre** les blancs d'œuf en **neige ferme** et **mettre de côté**. **Dans un autre** bol, battre les jaunes d'œuf et l'essence de citron en y **ajoutant** le sucre **lentement**. Battre **jusqu'à** ce que **vous obteniez** une couleur **jaune** pâle. Dans 4 tasses de farine, **mélanger** la poudre à pâte, le soda à pâte, le sel et la muscade. À la préparation de jaune d'œuf, ajouter la farine lentement en **alternant avec** la crème. **À l'aide** d'une spatule, **incorporer** lentement les blancs d'œuf en neige à la préparation. Ajouter de la farine **peu à peu afin que** la pâte **se roule bien**. **Laisser reposer** la pâte **recouverte** d'un papier film **environ deux heures** au refrigérateur.

Rouler la pâte environ 3/4 de **pouce** et **couper** avec **un coupe** beigne. **Préchauffer l'huile** dans **une friteuse** profonde à 350 degrés Fahrenheit. **Recouvrir** d'huile et faire frire **en remuant constamment** jusqu'à ce qu'ils prennent **une teinte dorée**. Après la friture, **laissez-les égoutter** pendant quelques secondes sur **des papiers absorbants**, puis **déposez-les** dans un sac plastique contenant du **sucre à glacer**. Fermez bien le sac et **remuez** les beignets afin de bien les recouvrir.

recette: recipe
beignes (un beigne): doughnuts
une pâtisserie: pastry
on peut se procurer: you can buy
les meilleurs: the best
faits à la maison: homemade
à partir de: from
les grand-mères: grandmothers
filles (une fille): their daughters
maintenant à vous: now to you

œufs (un œuf): eggs
tasses (une tasse): cups
le sucre blanc granulé: white granulated sugar
c.à thé (une cuillère à thé): teaspoon
le soda à pâte: baking soda
la poudre à pâte: baking powder
le sel: salt
la farine tout-usage: all-purpose flour
épaissir: to thicken
le citron: lemon
la muscade: nutmeg

séparer: separate
des jaunes: the egg yolks
battre: whisk
neige ferme: to form peaks
mettre de côté: set aside
dans un autre: in another
ajoutant (ajouter): adding (to add)
lentement: slowly
jusqu'à: until
vous obteniez (obtenir): you get (to get)
jaune: yellow
mélanger: to mix
alternant (alterner): alternating (to alternate)
à l'aide de: with the help of
incorporer: mix
peu à peu: gradually
afin que: so that
se roule (rouler): is rolled (to roll)
bien: well
laisser: to leave
reposer: to rest
recouverte (recouvert): covered
environ: about
deux heures (une heure): two hours

rouler: roll
un pouce: inch
couper: to cut
un coupe: knife
préchauffer l'huile: preheat the oil
une friteuse: deep fryer
recouvrir: cover
en remuant constamment: moving constantly
une teinte dorée: a golden color
laissez-les égoutter: let them drain
des papiers absorbants: paper towels
déposez-les (déposer): drop them (to drop)
sucre à glacer: powdered sugar
remuez (remuer): shake (to shake)

La bouillabaisse

Il existe une spécialité **réellement typique** de la culture régionale du France. Elle a **longtemps** fait l'objet de la curiosité des touristes. Directement **issue de** l'histoire de Marseille, la bouillabaisse **n'a pas fini de nous mettre l'eau à la bouche.**

Son **plus grand ancêtre a connu** une certaine popularité à **l'époque** de la fondation de **la ville**. Le plat **n'était** alors qu'un simple ragoût de **poissons appelé** le « Kakavia ». **Ce plat va évoluer** à travers les âges pour finalement **devenir** le plat que l'on connaît: **la vraie** bouillabaisse provençale connue alors sous **le nom** de « bolhabaissa », de bolh (**il bout**) et abaissa (**il abaisse**) **traduit** en français **par** : « **quand ça bout tu baisses** » (sous-entendu le **feu** de **cuisson**).

À l'origine, **il s'agissait** d'un plat très modeste. **Les pêcheurs conservaient** pour leur famille pour **les cuisiner en rentrant le soir**, certaines pièces de poissons qu'ils n'avaient pas pu **vendre durant la journée**. Après **avoir trié** le poisson, **ils faisaient chauffer un chaudron rempli** d'**eau de mer** et y **mettaient** tous les poissons **invendables, abîmés**.

Cela donnait un potage que l'**on dégustait** avec du **pain dur frotté** à **l'ail** (les croûtons). Les poissons **restants étaient** ensuite immergés dans la soupe qui **était mangée** avec de **la rouille** ou de **l'aïoli**.

Aujourd'hui, la bouillabaisse **a été intégrée** à la grande gastronomie bourgeoise provençale. Ce **qui nourrissait jadis** les familles **les plus pauvres** du sud de la France **est devenu** de **nos jours** un plat de grand choix que **ne peuvent se payer** que les personnes **les plus aisées**. **Il arrive malheureusement** assez fréquemment de **goûter** à une bouillabaisse **bon marché**, que des restaurants marseillais peu scrupuleux **proposent** aux touristes.

Une charte a donc **été créée** pour certifier de l'authenticité de la recette. **Elle renseigne** sur les poissons à utiliser, notamment au moins quatre des **espèces suivantes: rascasse**, rascasse blanche, **araignée** (vive), galinette (**rouget grondin**), saint-pierre, **baudroie** (lotte), congre ou scorpène. **Des langoustes** sont également incorporées au bouillon, **lui-même fait** à base de petits **poissons de roche**, **en remplacement des cigales de mer** (se faisant plus rares) **cuites** avec **les étrilles** et **les pommes de terre**. Elles **apportent** un parfum essentiel et très particulier à la préparation. Certains restaurants **parlent alors de** « bouillabaisse royale » et cela leur permet de faire **grimper** l'addition du **repas**. **Mais il ne faut pas s'y tromper**, la vraie bouillabaisse **contient bien** des cigales de mer.

Par ailleurs, la charte **nous instruit** du service que **se doit de suivre** le restaurateur vis-à-vis de son client. Ainsi, accompagné d'une sauce faite de rouille et de croûtons à l'ail, le poisson, servi entier dans **un deuxième** plat différent de celui du bouillon, **sera découpé** par le **serveur sous les yeux** du client.

Enfin les éléments essentiels sont l'extrême **fraîcheur** et la qualité du poisson. **Sans cela**, la bouillabaisse sera de mauvaise qualité. Au final, la bouillabaisse est une curiosité **qui revient assez cher**. Il est important de **savoir** que beaucoup de restaurants **en servent** à **des prix moins onéreux**. Mais **pour déguster** une vraie bouillabaisse provençale, **il faut compter au moins** 40 euros par personne. Une bouillabaisse **en dessous de** ce prix est un véritable **piège** à touristes.

---

aujourd'hui: today
a été intégrée (intégrer): has been integrated (to integrate)
qui nourrissait (nourrir): that fed (to feed)
jadis: formerly
les plus pauvres: the poorest
est devenu (devenir): has become (to become)
de nos jours: nowadays
ne peuvent pas (pouvoir): cannot (can, to be able to)
se payer: afford
les plus aisées: the wealthiest
il arrive (arriver): it happens (to happen)
malheureusement: unfortunately
goûter: to taste
bon marché: cheap
proposent (proposer): suggest (to suggest)

une charte: charter
a été créée (créer): has been created (to create)
elle renseigne sur (renseigner): it gives information about (to give information)
les espèces suivantes: following species
la rascasse: scorpion fish
l'araignée: spider crab
un rouget grondin: goatfish
une baudroie: monkfish
des langoustes (la langouste): spiny lobsters
lui-même fait: made itself
un poisson de roche: rockfish
en remplacement: replacing
des cigales de mer: slipper lobsters
cuites: cooked
les étrilles: small crabs
les pommes de terre: potatoes
elles apportent (apporter): they bring (to bring)
parlent de (parler): talk about (to talk)
grimper: to increase
un repas: meal
mais il ne faut pas s'y tromper: but make no mistake about it
contient bien: contains for sure

nous instruit (instruire): teaches us (to teach)
se doit de suivre (se devoir): has to follow (to have to)
un deuxième: second
(il) sera découpé par (découper): (it) will be cut by (to cut)
le serveur: the waiter
sous les yeux (un œil): under the eyes

la fraîcheur: freshness
sans cela: without that
qui revient assez cher: that is rather expensive
savoir: to know
en servent (servir): serve some (to serve)
des prix (un prix): prices
moins onéreux: less expensive
pour déguster: to taste
il faut compter: you will be charged
au moins: at least
en dessous de: below
un piège: trap

pays: country
chrétienne: Christian
on ne voudrait (vouloir): we wouldn't want
   to (to want)
manquer: to miss
pour rien: for nothing
monde: world
composé (composer): consisting of
   (to consist)
une pâte roulée: a rolled dough (to roll)
garnie de (garnir): garnished of (to garnish)
un appareil sucré: a sweet filling
la saveur: the flavor
demeurent souvent (demeurer): often stay
   (to stay)
bien gardé (garder): well kept (to keep)
un régal: a treat
on aime (aimer): we like (to like)
se remémorer: to remember
une année: year

que serait (être): what would be (to be)
qui vient couronner (couronner): which
   crowns (to crown)
un repas: a meal
qui nous laisse (laisser): which leaves us
   (to leave)
un peu hébétés (hébéter): a little dazed
   (to daze)
ravis (ravir): delighted (to delight)
nous nous pâmons (pâmer): we swoon
   (to swoon)
devant: over
qui a décoré (décorer): who decorated
   (to decorate)
les yeux: the eyes
le palais: the palate

pour faire: to make
tout devrait (devoir): everything should
   (must)
se manger (manger): be eaten (to eat)
la bûche: Yule log
qu'y a-t-il (avoir): what is (to be)
triste: sad
retrouver: to find
ce chef d'œuvre: this masterpiece
les enfants (un enfant): children
ne manquent (manquer): do not fail (to fail)
toutefois pas: however
lécher: to lick
une fois: one time
approbateurs: approving
attendris (attendrir): softened up
   (to soften up)

provenant (provenir): coming from
   (to come from)
un arbre fruitier: fruit tree
soit choisie (choisir): is chosen (to choose)
pour brûler (brûler): to burn (to burn)
l'âtre: hearth
les douze jours (le jour) the twelve days
des Fêtes (une fête): holidays

La bûche de Noël

Dans divers **pays** à prédominance **chrétienne**, la bûche de Noël représente une tradition que l'**on ne voudrait manquer pour rien** au monde. En effet, ce dessert savoureux **composé** d'**une pâte roulée garnie de** crème ou d'**un appareil sucré** dont **la saveur**, la composition et la consistance **demeurent souvent** un secret **bien gardé** par la cuisinière, constitue **un régal** que l'**on aime se remémorer d'une année** à l'autre.

Que serait Noël en effet sans cette apothéose finale **qui vient couronner un repas** gargantuesque **qui nous laiss**e **un peu hébétés** mais **ravis** ? À chaque année **nous nous pâmons devant** l'inventivité du chef **qui a décoré** la bûche d'une manière tout à fait originale, tant pour **les yeux** que pour **le palais**.

Car, **pour faire** bonne figure, **tout devrait** idéalement **se manger** dans **la bûche**. **Qu'y a-t-il** en effet de plus **triste** que de **retrouver** sur **ce chef d'œuvre** de la cuisine festive des décorations en plastique que **les enfants ne manquent toutefois pas** de **lécher** avec gourmandise, sous les regards pour **une fois** indulgents et **approbateurs** de leurs parents **attendris**.

À l'origine, la tradition voulait qu'une bûche naturelle **provenant** d'**un arbre fruitier soit choisie** minutieusement **pour brûler** dans **l'âtre** durant **les douze jours** du temps **des Fêtes**.

Mais le développement de l'architecture contemporaine, **qui laisse** peu de place à l'âtre, a fait **tomber** cette tradition dans **la désuétude**, du moins dans les grandes **villes**, pour la **remplacer par** le dessert que l'**on connaît**, mais **qui s'en plaindrait** ?

La bûche de Noël traditionnelle est **proposée** en divers parfums **qui incorporent** soit de la vanille, du café, du **sirop d'érable**, du chocolat, du Grand Marnier ou des pralines. **Toutefois**, **quel que soit** le choix **qui viendra chatouiller nos papilles** et **accorder** dans notre mémoire au dessert de Noël **une place prépondérante**, il ne faudra pas oublier de la décorer de divers éléments **qui ajoutent** au symbolisme de la fête. **Voici pour vous** une recette traditionnelle **qui sera sûrement** fort appréciée :

Pour le biscuit : 5 **œufs**, 50 g de **farine**, 50 g de **fécule** de **pomme de terre,** 170 g de **sucre**, 1 pincée de sel, 1 cuillérée à soupe d'**eau**, 1 **verre** à liqueur de rhum.

Pour la crème : 1 œuf entier, **un jaune d'œuf**, 4 barres de chocolat, 200 à 250 grammes de sucre, 1 demi-tasse de café, 1 tiers de verre d'eau.

Préparation : **Fouettez** les jaunes d'œufs avec le sel **assez longuement**, lorsque **le mélange** est **mousseux**, **ajoutez** l'eau et le rhum. **Puis ajoutez** la farine et la fécule et bien mélanger, enfin **incorporez** délicatement les blanc d'œufs **battus en neige**. **Étalez** la pâte dans **une lèchefrite** et **cuire pendant** 15 minutes à 350 degrés. **Faire un sirop épais** avec les ingrédients **qui restent**, puis **le laisser refroidir** au réfrigérateur. **Étendre** ensuite la crème sur la pâte puis **roulez-la sans trop serrer**. **Recouvrir** du reste de la crème et **décorez** votre bûche **selon** votre inspiration. En la garnissant d'**un père Noël** en sucre, **des lutins**, **des champignons** en chocolat, d'**une scie** ou d'**une hache**, on **rappellera** sa vocation première **qui était de réchauffer la maison** et **les cœurs**.

---

qui laisse (laisser): which leaves (to leave)
tomber (tomber): fall (to fall)
désuétude: (fall into) disuse
villes (la ville): cities
remplacer par: replace with
on connaît (connaître): we know (to know)
qui s'en plaindrait: who would complain

proposée (proposer): proposed (to propose)
qui incorporent (incorporer): which incorporate (to incorporate)
sirop d'érable: maple syrup
toutefois: even so
quel que soit: whatever
qui viendra chatouiller: that will tickle
nos papilles (la papilla): our taste buds
accorder (accorder): grant (to grant)
une place prépondérante: dominant place
il ne faudra pas oublier: we must not forget
qui ajoutent (ajouter): which add (to add)
voici pour vous: here for you is
qui sera sûrement: that will surely be

œufs (un œuf): eggs
une farine: flour
une fécule: starch
pomme de terre: potato
un sucre: sugar
une eau: water
un verre: glass

un jaune d'œuf: egg yolk

fouettez (fouetter): whip (to whip)
assez longuement: somewhat of a long time
le mélange: mix
mousseux: frothy
ajoutez (ajouter): add (to add)
incorporez (incorporer): incorporate (to incorporate)
battus en neige: stiff egg whites
étalez (étaler): spread (to spread)
une lèchefrite: grease tray
cuire pendant (cuire): bake for (to bake)
faire: make
un sirop épais: thick syrup
qui restent (rester): that are remaining (to remain)
le laisser refroidir: let it cool
étendre (étendre): spread out (to spread out)
roulez-la (rouler): roll it (to roll)
sans trop serrer: loosely
recouvrir: cover
décorez (décorer): decorate (to decorate)
selon: according to
un père Noël: Santa Claus
des lutins (un lutin): elves
champignons (un champignon): mushrooms
une scie: saw
une hache: ax
on rappellera (rappeler): we will remind (to remind)
qui était (être): which was
de réchauffer: warm up
la maison: house
les cœur (le cœur): hearts

apprête (apprêter): prepare (to prepare)
un mets: a dish
les repas: meals
fête: celebration
vois vaudra (valoir): it will be worth
  (to be worth)

gigot d'agneau: leg of lamb
ouvert en portefeuille: split open
réserver: set aside
les os (un os): bones
les parures: trimmings
grosse (gros): big
une gousse d'ail: garlic clove
une botte de chaque: bunch of each
asperges (une asperge): asparagus
navets (un navet): turnips
poireaux (un poireau): leeks
fraîches fèves: fresh fava beans
décortiquées (décortiqué): shelled
petits pois écossés: shelled peas
le persil: parsley
le romarin: rosemary
le beurre: butter
huile d'olive extra-vierge: extra-virgin olive oil
la fleur de sel: French sea salt
le poivre: pepper

une casserole: a saucepan
réunir: gather together
couvrir: cover
l'eau: water
faire cuire: cook
pour obtenir: to get, to obtain
un jus d'agneau: lamb gravy
préchauffer le four: preheat the oven
hacher: chop
finement: finely
farcir: stuff
le ficeler soigneusement: tie up carefully
saler: salt
poivrer: pepper
l'enduire: coat
à la broche: on a spit
cuisson: cooking, roasting
baisser: reduce
arroser: baste

éplucher les légumes: peel the vegetables
eau bouillante salée: boiling salted water
à forte ébullition: to a strong boil
la fraîcheur: freshness
dégraisser: skim the fat off
le passer: pass through, strain through
une étamine: cheesecloth
le faire réduire: let it reduce
sirupeuse (sirupeux): syrupy
enrober: coat
une noix de beurre: a pat of butter
rectifier: to adjust
l'assaisonnement: seasoning

laisser reposer: let rest
hors du four: outside the oven
trancher: slice
dresser: put
entouré: surrounded

Gigot d'agneau aux herbes

Cette recette traditionnelle originaire de Normandie **apprête** l'agneau d'une manière tout à fait succulente. Ce plat constituera **un mets** idéal pour **les repas** de **fête** et les grandes occasions et **vous vaudra** des compliments enthousiastes.

Ingrédients :

1 **gigot d'agneau** de 1 kg **ouvert en portefeuille**
  (**réserver les os** et **les parures**)

1 carotte

1 **grosse gousse d'ail**

1 **botte de chaque** : **asperges** vertes, asperges blanches, **navets**,
  carottes nouvelles, **poireaux**

250 g de **fèves fraîches décortiquées**, **petits pois écossés**

1 bouquet de **persil** plat

1 branche de thym et **romarin**

100 g de **beurre**

huile d'olive extra-vierge

fleur de sel et **poivre**

Dans **une casserole**, **réunir** les os et les parures de gigot, la carotte et l'ail, **couvrir** d'eau et **faire cuire** 1 heure **pour obtenir un jus d'agneau**. Préchauffer le four à 250 ° Celsius. **Hacher finement** les herbes et en **farcir** le gigot. **Le ficeler soigneusement**, **saler**, **poivrer**, **l'enduire** d'huile d'olive et le faire cuire 35 min au four, de préférence **à la broche**. Au bout de 5 min de **cuisson**, **baisser** la température du four à 200 °. **Arroser** avec le jus de cuisson.

Éplucher les légumes, faire cuire les asperges à **l'eau bouillante salée** et les autres légumes à l'étouffée avec un peu d'eau et de beurre, **à forte ébullition** pour conserver leur **fraîcheur**. **Dégraisser** le jus d'agneau, **le passer** à l'**étamine** et **le faire réduire** fortement à consistance **sirupeuse**. **Enrober** bien les petits légumes avec le jus, ajouter **une noix de beurre** et **rectifier l'assaisonnement**.

Laisser reposer le gigot 20 min **hors du four**. Puis le **trancher** et le **dresser** sur un grand plat, **entouré** de légumes.

Fondue au fromage classique

Cette recette de fondue au fromage **québécoise** est une version locale de la fameuse fondue au fromage classique très populaire en France. **Invitez quelques amis qui sauront sans doute apprécier** ce plat convivial que l'on accompagne d'**une miche** de **pain** et de fruits.

Ingrédients :
1/2 **livre** (225 g) d'**emmental**
1/2 livre (225 g) fromage gruyère
1 **gousse d'ail**
1 1/2 **tasse** (375 ml) de **vin blanc**
3 **cuillers à soupe (**45 ml) de kirsh
1 cuiller à soupe (15 ml) de **jus de citron**
3 cuiller à soupe (45 ml) de **farine tous usages**
Poivre, **au goût**

Râper et **mélanger** l'emmental et le gruyère. **Saupoudrer** de farine. **Frotter** l'intérieur du **caquelon** avec **l'ail coupé**, puis **jeter** l'ail. **Verser** le vin et le kirsh dans le caquelon et **chauffer à feu moyen** sans **qu'ils viennent à ébullition. Ajouter** le jus de citron.

Ajouter graduellement **des poignées** de fromage **en remuant** constamment avec **une cuillère en bois jusqu'à** ce que le fromage soit fondu et forme une sauce **onctueuse**.

Ajouter du poivre **si désiré. Amener à ébullition, retirer** le caquelon du feu et **déposer** sur **un réchaud allumé** sur la table. **Tremper** des croûtons de **pain**, **des légumes (pommes de terre, champignons,** brocolis, etc.) et des fruits (**pommes, poires** et raisins).

québécoise: from Quebec
invitez: invite
quelques amis: some friends
qui sauront sans doute: who will without
  a doubt
apprécier: appreciate
une miche: a loaf
pain: bread

livre: pound
emmental: *a cheese similar to Swiss*
une gousse d'ail: garlic clove
une tasse: cup
le vin blanc: white wine
cuillers à soupe: tablespoons
le jus de citron: lemon juice
la farine tous usages: all-purpose flour
le poivre: pepper
au goût: to taste

râper: grate
mélanger: blend
saupoudrer: sprinkle
frotter: scrub
un caquelon: fondue pot
l'ail coupé: the cut garlic
jeter: throw away
verser: pour
chauffer: warm
à feu moyen: medium heat
sans qu'ils viennent à ébullition (venir):
  without letting it come to a boil (to come)
ajouter: add

des poignées (une poignée): handfuls
en remuant: by stirring
une cuillère en bois: wooden spoon
jusqu'à: until
onctueuse (onctueux): creamy

si désiré: if desired
amener à ébullition: bring to a boil
retirer: take away
déposer: put
un réchaud: plate-warmer
allumé (allumer): lit (to light)
tremper: dip
le pain: bread
des légumes (un légume): vegetables
pommes de terre (une pomme de terre):
  potatoes
champignons (un champignon): mushrooms
pommes (une pomme): apples
poires (une poire): pears

Un goût très raffiné

La France est le premier producteur de foie gras au **monde puisqu'elle produit plus de** 80% de la production mondiale. **Depuis** la Monarchie, le foie gras fait partie de la culture française et de son héritage culinaire. Il est **fabriqué à partir de foies** de **canards** ou d'**oies**. Ces palmipèdes ont la particularité **d'emmagasiner la graisse** pour anticiper leur migration.

On compte de nombreuses variétés de foies gras **mais il faut bien faire** la distinction **entre** le foie gras de canard et le foie gras d'oie. Le premier **possède** un arôme **assez fort tandis que** le second est plus subtil et délicat. **On distingue** aussi les différents conditionnements: le foie gras **entier** et **le bloc** de foie gras, le premier **étant** de **meilleure** qualité. Ces appellations sont **régies par** une charte spécifique et sont rigoureusement contrôlées par les autorités concernées. **Vous pouvez** aussi **préparer votre propre** foie gras à base de foies **frais**. Le foie gras **fourré** aux truffes est une autre grande spécialité.

En France, la majorité du foie gras est produit dans **le sud-ouest, c'est-à-dire** le Périgord, le Gers et les Landes, **même** si l'Alsace est aussi une région très productive. La cuisine française **étant intimement liée à** sa culture, **un séjour** dans le Périgord, dans l'un des Plus Beaux Villages de France, **ne pourra que vous convaincre** de la richesse et de l'authenticité de cette région.

Finalement, le foie gras **révèle** toute ses saveurs et arômes **grâce au vin**, particulièrement les vins **blancs liquoreux** et fruités comme le Sauternes, le Monbazillac ou **encore** le Champagne. **Pas d'inquiétude** pour votre **santé** : la consommation de confits, foies gras, graisses de canard ou d'oie est bénéfique pour la santé et **prévient** des insuffisances cardio-vasculaires !

Le diamant noir

La complexité olfactive **des truffes** en **a fait** leur **célébrité partout** dans **le monde**. **En outre**, la truffe est **un produit** rare et son apparition **reste toujours** mystérieuse. C'est la raison pour laquelle, la truffe est **souvent appelée** le « **diamant noir** ». Il existe de nombreuses différentes sortes de truffes, **au-delà de** la distinction **blanches** et noires.

Chaque variété **possède** des qualités gustatives différentes. Les truffes **se rencontrent** principalement dans **le sud** de la France, spécialement dans le Perigord, la Provence - où la truffe est appelée « rabasse » - et la Bourgogne. Comme **un champignon**, **qui vit** en symbiose avec la faune et la flore, la truffe **a besoin** de conditions particulières pour **pousser** : **le chêne en fait partie** et **même**, mais plus rarement le thym et la lavande. La truffe représente aussi l'art de **vivre** à la Française.

La récolte de la truffe est une tradition **vieille** de cent **ans**. Il existe deux manières principales de la récolter: **les chiens** et **les cochons**. Le cochon **adore** les truffes, **il les repère** avec son **fin odorat**, **cherche** dans **la terre** avec son **groin jusqu'à** ce qu'**il déterre** le champignon. Le chien **doit être entraîné** pour **devenir un chasseur** de truffes.

Ensuite, les truffes **sont vendues** dans **les marchés locaux** typiques **qui ont lieu** dans les villages, où le cérémonial et le professionalisme **règnent** à cause de la grande **valeur** des truffes. **Comptez environ** 1500 Euros par kilo !

Enfin, **la meilleure façon** d'apprécier la truffe est de **la goûter**. La gastronomie française possède de nombreuses **recettes** à base de truffes. La plus simple est souvent la meilleure: **vous allez parfaitement** apprécier la grande saveur de la truffe dans une omelette. **Cependant**, les truffes **s'adaptent** parfaitement à une cuisine **plus recherchée** comme le foie gras.

des truffes: truffles
fait (faire): have done (to do)
célébrité: popularity
partout: everywhere
le monde: the world
en outre: moreover
un produit (des produits): a product
reste toujours (rester): always stays (to stay)
souvent: often
appelée (appeler): called (to call)
diamant noir: black diamond
au-delà de: beyond
blanches: white
noires: black

chaque: each
possède (posséder): possesses (to possess)
se rencontrent (rencontrer): can be found (to find)
le sud: the South
un champignon: a mushroom
qui vit (vivre): that lives (to live)
a besoin: needs
pousser: to grow
le chêne: the oak
en fait partie: is a part of
même: even
vivre (vivre): live (to live)

la récolte: the harvest
vieille: old
ans (un an): years
les chiens (le chien): dogs
les cochons (le cochon): pigs
adore (adorer): love (to love)
il les repère (repérer): it locates them (to locate)
fin odorat: fine sense of smell
cherche (chercher): look for (to look for)
la terre: the ground
groin: snout
jusqu'à: until
qu'il déterre (déterrer): it digs up (to dig up)
doit être entraîné: must be trained
devenir: become
un chasseur: a hunter

ensuite: next, then
sont vendus (vendre): are sold (to sell)
les marchés locaux: the local markets
qui ont lieu (avoir lieu): that take place (to take place)
règnent (régner): reign (to reign)
valeur: value
comptez (compter): count (to count)
environ: about

la meilleure façon: the best way
la goûter (goûter): taste it (to taste)
recettes (une recette): recipes
vous allez parfaitement: you will fully
cependant: meanwhile
s'adaptent (adapter): adapt themselves (to adapt)
plus recherchée: very special

La cuisine sénégalaise

Si l'on **compare** la cuisine sénégalaise **aux autres traditions culinaires** du continent africain, c'est **sans doute** celle **qui a subit** le plus l'influence de cuisines **étrangères** et traditionnelles, en particulier à Dakar. La capitale du Sénégal est **une ville** multiethnique, multiculturelle et **ouverte sur l'extérieur**.

À Dakar, **les recettes** du **terroir ont tendance à céder** la place à **des mets** européens, **moyen-orientaux** et asiatiques. **Sans renoncer** toutefois aux modes de préparation et de consommation traditionnels, ces plats sont adaptés aux **habitudes** culinaires locales. **Par ailleurs**, si les restaurants **proposent** des plats sénégalais traditionnels, **on trouve** aussi souvent au menu des plats de différents **pays**, **y compris** du continent africain (Bénin, Cameroun), **valorisant** ainsi la diversité des produits **disponibles** sur **le marché**.

Le voyageur un peu curieux découvrira à Dakar toute **une panoplie** de **goûts**, de **saveurs** et d'odeurs issus de ce **mélange** de produits locaux et importés. Dans les provinces sénégalaises, **il trouvera** des plats plus traditionnels, spécifiques à certains terroirs ou ethnies, que **les femmes auront plaisir** à **préparer** pour **montrer** à l'étranger leurs talents culinaires et la richesse des produits de leur région…

---

on compare (comparer): we compare (to compare)

aux autres: with other

traditions culinaires: culinary traditions

sans doute: certainly

qui a subit (subir): has been subjected to (to be subjected to)

étrangères: foreigners

une ville: city

ouverte (ouvert): open

sur l'extérieur: to the outside

les recettes (une recette): recipes

terroir: land

(elles) ont tendance à (avoir tendance à): (they) tend to (to tend to)

céder: to give up, give way

des mets (un mets): dishes, foods

moyen-orientaux: Middle East

sans renoncer: without giving up

habitudes: habits

par ailleurs: in addition

proposent (proposer): offer (to offer)

on trouve (trouver): we find (to find)

pays: countries

y compris: including

valorisant: promoting

disponibles (disponible): available

le marché: the market

la voyaguer: the traveler

un peu curieux: a little bit curious

(il) découvrira (decouvrir): (he) will discover (to discover)

une panoplie: range

goûts (un goût): tastes

saveurs (une saveur): flavors

un mélange: blend

il trouvera (trouver): he will find (to find)

les femmes (une femme): women

(elles) auront plaisir à: (they) will take pleasure in

préparer: preparing

montrer: showing

Bien sûr, certains produits aux saveurs **fortes**, à la texture inhabituelle, pourront **étonner le palais** des « toubabs », mais **cela fait partie** du jeu de la découverte. La surprise de **la nouveauté fait** ensuite **place à un attrait** pour une cuisine souvent accessible, originale **sans être trop étrangère**, que vous aurez plaisir à **reproduire** de **retour** dans votre pays. **Les livres** de recettes vous y **aideront** et les Sénégalaises, **fières** de leurs **savoir-faire, seront prêtes à vous apprendre** à cuisiner **vos plats favoris.**

Vous n'aurez sans doute **pas** l'occasion de découvrir l'alimentation **quotidienne** de la grande majorité des Sénégalais, **moins riche** et **moins variée**, que celle du restaurant ou de la gargote. L'état de **pauvreté** des familles urbaines et rurales **ne leur permet pas** toujours de préparer **deux repas par jour** ni de diversifier leur alimentation.

Elles se contentent ainsi souvent **d'un bol de riz** ou de **mil**, **agrémenté parfois** de quelques **légumes**, d'un peu de **poisson**, d'**un morceau** de **viande à partager entre** les nombreux membres de la famille. **Sachez** donc qu'un plat **bien garni** est un privilège, **un cadeau offert** par votre hôtesse en signe d'hospitalité, qu'**il faut savoir apprécier même si parfois nos habitudes alimentaires** sont très différentes.

bien sûr: of course
fortes (fort): strong
étonner: to surprise
le palais: the palate
cela fait partie: it is part of
le jeu: game
la découverte: discovery
la nouveauté: the novelty
(elle) fait place à (faire): (it) makes way for (to make)
un attrait: attraction
sans être: without being
trop étrangère: too foreign
reproduire: to reproduce
retour: to come back
les livres (un livre): the books
(ils) aideront (aider): (they) will help (to help)
fières (fier): proud
un savoir-faire: know-how
seront prêtes (être): they will be ready (to be)
vous apprendre: to teach you
vos plats favoris: your favorite dishes

vous n'aurez pas: you will not have
quotidienne (quotidien): daily
moins riche: less rich
moins variée: less varied
pauvreté: poverty
ne leur permet pas (permettre): does not allow them (to allow)
deux repas (un repas): two meals
par jour: per day

elles se contentent de: they are content with
un bol de riz: a bowl of rice
le mil: millet
agrémenté: accompanied
parfois: sometimes
les légumes (un légume): vegetables
le poisson: fish
un morceau: a piece
la viande: meat
à partager: to share
entre: between
(vous) sachez (savoir): you know (to know)
bien garni: full
un cadeau: a gift
offert (offrir): given
il faut savoir (falloir): it is necessary to know (to be necessary)
apprécier: to appreciate
même si: even if
parfois: sometimes
nos habitudes (une habitude): our habits
alimentaires (alimentaire): dietary

la fête: celebration	
appelée (appeler): named (to name, to call)	
de nos jours: nowadays	
se régaler: to enjoy	
entre: between	
les amis: friends	
autour de: around	

la pâte: dough
environ: about
tout d'abord: first
versez (verser): pour (to pour)
la farine: flour
un saladier: a bowl
une cuillère: a spoon
creusez (creuser): dig (to dig)
délayez (délayer): mix (to mix)
un demi-litre: half a liter
le lait: milk
un fouet: whisk
une fourchette: fork
un mélange: mixture
sans grumeaux (un grumeau): without lumps
vous pouvez utiliser (pouvoir): you can use
  (can, to be able to)
une fois: once
obtenue: obtained
bien lisse: very smooth
ajouter: to add
œufs (un œuf): eggs
cuillères à soupe: tablespoons
le sucre: sugar
le sel: salt
laissez reposer: let it rest
sortez (sortir): get out (to get out)
mélangez (mélanger): mix (to mix)
un demi-verre: half a glass
l'eau: water
rendre: to make
moins épaisse: less thick

la cuisson: the cooking
un pinceau: brush
une demi pomme de terre: half a potato
graissez légèrement: oil lightly
une huile: oil
neutre: neutral
le tournesol: sunflower
répétez (répéter): repeat (to repeat)
éviter: to avoid
la poêle: the pan

faites chauffer (faire): make hot (to make)
chaude (chaud): warm
une louche: ladle
en faisant tourner: by making turn
cuire: to cook
les bords (un bord): edges
se décollent (décoller): come off (to come off)

saupoudrez (saupoudrer): sprinkle
  (to sprinkle)
sucre en poudre: powdered sugar
étalez (étaler): spread (to spread)
la confiture: jam
dégustez (déguster): enjoy (to enjoy)

Le 2 février, c'est la Chandeleur. Cette **fête** judéo-chrétienne, anciennement **appelée** la Chandeleuse, est **de nos jours** l'occasion de **se régaler** en famille ou **entre amis autour de** bonnes crêpes.

Préparation de **la pâte** pour 10 crêpes **environ** :

Tout d'abord, **versez** 250 grammes de **farine** dans **un saladier**. À l'aide d'**une cuillère**, **creusez** un puits au centre et **délayez** progressivement **un demi-litre** de **lait** avec **un fouet** ou **une fourchette**. Pour **un mélange sans grumeaux vous pouvez utiliser** un batteur électrique. **Une fois** que la pâte **obtenue** est **bien lisse**, ajouter 3 **œufs**, 2 **cuillères à soupe** de **sucre**, une pincée de **sel** et 3 cuillères à soupe de rhum. **Laissez reposer** la pâte au réfrigérateur. Au bout d'une heure, **sortez** la pâte, **mélangez** et ajoutez **un demi-verre** d'**eau** pour **rendre** la pâte **moins épaisse**.

La cuisson des crêpes :

À l'aide d'**un pinceau**, d'un papier absorbant, ou d'**une demi pomme de terre**, **graissez légèrement** une crêpière avec un peu d'**huile**, utilisez de préférence une huile **neutre** tel le que l'huile de **tournesol**. **Répétez** cette opération avant la cuisson de chaque crêpe pour **éviter** que la pâte attache à **la poêle**.

Faites chauffer la crêpière. Une fois que la poêle est bien **chaude**, versez **une louche** de pâte dans la poêle. Répartissez uniformément la pâte **en faisant tourner** la poêle. Laisser **cuire** environ 2 minutes et dès que **les bords se décollent**, retournez la crêpe à l'aide d'une spatule.

Saupoudrez la crêpe de **sucre en poudre** ou bien **étalez** un peu de **confiture**. **Dégustez** chaude de préférence. Bon appétit !

Coq au vin

Ce mets délicieux et traditionnel **connaît** ses **inconditionnels** qui se font un plaisir de le cuisiner régulièrement pour le plaisir **gustatif** de leur famille ou de leurs **amis**.

Ingrédients :
Idéalement un **coq**, ou 1 ou 2 **poulets** (1,5 kg),
  coupé en 8 **morceaux ou plus**
1/2 **bouteille vin rouge corsé** type bourgogne
150 g lard, **en cube**
250 g **champignons** de Paris
une douzaine de **petits oignons blancs**
2-3 **gousses d'ail**, **hachées**
2 carottes, **pelées**, **coupées en quartier**
Huile de tournesol, **beurre non salé**
Bouquet d'herbes: 2 **brins** de thym et 1 **feuille de laurier**, **persil**
Sel et **poivre**

Un jour en avance, **nettoyer** et **couper** le poulet en 8 morceaux ou plus. **Verser** une demi-bouteille de bourgogne rouge sur le poulet **Ajouter** les petits oignons blancs, les carottes et les herbes, **couvrir** et **mettre** au réfrigérateur.

Le jour **suivant**, **retirer** et **égoutter** le poulet et **les légumes**. **Garder** le vin pour **plus tard**. **Faire brunir** le poulet avec de l'huile dans une poêle. **En utilisant** la **même** poêle, ajouter de l'ail aux légumes et **chauffer pendant quelques** minutes. Mettre le poulet et les légumes dans **une cocotte** ou une grande casserole. Verser le vin et du sel et poivre. **Amener à ébullition à feu moyen**. Couvrir et **cuire à feux doux** pendant une ou deux **heures**.

Faire brunir à la poêle : lard, oignon et champignons pendant 10 minutes environ. Quand le poulet est **prêt**, ajouter le lard, oignon et champignons dans la cocotte et **remuer** pendant 2 à 3 minutes. **Goûter** et **corriger** le sel et le poivre éventuellement. Ajouter du persil. Préparer du **riz** ou **des pommes de terre comme garniture**.

---

ce mets: this dish
connaît: known
inconditionnels: devotees, loyals
gustatif: taste
amis: friends

un coq: rooster
poulets (le poulet): chickens
coupé: cut
morceaux (un morceau): pieces
ou plus: or more
une bouteille: bottle
le vin rouge: red wine
corsé: strong
en cube: cubed
champignons (un champignon): mushrooms
petits oignons blancs: small white onions
gousses d'ail: cloves of garlic
hachées (hacher): minced (to chop, mince)
pelées (peler): peeled (to peel)
coupées en quartier: quartered
huile de tournesol: sunflower oil
le beurre: butter
non salé: unsalted
brins (un brin): sprigs
une feuille de laurier: bay leaf
le persil: parsley
le sel: salt
le poivre: pepper

un jour en avance: one day before
nettoyer: clean
couper: cut
verser: pour
ajouter: add
couvrir: cover
mettre: put

suivant: following
retirer: remove
égoutter: drain
les légumes (un légume): vegetables
garder: keep
plus tard: later
faire brunir: brown
en utilisant: by using
même: same
chauffer: warm up
pendant quelques minutes: for a few minutes
une cocotte: pot
amener à ébullition: bring to a boil
à feu moyen: at medium heat
cuire: cook
à feux doux: at low heat
heures (une heure): hours

prêt: ready
remuer: stir
goûter: taste
corriger: correct, adjust
le riz: rice
des pommes de terre: potatoes
comme garniture: as a side dish

Saveurs des Antilles

en matière de goût: in terms of taste
sont associées: are associated with
le rhum: rum
épices (une épice): spices
la douceur: the sweetness
que l'on ne trouve que rarement: that one can rarely find
la métropole: Metropolitan France
le prix: price
exorbitants (exorbitant): exorbitant
un ananas: pineapple
la mangue: mango
la goyave: guava
la grenade: pomegranate
la papaye: papaya
le fruit de la passion: passion fruit
un avocat: avocado
la noix de coco: coconut
la patate douce: sweet potato
les légumes (un légume): vegetables
mais aussi: but also
le gingembre: ginger
la cannelle: cinnamon

bien sûr: of course
réputés (réputé): well-known, famous
des mélanges (un mélange): blends, mixtures
un goût doux et sucré: sweet taste
mais qui font également bien: but that do equally well
tourner la tête: to turn the head (to make drunk)
saveurs: flavors
elles évoquent (évoquer): that evoke (to evoke)
le soleil: sun
exotisme: exoticism

en raison de: because of
nombreuses (nombreux): numerous
telles que (tel que): such as
le safran: saffron
très connue: very well known
utilisée comme: used as
le plat: dish, meal
portant ce même nom: named the same way
plusieurs: several
la moutarde: mustard
le poivre noir: black pepper
le clou de girofle: clove

En matière de goût, les Antilles **sont associées** au **rhum,** aux **épices** et à **la douceur** des fruits **que l'on ne trouve que rarement** en **métropole** (ou à des **prix exorbitants**). Ananas, **mangue,** **goyave,** **grenade,** **papaye,** litchi, maracudja (**fruits de la passion**), **avocat** et **noix de coco** pour les fruits, manioc, cristophine, ou **patate douce** pour **les légumes, mais aussi le gingembre, la cannelle,** le curry, la vanille pour les épices.

Et **bien sûr** les **réputés** rhums, ou punchs qui sont **des mélanges** de rhum et de fruits d'**un goût doux et sucré,** (**mais qui font également bien tourner la tête**), sont des **saveurs qui évoquent soleil** et **exotisme.**

La cuisine créole est riche en goût et en couleur **en raison de** différentes et **nombreuses** épices utilisées **telles que le safran** (curcuma), les piments, le gingembre, ou la **très connue** « colombo » **utilisée comme** base du **plat portant ce même nom** (colombo de poulet, d'agneau ou de porc), et qui est un mélange de **plusieurs** épices (curcuma, coriandre, cumin, **moutarde,** fenugrec, **poivre noir, clous de girofle**).

Les plats **sont composés de** nombreux **fruits de mer**, de **poissons**, de **poulet grillé** mais **on peut également trouver des boudins savoureux**, blanc ou **noir**: une spécialité, **toujours très bien préparée**, même **dans les** « baraques ».

Les plats **les plus connus** de la cuisine créole sont le « rougail saucisse » ou le « cari poulet ». **Les beignets de morue appelés** « accras » sont également très réputés et font **le délice des apéritifs** avec les petits boudins créoles.

En boisson, les Antilles **offrent un large éventail** de fruits **permettant d'apprécier** des saveurs incomparables. Consommés tout simplement **purs**, **pressés** en **jus** de fruits, ou mélangés au rhum pour **créer** des punchs, c'est un cocktail de vitamine **qui régale le palais**. Les fruits sont également utilisés en cuisine dans **la confection** des plats, mélangés avec **la viande** ou le poisson, **effectuant ainsi** un mélange **sucré-salé très goûteux**.

Le lait de coco, initialement employé en boisson, mélangé avec du rhum, est également utilisé dans la confection des plats. La cuisine créole est **un vrai régal** pour le palais **comme pour les yeux**.

---

sont composés de: are made of
fruits de mer: seafood
poissons (un poisson): fish
le poulet grillé: roasted chicken
on peut également: one can also
trouver: find
des boudins (un boudin): blood sausages
savoureux: tasty
blanc: white
noir: black
toujours: always
très bien préparée: very well prepared
même dans: even in
les baraques (une baraque): shacks

les plus connus: the most famous
les beignets de morue: cod fritters
appelés (appeler): called (to call)
le délice: delight
des apéritifs (un apéritif): appetizers

offrent (offrir): offer (to offer)
large: wide
un éventail: range
permettant de: allowing
apprécier: to appreciate
purs (pur): pure
pressés (pressé): squeezed
jus: juice
créer: to create
qui régale (regaler): that delights (to delight)
le palais: palate
la confection: making
la viande: meat
effectuant (effectuer): making (to make)
ainsi: this way, thus
sucré-salé: sweet and salty
très goûteux: very tasty

le lait de coco: coconut milk
initialement: initially
employé: used
un vrai régal: a real feast
comme pour: as well as for
les yeux: the eyes

Évaluez votre compréhension

Le pain français, page 184

1. Walking down the streets of Paris, what might you expect to see?

2. Why did a long loaf of bread work better than a round loaf?

3. How many types of regional bread exist in France?

La bouillabaisse, page 186

1. *Bouillabaisse* originates from what city?

2. What was *bouillabaisse* originally made with, and what was it called?

3. What does the real *bouillabaisse* contain "for sure"?

Gigot d'agneau aux herbes, page 190

1. What does this recipe tell you to set aside?

2. How do you create the lamb gravy?

3. How do you remove the fat from the lamb gravy?

Un goût très raffiné, page 192

1. How much of the world production of *foie gras* comes from France?

2. What is *foie gras* made from?

3. What is the distinction between duck *foie gras* and goose *foie gras*?

Test your comprehension

Le diamant noir, page 193

1. What are the two types of truffles?

2. In what region are truffles found?

3. What two animals are used to hunt for truffles?

Coq au vin, page 197

1. How many small white onions does this recipe call for?

2. After bringing the *coq au vin* to a boil, how long should you cook it at low heat?

3. What two sides are suggested for this dish?

La cuisine sénégalaise, page 194

1. What will the curious traveler discover?

2. Poverty in some neighborhoods affects daily meals in what way?

3. If your plate is full, what is this a sign of?

Saveurs des Antilles, page 198

1. What is one speciality that you can always find well prepared?

2. What are *accras*?

3. Mixing fruit with meat dishes creates what type of flavor?

Réponses

Culture   **Un dimanche en France, page 4** 1. bakeries and florists 2. a family meal at grandmother's house. 3. seafood, meats, cheese, vegetables, salads, and dessert **Parfum de nos enfances, page 6** 1. It was used by the Romans during baths and during medieval times for its medicinal qualities. 2. July 15–August 15 3. Real lavender grows wild and reproduces naturally. It is recognizable by its color, more mauve. *Lavindin* is more violet. **Les marchés du Sénégal, page 8** 1. Kermel market; in the heart of Dakar. 2. Casamanc market 3. weekly markets outside the city limits, in the bush; buy, sell, and trade **Les mois du camping et du crabe, page 10** 1. toilets and showers 2. mangrove swamps, humid places; vegetation and small crabs and fish 3. so that it can grow to maturity and so that it does not go extinct or become endangered **Les vendanges, page 12** 1. between the end of August/beginning of September through October 2. students 3. Workers sign a contract; work cannot last longer than a month; with two contracts together work cannot exceed two months. 4. You can harvest day and night; it takes less time and costs about 50% less than by hand. **Noël sur les marchés, page 14** 1. Germany and Alsace 2. waffles, hot wine, crepes, grilled chestnuts 3. Christmas figurines and ornaments, pottery, candles, jewelry, artwork, mittens **Francophonie canadienne, page 18** 1. 1974 2. poutine, French fries covered with sauce **La mode, reflet de la culture, page 19** 1. Coco Chanel 2. simplified styles, masculine styles for women and getting rid of the corset

Voyages   **La grande et la merveilleuse, page 24** 1. French literature 2. milk cakes **Les pâtisseries de Paris, page 25** 1. Choose one that is brown on top and caramelized. 2. Blé Sucré; perfect for a late afternoon snack **Le visage unique de Montréal, page 26** 1. 1642; fur trading 2. the contrast between the buildings' old architecture and modern architecture 3. They allow you to shop without braving the cold of winter. 4. being welcoming and open-minded **Des îles pleines de richesses, page 28** 1. 1503; it was discovered by Christopher Columbus in 1498. It was populated by the French and in 1792 became a labor camp and exile for criminals. 2. Touloulous; women disguised and not recognizable (even by their husbands) who play a game asking men to dance **Le quartier de la Croix-Rousse, page 32** 1. between the Saone and the Rhone rivers; it is a hill north of Lyon. 2. hot candy, cotton candy, and riding bumper cars 3. an enormous rock that was dug up in 1892 during the construction of the cable car **Le vieux Marseille : le panier, page 34** 1. the aroma of soap 2. orphanage; art center/museum 3. The French series *Plus Belle La Vie* was filmed here. **Belle-Île-en-Mer, page 36** 1. the citadelle 2. by foot; good shoes, a picnic basket, a bottle of water, sunglasses, and a windbreaker 3. You go down some very steep steps. **Saint Tropez, page 38** 1. Saint-Tropez church, Sainte-Anne chapel, Annonciade chapel 2. twelve

Answers

Tradition

Un jour, un chocolat, page 44 1. Germany, 19th century 2. They drew lines with chalk. **Les vacances à la française, page 45** 1. The idea to start getting paid for vacations came to fruition. 2. They went on strike, almost paralyzing the country. 3. They have increased exponentially. **Le temps des sucres, page 46** 1. a maple cabin; families go to the cabin to enjoy a big meal, harvest maple syrup, and make maple candy. 2. with snow 3. Make a jag/hole in the ground for a blowtorch; this boils the syrup; the syrup is filtered and emptied into an evaporator. **Le réveillon de la Saint Sylvestre, page 48** 1. coins and medals 2. the opulence of the year 3. so that the meal lasts until midnight **Des chants sacrés, page 50** 1. tubers with rice and pigeon peas 2. Christmas carols 3. People come together to sing Christmas Carols; end of November–Christmas Eve **La tradition du pastis, page 52** 1. anise 2. A law was passed prohibiting the consumption of absinthe. 3. at the end of the afternoon **Le vin et le fromage français, page 54** 1. quality, authenticity, and origin of wine (and cheese) 2. It guarantees that a certain type of wine (from the same terrain) will have the same general characteristics. 3. nine **La cérémonie du mariage, page 58** 1. the exchanging of "consents" or vows 2. lively and happy 3. June–August; mild weather and the days are longer, move favorable for a party

Célébration

La fête du Travail, page 65 1. lily of the valley 2. It started in 1561 because King Charles IX received a sprig of lily and decided to give it to the ladies to bring them good luck. 3. Be careful when you give this flower to friends and family because it is toxic. **Le carnaval aux Antilles, page 66** 1. their song and dance 2. very colorful, made with feathers and shimmering fabrics 3. children all in the same costume, the same color, with masks of monkeys or witches **Faites de la musique !, page 68** 1. more than 340 2. summer solstice; to celebrate the arrival of summer 3. Alcohol became a problem and car accidents increased because of alcohol being sold to young people. Free public transportation encouraged people not to drink and drive. **Poisson d'avril !, page 70** 1. January 1st 2. attaching a paper fish to someone's back 3. April 1st marks the end of Lent, and during Lent eating meat is replaced by eating only fish. The fake fish marks the end of eating fish and the return to eating meat. **Le 14 juillet, page 72** 1. patriotism; the date commemorates the storming of Bastille and is the symbol of the revolution. 2. to beat the crowds and find a good place to watch the parade 3. The planes release white, blue, and red smoke, to symbolize the three colors of the French flag. **Jours de mémoire, page 78** 1. All Saints' Day; to acknowledge the Saints recognized by the Catholic Church 2. Day of the Dead; people remember the people they have lost; they go to the cemeteries and clean up the graves, leave flowers, and reminisce and talk about the good times. 3. chrysanthemum **La fête des Rois en France, page 80** 1. January 6th 2. A charm is hidden in the cake, and the person who finds it is crowned queen or king for the day and he/she gets to pick a "royal partner." 3. The north of the country makes its cake with a puff pastry filled with "frangipane" cream. The south makes a brioche in the form of a crown decorated with dried fruit and sugar. **Noël en Provence, page 82** 1. The crops will be good. 2. The youngest and oldest child light the Yule log together. 3. meat; the 13 people at "The Last Supper"

Réponses

Biographie

Ingénieur français célèbre, page 88 1. Charles Nepveu 2. Statue of Liberty 3. viaducts, bridges, train stations, churches **Cinéaste français, page 92** 1. to use natural lighting and new equipment that is lighter and less noisy so you can follow the characters and film more closely 2. The characters and emotions feel more realistic. 3. Life is too precious not to be lived fully. **Écrivain et philosophe français, page 94** 1. His father died when he was two years old. 2. He didn't get married or have children. 3. He failed the exam that would have allowed him to start teaching. **Prix Nobel de médecine, page 95** 1. insulin 2. religious studies 3. orthopedic surgery **La Môme, page 96** 1. Billie Holiday 2. Her father came and took her to work with a traveling circus. 3. because she was very small, like a little bird **Écrivaine acadienne, page 98** 1. mainly female, with a vast array of emotions ranging from humor to rage 2. history of Acadie 3. more than forty **Une personnalité fondamentale, page 100** 1. taking the people's local culture and their identity away 2. He took a stand for their country to fight against oppression. His name and writings began to "cross borders," and he became more popular and better known in other countries. 3. He became Mayor. **Les débuts de Coco Chanel, page 102** 1. Arthur Capel; Boy 2. fluid fabrics like jersey 3. the little black dress; straight sheath dress, collarless with three-quarters-length sleeves

Coutumes

Bises ou pas bises ?, page 108 1. You should maintain a certain distance and shake his/her hand. 2. a kiss 3. shaking the hand **Ne pas avoir l'air d'un touriste, page 110** 1. You should learn to speak French, even if it's just a few words or phrases. 2. people approaching them and asking for help in English without even trying to speak French 3. The tip is usually included in the check, but if there is change left over you can leave this for the tip. **L'étiquette professionnelle, page 112** 1. lunch break; noon to 2PM 2. in business settings, the spontaneous use of "tu" 3. Madame 4. five minutes early; between 8PM–11PM **La bienséance autour d'une table, page 114** 1. They are a time for family and friends to come together and share and talk. 2. The hostess generally assigns the seats, alternating male and female guests. 3. Do not talk with your mouth full, do not eat with your mouth open, don't make loud noises when chewing, don't lean your elbows on the table or hold your head in your hands with your elbows on the table. 4. Use them in the order from exterior to interior. **La signification des gestes, page 116** 1. amazement or impatience; biting your lower lip and shaking your hand from left to right 2. something has gone wrong; placing one hand on your forehead 3. "J'ai sommeil ou je suis fatigué"; placing two hands, palms together, against the side of your face 4. "C'est délicieux!"; kissing the tops of your fingers closed together and then opening your hand

Les Arts

Les Petits Rats, page 125 1. a ballet school; the noise of the scampering feet learning to dance 2. height and weight restrictions 3. only four or five **L'art public à Montréal, page 126** 1. three hundred 2. La Croix du Mont-Royal (the cross on Mont-Royal) 3. the fountain La Joute, a sculpture of a bronze cow **La musique guadeloupéenne, page 128** 1. accordion, violin, maracas, and drum 2. It was used as a way for the slaves to secretly communicate with each other. 3. Zouk; Kassav' **Les splendeurs de Versailles, page 130** 1. It is filled with three hundred fifty-seven mirrors. 2. Marie Antoinette; to escape the rigor and etiquette of the court 3. an exhibit dedicated to Louis XIV called "the man and the king" **Le théâtre français, page 132** 1. Greece 2. Christmas and Easter 3. misunderstandings between the characters, characters being silly and acting like "idiots" **Les troubadours au Moyen Âge, page 135** 1. at lordly courts in castles in the medieval era 2. emotions of the heart and soul, tribulations of the heart 3. *la chanson en cinq ou six couplets* (a song in five or six verses), *la sérénade du chevalier amoureux* (the serenade of the chivalrous knight), *la pastourelle* (shepherdess song) **Les musées parisiens, page 136** 1. a train station; built in 1900 for The World Fair 2. an oil refinery 3. Camille Claudel's **Un symbole de la culture, page 138** 1. Guignol 2. glove 3. a wooden head, smile on his face, black eyes, dimples, a jacket with a red bowtie

Answers

Histoire

La fleur de lys, page 146 1. purity 2. royal power 3. Philippe Auguste **Historique du drapeau français, page 147** 1. white, blue, red; white 2. faith and liberty 3. rooster emblem **À la découverte de la Martinique, page 148** 1. island of flowers 2. France and England; 1814 3. the eruption of the volcano Pelée **La Nouvelle-France, page 150** 1. Quebec 2. its natural resources and its relevance for the fur trade 3. the battle fought on the Plaines d'Abraham **Les sans-culottes, page 152** 1. lower social classes, arts industries 2. someone who doesn't wear culottes, which were worn by the nobles and aristrocrats; for being free men who claimed their liberty and fought for the rights of all citizens 3. red; liberty **L'Arc de Triomphe, page 154** 1. the different stages of war 2. The Tomb of the Unknown Soldier **Histoire de France, page 156** 1. the end of the monarchy and the beginnings of a democratic republic in France 2. Austria 3. She wore fancy outfits, organized big parties, and loved music and dancing. **Jeanne d'Arc, page 158** 1. la Pucelle d'Orléans (The Virgin of Orleans); she is one of three patron saints of France 2. so she could travel incognito 3. She was bought by the English for ten thousand pounds. She was accused of heresy by the church. She was burned at the stake in 1431.

Géographie

Les trois fleuves de France, page 166 1. the Seine, the Loire, and the Rhone 2. Lake Leman 3. castles **Les plages françaises, page 168** 1. the English Channel and the Mediterranean; Atlantic Ocean 2. scuba diving and observing the sea life 3. chalk cliffs **Les Alpes, page 170** 1. eight 2. Grenoble 3. Edelweiss, étoile des glaciers (star of the glaciers) **Sur la route des baleines, page 172** 1. Saguenay and Saint-Laurent 2. whale watching, and it is the first establishment for the colony of Nouvelle-France 3. because of the sounds they make to communicate with each other **Les pays de mer et de montagne, page 174** 1. cliffs and coastline 2. the mixture of salt water and fresh water 3. a known landmark that is a large rock with steep sides that stands on the shore of the river and makes a natural arch **Des fleurs et encore des fleurs, page 176** 1. rains and soil 2. the fern 3. the mangrove tree **Un pays aux contrastes, page 177** 1. Gulf of Guinea 2. fishing and cotton 3. the river Mono **Le Lac Léman, page 178** 1. crescent or comma 2. algae 3. maples, beech, poplar, ash

Gastronomie

Le pain français, page 184 1. a child leaving a bakery eating a piece of a baguette 2. It would fit better in the pockets of soldiers. 3. eighty **La bouillabaisse, page 186** 1. Marseille 2. fish; Kakavia 3. slipper lobster **Gigot d'agneau aux herbes, page 190** 1. bones and trimmings 2. cover the bones and trimmings with water and let cook for one hour 3. pass through a cheesecloth **Un goût très raffiné, page 192** 1. more than 80% 2. duck or goose liver 3. Duck has a strong aroma, and goose is more subtle and delicate. **Le diamant noir, page 193** 1. black and white 2. the South of France 3. pigs and dogs **La cuisine sénégalaise, page 194** 1. that Dakar is filled with a wide range of tastes and flavors 2. They can't always prepare two meals a day. 3. It is a gift offered by the hostess, and it is a sign of hospitality. **Coq au vin, page 197** 1. a dozen 2. one or two hours 3. rice and potatoes **Saveurs des Antilles, page 198** 1. blood sausage 2. cod fritters 3. sweet and salty

Audio Recordings

Recordings of the following twenty-five passages are available via the online and mobile McGraw-Hill Education Language Lab app (see page iv for details).

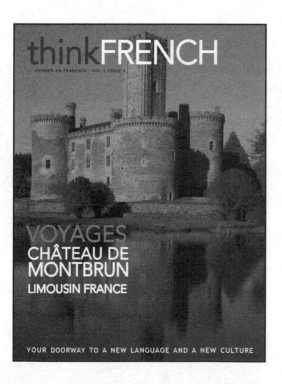

CONSERVATION HUNTING

People and Wildlife in Canada's North

Milton M.R. Freeman, Robert J. Hudson and
Lee Foote
(editors)

Library and Archives ⌐ ⌐ ⌐ ⌐ guing in Publication

Conservation hunting : people and wildlife in Canada's north /
Milton M.R. Freeman, Robert J. Hudson and A. Lee Foote (editors).

(Occasional publication series ; 56)

Papers from a conference titled: People, wildlife and hunting:
emerging conservation paradigms, held in Edmonton, Oct. 24-26,
2004.

ISBN 1-896445-35-7

1. Wildlife management--Canada, Northern--Congresses.
2. Hunting--Canada, Northern--Congresses. 3. Rural
development--Canada, Northern--Congresses. I. Freeman, Milton
M. R., 1934- II. Hudson, Robert J. III. Foote, A. Lee IV. Canadian
Circumpolar Institute V. Series: Occasional publication series
(Canadian Circumpolar Institute) ; 56.

SK471.N6C65 2005   333.95'4'09719   C2005-902590-5

ISSN 0068-0303

Cover photo courtesy Dept of Environment, Government of Nunavut
Cover design by Art Design Printing Inc.
Printed in Canada by Art Design Printing Inc.